CHINA RURAL STATISTICS 1988

THE CHINA STATISTICS SERIES

China Statistical Abstract 1988

China Social Statistics 1986

China Trade and Price Statistics 1988

China Rural Statistics 1988

The China Statistics Series publishes revised English language editions of China Statistics prepared by the State Statistical Bureau of the People's Republic of China (SSB). The English Language Editorial Board, composed of representatives of the China Statistical Information and Consultancy Service Center, an affiliate of the SSB, and the China Statistics Archives, a research center of the University of Illinois at Chicago, is responsible for the translation and revision of these volumes.

CHINA RURAL STATISTICS 1988

Compiled by the State Statistical Bureau
of the People's Republic of China

THE CHINA STATISTICS SERIES

William T. Liu, *Series Editor*

PRAEGER

New York
Westport, Connecticut
London

ISBN: 0-275-93346-6
ISSN: 1040-7979

First published in 1989

Praeger Publishers, One Madison Avenue, New York, NY 10010
A division of Greenwood Press, Inc.

Printed in the United States of America

The paper used in this book complies with the
Permanent Paper Standard issued by the National
Information Standards Organization (Z39.48-1984).

10 9 8 7 6 5 4 3 2 1

UIC

The University of Illinois at Chicago

China Statistics Archives
Suite 700 South
1033 West Van Buren Street
Chicago, Illinois 60607-9940

CSICSC

China Statistical Information and
Consultancy Service Center

38 Yuetan Nanjie, Sanlihe,
Beijing, People's Republic of China

TABLE OF CONTENTS

Section II
Total Output Value of Rural Society

Section VI
Rural Financial Statistics

Section VII
Income and Living Expenditure of Rural Households

Section VIII
Rural Production Conditions

Section III

Output of Major Farm Crops, Livestock, and Township and Village Enterprises' Industrial Products

Section IX
Rural Culture, Education, Health Care and Social Welfare

Section X
The Ranking of Regions by Selected Indicators

Section XI
Selected Indicators at County Level

PREFACE AND ACKNOWLEDGMENTS

China Rural Statistics 1988 was compiled to offer essential basic information on China's rural economic and social development and the outcome of rural reform. There are eleven sections: Rural Basic Statistics; Total Output Value of Rural Society; Output of Major Farm Crops; Livestock; and Township and Village Enterprises' Industrial Products; Rural Commerce; Rural Economic Efficiency; Rural Financial Statistics; Income and Living Expenditure of Rural Households; Rural Production Conditions; Rural Culture; Education; Health Care; and Social Welfare; The Ranking of Regions by Selected Indicators; and Selected Indicators at County Level.

Compared with the **China Rural Statistics** for the previous years (Chinese edition), the data in this volume has increased substantially, and the presentation has been improved. The regional and county level data in the last two sections are provided for the first time.

Statistical Bureau of the People's Republic of China

China Rural Statistics 1988 is a revised and improved English language edition of the official China Statistical Abstract published by the State Statistical Bureau of the People's Republic of China (SSB). The SSB compiled the statistics contained in this volume. The English Language Editorial Board was responsible for the translation and annotation of this volume. The English Language Editorial Board is composed of representatives of the China Statistical Information and Consultancy Service Center, an affiliate of the SSB, and the China Statistics Archives, a research center at the University of Illinois at Chicago.

This is the fourth volume in a series of statistical annuals which are published by Praeger Publishers. The volumes published or in print are **China Statistics Abstract 1988**, **China Social Statistics 1986**, and **China Trade and Price Statistics 1988**. Other volumes will include the **China Urban Yearbook 1988**, and **China Industrial Yearbook 1988**.

The China Statistics Archives also publishes **China Statistics Monthly**, which is available on a quarterly diskette.

English Language Editorial Board

CHINA

RURAL

STATISTICS

1988

Section I

RURAL BASIC STATISTICS

1.1 *RURAL GRASS ROOTS UNITS*

Item	Unit	1986	1987
Number of Rural Townships and Towns		71521	68490
Township Governments		61766	58210
Minority Autonomous Governments		3746	3248
Town Governments		9755	10280
Minority Autonomous Governments		113	174
Village Boards*		847894	830302
Rural Households, Population and Labor Force			
Number of Rural Households	1,000	195750	201683
Total Rural Population	1,000	850070	857131
Rural Labor Force	1,000	379900	390004

Note:
*** The village boards are organized by village residents voluntarily for handling local problems, such as security and disputes among residents.**

1.2 *NUMBER OF STATE-RUN AGRICULTURAL INSTITUTIONS*

Year	Agricultural Technical Stations	Livestock Breeding Stations	Livestock Veterinary Stations	Seed Stations and Seed Companies	Demonstration and Breeding Farms for Improved Seed Strains
1980	15114	533	5530	2436	2404
1985	14242	793	8020	2487	2363
1986	14425	552	7273	2582	2356
1987	15167	443	7243	2644	2331

1.3 NUMBER OF RURAL GRASS ROOTS UNITS BY REGION 1987

Region	Rural Townships and Towns	Township Governments		Town Governments		Village Boards	Households (1,000)	Total Rural Population (1,000)	Rural Labor Force (1,000)
		Total	Minority Autonomous Governments	Total	Minority Autonomous Governments				
Total	**68490**	**58210**	**3248**	**10280**	**174**	**830302**	**201683**	**857131**	**390004**
Beijing	290	279	4	11		4167	1157	3889	1898
Tianjin	222	198		24		3876	976	3831	1762
Hebei	3674	3108	269	566	14	50459	12043	48776	21642
Shanxi	1928	1441		487		32370	5340	21179	8228
Inner Mongolia	1533	1308	24	225	1	13690	3122	13887	5158
Liaoning	1220	804	140	416	55	15672	5589	22042	8298
Jilin	908	640	26	268	4	10190	3209	14469	5147
Heilongjiang	1172	827	50	345	2	14511	3889	18422	4882
Shanghai	210	197		13		3028	1368	4232	2599
Jiangsu	1902	1594		308		36101	13763	51787	26910
Zhejiang	3213	2568	16	645	1	43468	9593	34666	19551
Anhui	3389	3025	3	364		31417	10686	45342	20812
Fujian	972	755	11	217		14659	5029	23503	9259
Jiangxi	1949	1755	2	194		20204	5777	28709	12769
Shandong	2481	1670	4	811	3	89294	17148	68058	31496
Henan	2112	1826	12	286	8	46976	15531	69473	30963
Hubei	2075	1250	9	825	2	32754	9177	39591	16992
Hunan	3310	2896	84	414		48117	12773	49909	23893
Guangdong	1945	479	70	1466	51	25440	11270	53076	23806
Guangxi	1340	1060	60	280		14665	6888	35316	16373
Sichuan	8564	7948	111	616	6	76204	23081	90738	45513
Guizhou	3864	3535	537	329	10	25831	5635	26784	12044
Yunnan	12513	12030	1677	483	6	102318	6143	30791	15207
Tibet	2079	2071	8	8	8	10149	326	1794	902
Shaanxi	2611	2231		380		32506	5884	25481	10969
Gansu	1511	1354	45	157		17479	3518	17546	7602
Qinghai	429	404	46	25	1	3970	525	2911	1246
Ningxia	281	246		35		2445	610	3266	1288
Xinjiang	793	711	40	82	2	8342	1636	7663	2795

1.4 *NUMBER OF STATE-RUN AGRICULTURAL INSTITUTIONS BY REGION* *1987*

Region	Agricultural Technical Stations	Livestock Breeding Stations	Veterinary Stations	Seed Stations and Seed Companies	Seed Demonstration and Breeding Farms
National Total	**15167**	**443**	**7243**	**2644**	**2331**
Beijing	4	6	16	15	13
Tianjin	12	5	12	12	7
Hebei	325	94	242	163	154
Shanxi	119	9	29	119	110
Inner Mongolia	263	22	344	98	62
Liaoning	718	3	162	72	63
Jilin	924	20	66	51	48
Heilongjiang	1197	18	985	115	117
Shanghai	18		11	11	14
Jiangsu	152	1	89	80	125
Zhejiang	559	16	116	85	84
Anhui	663	9	122	121	143
Fujian	1026	5	938	87	66
Jiangxi	170	4	98	87	92
Shandong	193	34		140	142
Henan	1313	70	611	305	125
Hubei	1475	7	294	154	110
Hunan	1246	3	48	52	87
Guangdong	1504	13	130	24	92
Guangxi	1275	12	479	96	77
Sichuan	480	3	229	206	171
Guizhou	688	21	571	94	64
Yunnan	177	24	230	127	79
Tibet			54	2	1
Shaanxi	336	16	193	119	109
Gansu	94	4	239	88	87
Qinghai	32		241	13	19
Ningxia	25	1	41	19	20
Xinjiang	179	23	653	89	50

1.5 NUMBER OF STATE FARMS, AND STAFF AND WORKERS UNDER LAND RECLAMATION AGENCY BY REGION

	Number of Farms			Number of Staff and Workers (1,000)		
Region	1980	1986	1987	1980	1986	1987
Total	**2093**	**2069**	**2124**	**4586**	**5095**	**5130**
Beijing	16	16	16	43	60	61
Tianjin	15	16	17	16	27	28
Hebei	33	32	32	123	128	136
Shanxi	34	31	30	09	09	09
Inner Mongolia	127	118	118	154	184	194
Liaoning	124	121	123	290	316	315
Jilin	134	141	143	68	79	83
Heilongjiang	103	101	106	653	757	746
Shanghai	30	28	28	186	138	129
Jiangsu	32	31	31	147	165	167
Zhejiang	70	66	66	42	37	39
Anhui	25	25	25	72	75	72
Fujian	124	122	123	69	74	74
Jiangxi	158	142	142	248	233	246
Shandong	18	17	17	12	08	08
Henan	94	94	94	40	41	40
Hubei	48	49	49	385	400	403
Hunan	88	81	81	224	242	254
Guangdong	145	156	152	573	693	689
Guangxi	49	49	49	81	81	83
Sichuan	140	135	134	27	28	29
Guizhou	41	46	46	13	15	13
Yunnan	35	44	45	130	131	134
Tibet	9	5		19	06	
Shaanxi	18	19	20	17	23	22
Gansu	26	18	18	34	37	40
Qinghai	20	16	15	10	08	07
Ningxia	14	15	15	37	44	44
Xinjiang	323	335	389	864	1056	1063

1.6 *NUMBER AND EMPLOYMENT OF NEW RURAL ECONOMIC ASSOCIATIONS* BY SECTOR*

Sector	Number of Associations (1,000)		Employment (1,000)	
	1986	1987	1986	1987
Total	478.1	484.1	4224.8	4267.2
Farming	11.0	9.7	84.9	72.4
Forestry	4.5	4.3	33.5	33.2
Animal Husbandry	4.4	4.5	22.3	20.2
Fishery	58.8	65.3	341.2	366.0
Industry	230.4	236.3	2542.2	2595.6
Construction	34.2	34.7	598.5	589.7
Transportation	70.1	63.6	256.2	249.8
Commerce, Food Services and Service Trade	47.9	48.6	224.2	226.1
Other	16.8	17.1	121.8	114.2

Note:
*** Rural economic associations (Nongchun Xin Jingji Lianheti) refer to the economic organizations that farmers voluntarily joined since 1979, to deal with farm crops production, processing farm crops, selling products and other business. The members of these associations jointly manage the associations and share the costs and benefits.**

1.7 NUMBER AND EMPLOYMENT OF NEW RURAL ECONOMIC ASSOCIATIONS BY REGION

Region	Number of Associations		Employment (person)	
	1986	1987	1986	1987
Total	**478134**	**404050**	**4224788**	**4267222**
Beijing	211	195	2983	2019
Tianjin	5956	6103	60772	50630
Hebei	108229	114122	865956	959814
Shanxi	7523	6407	94648	86215
Inner Mongolia	1538	1653	17907	22591
Liaoning	13788	10540	97451	75997
Jilin	2094	1713	17742	15083
Heilongjiang	1436	942	13842	10753
Shanghai	120	123	2041	1890
Jiangsu	16325	14883	130792	120010
Zhejiang	44487	47218	376728	365341
Anhui	22869	22730	196066	204886
Fujian	25822	35354	212641	257570
Jiangxi	10009	10073	78121	74764
Shandong	48488	46323	425969	365984
Henan	46391	47754	522306	563721
Hubei	9970	7356	87650	65753
Hunan	14486	13872	121280	122590
Guangdong	41225	45136	345716	379480
Guangxi	4127	4086	43367	45174
Sichuan	25084	22096	195124	185106
Guizhou	3366	3724	38352	39103
Yunnan	7311	5534	65148	
Tibet				
Shaanxi	9305	9010	107891	113493
Gansu	7273	6467	92221	76072
Qinghai	268	205	4226	3016
Ningxia	284	295	5012	4045
Xinjiang	149	136	2836	2478

1.8 NUMBER AND EMPLOYMENT OF TOWNSHIP AND VILLAGE-RUN ENTERPRISES

Item	1980	1985	1986	1987	1987 as Percentage of 1986
Total Number of Enterprises	1425	1569	1517	1579	104.0
Agriculture	378	224	240	231	96.4
Industry	758	855	878	969	110.5
Transportation	90	106	79	69	87.3
Construction	51	83	76	74	96.8
Others	148	301	245	235	95.9
Township-run Enterprises					
Agriculture	54	33	32	31	96.9
Industry	199	239	256	257	100.4
Transportation	27	25	23	20	87.0
Construction	24	36	36	35	97.2
Others	33	86	79	76	96.2
Total Employment	29997	41521	43915	47025	107.1
Agriculture	4561	2524	2408	2441	101.4
Industry	19423	27821	30413	33390	109.8
Transportation	1136	1142	1098	1066	97.1
Construction	3346	7899	8069	8284	102.7
Others	1530	2135	1927	1844	95.7
Township-run Enterprises					
Agriculture	1207	622	595	592	99.5
Industry	9125	13277	14736	15742	106.8
Transportation	627	624	638	599	93.9
Construction	2504	5740	5962	6146	103.1
Others	475	844	818	766	93.6

1.9 *NUMBER AND EMPLOYMENT OF TOWNSHIP AND VILLAGE-RUN ENTERPRISES BY REGION*

	Number of Enterprises (1,000)			Employment (1,000)		
Region	1980	1986	1987	1980	1986	1987
Total	**1424.7**	**1517**	**1579**	**29997**	**43915**	**47025**
Beijing	5.3	16	17	314	819	843
Tianjin	4.0	10	11	302	648	693
Hebei	113.3	87	85	1886	2366	2532
Shanxi	75.1	59	57	883	1245	1269
Inner Mongolia	16.2	29	11	65	312	301
Liaoning	33.2	53	54	1117	1965	2020
Jilin	16.7	21	24	378	540	600
Heilongjiang	20.0	24	27	485	586	621
Shanghai	5.2	13	11	699	1359	1300
Jiangsu	75.6	104	125	3886	6756	7298
Zhejiang	78.0	99	94	2349	3971	4027
Anhui	43.5	57	58	864	1558	1678
Fujian	42.0	61	53	1174	1307	1349
Jiangxi	43.8	55	56	838	943	960
Shandong	187.5	209	182	3343	4975	5334
Henan	70.8	63	78	1608	2168	2496
Hubei	111.8	122	133	1527	1967	2078
Hunan	126.0	107	111	1994	2055	2220
Guangdong	86.4	86	122	2008	2594	3144
Guangxi	31.3	22	25	593	487	514
Sichuan	119.3	122	127	1730	2646	2864
Guizhou	17.5	12	11	201	258	262
Yunnan	20.8	17	33	421	564	724
Tibet		1			5	
Shaanxi	42.1	43	49	628	953	1030
Gansu	18.2	12	13	226	500	534
Qinghai	3.3	2	2	38	74	65
Ningxia	5.7	3	3	51	73	76
Xinjiang	12.1	9	9	194	223	192

1.10 *NUMBER AND EMPLOYMENT OF REGISTERED HOUSEHOLDS INDIVIDUALLY RUNNING NON-AGRICULTURAL BUSINESSES*

(1,000)

Item	1981	1985	1986	1987	1988
Total Number of Households	961	8916	9201	10342	1224
Total Employment	1219	13823	14383	16660	1158
Industry					
Number of Households	125	1249	1262	1467	1162
Employment	172	2549	2684	3436	1280
Commerce					
Number of Households	380	4645	4809	5400	1123
Employment	446	6363	6640	7597	1144
Food Services					
Number of Households	186	771	810	890	1099
Employment	277	1393	1489	1677	1126
Transportation					
Number of Households	8	881	900	1116	1240
Employment	10	399	1389	1640	1180
Other Businesses					
Number of Households	262	1370	1420	1469	1035
Employment	314	2119	2181	2309	1059

1.11 SELECTED RURAL AGGREGATE INDICATORS

Year	Rural Total Output Value of Society (1,000,000,000 yuan)	As Percentage of National Total Output Value	Gross Output Value of Agriculture (1,000,000,000 yuan)	As Percentage of Gross Output Value of Industry and Agriculture
1980	279.212	32.7	192.260	27.2
1985	634.004	38.9	361.949	27.1
1986	755.423	39.8	401.301	26.4
1987	943.161	40.9	467.600	25.3

SELECTED RURAL AGGREGATE INDICATORS
(continued)

Year	Net Output Value (1,000,000,000 yuan)	As Pecentage of National Income	Agricultural Taxes (1,000,000,000 yuan)	As Percentage of Total Government Revenue	Value of Rural Retail Sales (1,000,000,000 yuan)	As Percentage of Total Retail Sales of Society
1980	249.17	36.5	2.77	2.6	118.97	55.6
1985	272.01	34.9	4.21	2.3	251.70	58.5
1986	315.39	33.9	4.45	2.0	285.60	57.7
1987			4.97	2.1	335.00	57.6

Section II

TOTAL OUTPUT VALUE OF RURAL SOCIETY

2.1 *TOTAL OUTPUT VALUE OF RURAL SOCIETY AND ITS COMPOSITION*

(at current prices) (1,000,000,000 yuan)

	National Total		East Economic Zone***		Middle Economic Zone***		West Economic Zone***	
Year	1980	1987	1980	1987	1980	1987	1980	1987
Total Rural Output Value of Society	279.212	943.161	137.896	534.545	93.374	276.539	47.942	132.077
Gross Output Value of Agriculture	192.260	467.570	84.383	215.838	69.384	163.335	38.493	88.397
Gross Output Value of Rural Industry*	54.396	328.486	36.362	237.048	13.207	66.642	4.827	24.796
Gross Output Value of Rural Construction	17.997	72.331	9.290	43.661	6.243	20.587	2.464	8.083
Gross Output Value of Rural Transportation	4.714	33.447	2.402	15.848	1.666	12.836	0.646	4.763
Gross Output Value of Rural Commerce**	9.845	41.327	5.459	22.150	2.874	13.139	1.512	6.038
Percentage								
Total Rural Output Value of Society	100.0	100.0	100.0	100.0	100.0	100.0	100.0	100.0
Gross Output Value of Agriculture	68.9	49.6	61.2	40.4	74.3	59.1	80.3	66.9
Gross Output Value of Rural Industry*	19.5	34.8	26.4	44.3	14.1	24.1	10.1	18.8
Gross Output Value of Rural Construction	6.4	7.7	6.7	8.2	6.7	7.4	5.1	6.1
Gross Output Value of Rural Transportation	1.7	3.5	1.7	3.0	1.8	4.6	1.3	3.6
Gross Output Value of Rural Commerce**	3.5	4.4	4.0	4.1	3.1	4.8	3.2	4.6

Note:
*** Including village run industrial enterprises.**

**** Including food services.**

***** The east economic zone includes Beijing, Tianjin, Hebei, Liaoning, Shanghai, Jiangsu, Zhejiang, Fujian, Shandong, Guangdong and Guangxi. The middle economic zone includes Shanxi, Inner Mongolia, Jilin, Heilongjiang, Anhui, Jiangxi, Henan, Hubei and Hunan. The west economic zone includes Sichuan, Guizhou, Yunnan, Tibet, Shaanxi, Gansu, Qinghai, Ningxia and Xinjiang.**

2.2 *RURAL TOTAL OUTPUT VALUE BY REGION*
(at current prices) (1,000,000,000 yuan)

Region	1980	1985	1987
Total	**279.212**	**755.423**	**943.161**
Beijing	3.040	9.818	12.413
Tianjin	2.013	8.633	11.854
Hebei	15.148	37.830	47.700
Shanxi	6.580	15.291	16.617
Inner Mongolia	4.023	9.542	11.124
Liaoning	11.320	31.804	40.835
Jilin	6.403	15.058	19.721
Heilongjiang	10.135	20.240	22.280
Shanghai	5.425	16.401	21.644
Jiangsu	27.408	96.386	124.503
Zhejiang	15.487	54.732	70.572
Anhui	11.019	33.504	40.437
Fujian	6.407	19.110	24.242
Jiangxi	9.279	19.126	22.311
Shandong	25.765	68.776	87.084
Henan	19.171	46.016	60.432
Hubei	12.602	35.961	42.843
Hunan	14.162	33.666	40.774
Guangdong	18.096	56.674	75.356
Guangxi	7.787	15.859	18.342
Sichuan	22.783	51.700	61.786
Guizhou	4.309	10.796	12.156
Yunnan	5.965	12.876	15.092
Tibet	0.564	1.073	1.131
Shaanxi	5.643	15.095	18.507
Gansu	3.296	7.974	9.550
Qinghai	1.003	1.853	2.004
Ningxia	0.804	1.919	2.124
Xinjiang	3.575	7.910	9.727

2.3 *GROSS OUTPUT VALUE OF AGRICULTURE BY REGION*
(at current prices) (1,000,000,000 yuan)

Region	1980	1985	1987
Total	**192.260**	**401.301**	**467.570**
Beijing	1.430	2.814	3.442
Tianjin	0.768	2.692	3.293
Hebei	9.779	17.438	20.066
Shanxi	3.823	5.882	6.142
Inner Mongolia	3.078	7.725	8.774
Liaoning	7.356	14.203	16.922
Jilin	4.827	9.843	12.081
Heilongjiang	8.561	13.717	13.700
Shanghai	1.874	3.376	3.884
Jiangsu	13.845	33.267	38.025
Zhejiang	9.280	19.204	22.812
Anhui	8.463	22.192	25.534
Fujian	4.548	10.707	13.297
Jiangxi	6.815	12.479	14.435
Shandong	17.342	36.118	41.318
Henan	13.291	25.949	32.362
Hubei	9.412	21.910	24.968
Hunan	11.114	22.268	25.339
Guangdong	11.931	31.486	38.987
Guangxi	6.230	11.869	13.792
Sichuan	18.271	33.898	38.894
Guizhou	3.604	7.931	9.225
Yunnan	4.592	9.601	11.125
Tibet	0.559	0.992	1.029
Shaanxi	4.230	8.720	10.339
Gansu	2.729	5.640	6.551
Qinghai	0.778	1.411	1.594
Ningxia	0.642	1.416	1.476
Xinjiang	3.088	6.553	8.164

2.4 GROSS OUTPUT VALUE OF RURAL INDUSTRY BY REGION

(at current prices) (1,000,000,000 yuan)

Region	1980	1985	1987
Total	**54.396**	**238.079**	**328.486**
Beijing	1.080	4.905	6.490
Tianjin	1.021	4.624	6.798
Hebei	3.342	14.532	20.368
Shanxi	1.699	6.268	6.949
Inner Mongolia	0.400	0.727	0.928
Liaoning	2.692	13.056	18.138
Jilin	0.822	2.842	4.433
Heilongjiang	1.061	3.304	4.318
Shanghai	2.836	10.759	14.430
Jiangsu	10.928	50.141	69.724
Zhejiang	3.988	27.883	37.689
Anhui	1.092	6.718	8.859
Fujian	1.119	5.276	7.135
Jiangxi	1.065	3.803	4.281
Shandong	4.955	21.709	32.329
Henan	3.243	12.047	16.720
Hubei	1.781	8.128	10.815
Hunan	2.044	6.380	9.339
Guangdong	3.652	14.202	21.627
Guangxi	0.749	1.678	2.320
Sichuan	2.634	10.569	14.091
Guizhou	0.237	1.410	1.582
Yunnan	0.561	1.520	1.893
Tibet	0.005	0.012	0.032
Shaanxi	0.713	3.702	4.792
Gansu	0.316	1.047	1.380
Qinghai	0.060	0.147	0.169
Ningxia	0.083	0.224	0.309
Xinjiang	0.218	0.466	0.548

2.5 GROSS OUTPUT VALUE OF RURAL CONSTRUCTION BY REGION

(at current prices) (1,000,000,000 yuan)

Region	1980	1985	1987
Total	**17.997**	**59.193**	**72.331**
Beijing	0.160	1.151	1.058
Tianjin	0.073	0.461	0.623
Hebei	1.155	3.402	3.904
Shanxi	0.552	1.220	1.309
Inner Mongolia	0.245	0.462	0.605
Liaoning	0.425	1.694	2.150
Jilin	0.340	1.127	1.377
Heilongjiang	0.264	1.394	1.675
Shanghai	0.451	1.445	2.261
Jiangsu	1.455	7.696	9.935
Zhejiang	1.488	4.360	6.350
Anhui	0.939	2.360	2.805
Fujian	0.307	1.273	1.533
Jiangxi	1.118	1.543	1.807
Shandong	2.319	6.434	7.687
Henan	1.674	3.849	4.930
Hubei	0.823	2.771	3.218
Hunan	0.288	2.479	2.861
Guangdong	1.114	5.428	7.182
Guangxi	0.343	1.197	0.978
Sichuan	0.872	3.339	3.821
Guizhou	0.293	0.709	0.481
Yunnan	0.436	0.910	0.995
Tibet		0.023	0.020
Shaanxi	0.366	1.214	1.377
Gansu	0.183	0.588	0.739
Qinghai	0.125	0.144	0.102
Ningxia	0.045	0.079	0.092
Xinjiang	0.144	0.441	0.456

2.6 GROSS OUTPUT VALUE OF RURAL TRANSPORTATION BY REGION

(at current prices) (1,000,000,000 yuan)

Region	1980	1985	1987
Total	**4.714**	**24.540**	**33.447**
Beijing	0.260	0.498	0.733
Tianjin	0.100	0.569	0.704
Hebei	0.324	0.548	1.278
Shanxi	0.263	1.315	1.478
Inner Mongolia	0.123	0.313	0.399
Liaoning	0.384	1.370	1.701
Jilin	0.135	0.530	0.865
Heilongjiang	0.029	1.095	1.558
Shanghai	0.094	0.225	0.316
Jiangsu	0.309	2.544	3.306
Zhejiang	0.156	1.288	0.480
Anhui	0.088	0.806	1.520
Fujian	0.081	0.898	1.147
Jiangxi	0.172	0.637	0.797
Shandong	0.228	1.634	2.214
Henan	0.314	2.034	3.258
Hubei	0.099	1.275	1.595
Hunan	0.443	1.053	1.366
Guangdong	0.340	1.931	2.576
Guangxi	0.126	0.339	0.393
Sichuan	0.195	1.537	2.033
Guizhou	0.039	0.320	0.374
Yunnan	0.184	0.329	0.455
Tibet		0.023	0.021
Shaanxi	0.135	0.712	0.980
Gansu	0.033	0.307	0.428
Qinghai	0.012	0.077	0.074
Ningxia	0.005	0.154	0.188
Xinjiang	0.043	0.179	0.210

2.7 GROSS OUTPUT VALUE OF RURAL COMMERCE BY REGION

(at current prices) (1,000,000,000 yuan)

Region	1980	1985	1987
Total	**9.845**	**32.310**	**41.327**
Beijing	0.110	0.450	0.690
Tianjin	0.051	0.287	0.436
Hebei	0.548	1.910	2.084
Shanxi	0.243	0.606	0.739
Inner Mongolia	0.177	0.315	0.418
Liaoning	0.463	1.481	1.924
Jilin	0.279	0.716	0.965
Heilongjiang	0.220	0.730	1.029
Shanghai	0.170	0.596	0.753
Jiangsu	0.871	2.738	3.513
Zhejiang	0.575	1.997	2.241
Anhui	0.437	1.228	1.719
Fujian	0.352	0.956	1.130
Jiangxi	0.109	0.664	0.991
Shandong	0.921	2.881	3.536
Henan	0.649	2.137	3.162
Hubei	0.487	1.877	2.247
Hunan	0.273	1.486	1.869
Guangdong	1.059	3.627	4.984
Guangxi	0.339	0.776	0.859
Sichuan	0.811	2.357	2.947
Guizhou	0.136	0.426	0.494
Yunnan	0.192	0.516	0.624
Tibet		0.023	0.029
Shaanxi	0.199	0.747	1.019
Gansu	0.035	0.392	0.452
Qinghai	0.028	0.074	0.065
Ningxia	0.029	0.046	0.059
Xinjiang	0.082	0.271	0.349

2.8 *OUTPUT VALUE OF AGRICULTURE BY ECONOMIC ZONE*
(at current prices) (1,000,000,000 yuan)

	National Total		East Economic Zone*		Middle Economic Zone*		West Economic Zone*	
	1980	1987	1980	1987	1980	1987	1980	1987
Gross Agricultural Output Value	401.301	467.570	183.174	215.838	141.965	163.335	76.162	88.397
Crop Farming	249.830	283.793	109.366	125.533	94.053	105.738	46.411	52.522
Forestry	20.119	22.198	8.657	9.687	7.150	7.972	4.312	4.539
Animal Husbandry	87.354	106.578	38.935	47.173	28.981	34.963	19.438	24.442
Sideline Occupation	27.562	32.515	13.752	16.136	8.410	10.280	5.400	6.099
Fishery	16.436	22.486	12.464	17.309	3.371	4.382	0.601	0.795
Percentage								
Gross Agricultural Output Value	100.0	100.0	100.0	100.0	100.0	100.0	100.0	100.0
Crop Farming	62.2	60.7	59.7	58.1	66.3	64.7	60.9	59.4
Forestry	5.0	4.7	4.7	4.5	5.0	4.9	5.7	5.1
Animal Husbandry	21.8	22.8	21.3	21.9	20.4	21.4	25.5	27.7
Sideline Occupation	6.9	7.0	7.5	7.5	5.9	6.3	7.1	6.9
Fishery	4.1	4.8	6.8	8.0	2.4	2.7	0.8	0.9

Note:
***The east economic zone includes Beijing, Tianjin, Hebei, Liaoning, Shanghai, Jiangsu, Zhejiang, Fujian, Shandong, Guangdong and Guangxi. The middle economic zone includes Shanxi, Inner Mongolia, Jilin, Heilongjiang, Anhui, Jiangxi, Henan, Hubei and Hunan. The west economic zone includes Sichuan, Guizhou, Yunnan, Tibet, Shaanxi, Gansu, Qinghai, Ningxia and Xinjiang.**

2.9 *OUTPUT VALUE OF AGRICULTURE BY REGION*

(at current prices) (1,000,000,000 yuan)

	Gross Output Value of Agriculture					
	Total		Crop Farming		Forestry	
Region	*1986*	*1987*	*1986*	*1987*	*1986*	*1987*
Total	**401.301**	**467.570**	**249.830**	**283.793**	**20.119**	**22.198**
Beijing	2.814	3.442	1.631	1.912	0.080	0.080
Tianjin	2.692	3.293	1.714	2.024	0.032	0.037
Hebei	17.438	20.066	12.524	13.780	0.582	0.683
Shanxi	5.882	6.142	4.224	4.236	0.362	0.337
Inner Mongolia	7.725	8.774	4.028	4.506	0.437	0.363
Liaoning	14.203	16.922	8.447	9.610	0.419	0.486
Jilin	9.843	12.081	7.070	8.612	0.294	0.293
Heilongjiang	13.717	13.700	10.167	9.975	0.636	0.669
Shanghai	3.376	3.884	1.683	1.769	0.024	0.034
Jiangsu	33.267	38.025	21.151	22.811	0.515	0.602
Zhejiang	19.204	22.812	10.100	11.391	0.926	1.161
Anhui	21.192	25.534	15.587	17.615	0.899	1.088
Fujian	10.707	13.297	4.972	6.003	1.029	1.357
Jiangxi	12.479	14.435	6.970	7.976	0.966	1.087
Shandong	36.118	41.318	25.592	29.905	1.267	1.211
Henan	25.949	32.362	18.365	22.974	1.292	1.324
Hubei	21.910	24.968	14.679	16.013	0.875	0.997
Hunan	22.268	25.339	12.963	13.831	1.389	1.814
Guangdong	31.486	38.987	15.428	18.994	2.749	3.082
Guangxi	11.869	13.792	6.124	7.334	1.034	0.954
Sichuan	33.898	38.894	20.650	22.722	1.737	1.773
Guizhou	7.931	9.225	4.437	5.153	0.527	0.550
Yunnan	9.601	11.125	5.179	6.175	0.740	0.885
Tibet	0.992	1.029	0.353	0.364	0.016	0.015
Shaanxi	8.720	10.339	5.945	6.929	0.560	0.613
Gansu	5.640	6.551	3.729	4.184	0.314	0.345
Qinghai	1.411	1.594	0.633	0.703	0.070	0.066
Ningxia	1.416	1.476	1.007	1.040	0.065	0.044
Xinjiang	6.553	8.364	4.478	5.252	0.256	0.248

OUTPUT VALUE OF AGRICULTURE BY REGION

(at current prices) (1,000,000,000 yuan) (continued)

	Gross Output Value of Agriculture					
	Animal Husbandry		Sideline Production		Fishery	
Region	*1986*	*1987*	*1986*	*1987*	*1986*	*1987*
Total	**87.354**	**106.578**	**27.562**	**32.515**	**16.436**	**22.486**
Beijing	0.939	1.224	0.095	0.121	0.069	0.105
Tianjin	0.567	0.722	0.165	0.223	0.214	0.287
Hebei	3.328	4.363	0.718	0.811	0.286	0.429
Shanxi	1.023	1.236	0.263	0.319	0.010	0.014
Inner Mongolia	2.399	2.902	0.807	0.938	0.054	0.065
Liaoning	3.231	3.958	1.051	1.226	1.055	1.642
Jilin	1.855	2.340	0.540	0.708	0.084	0.128
Heilongjiang	2.236	2.282	0.476	0.520	0.202	0.254
Shanghai	1.275	1.548	0.049	0.054	0.345	0.479
Jiangsu	6.947	8.745	2.293	3.029	2.261	2.838
Zhejiang	4.003	4.945	2.203	2.724	1.972	2.591
Anhui	4.119	4.933	1.046	1.168	0.541	0.730
Fujian	2.198	2.771	1.108	1.209	1.400	1.957
Jiangxi	2.911	3.433	1.205	1.416	0.427	0.523
Shandong	6.282	6.413	1.360	1.473	1.617	2.316
Henan	4.212	5.111	1.930	2.762	0.150	0.191
Hubei	4.386	5.486	0.893	1.053	1.077	1.419
Hunan	5.840	7.240	1.250	1.396	0.826	1.058
Guangdong	6.841	8.532	3.611	4.208	2.857	4.171
Guangxi	3.324	3.952	0.999	1.058	0.388	0.494
Sichuan	9.408	11.848	1.690	2.015	0.413	0.536
Guizhou	2.003	2.419	0.916	1.046	0.048	0.057
Yunnan	2.614	2.942	0.996	1.028	0.072	0.095
Tibet	0.536	0.562	0.087	0.088		
Shaanxi	1.395	1.881	0.797	0.879	0.023	0.037
Gansu	1.253	1.585	0.315	0.431	0.002	0.006
Qinghai	0.501	0.684	0.052	0.139	0.005	0.002
Ningxia	0.282	0.322	0.051	0.051	0.011	0.019
Xinjiang	1.336	2.199	0.455	0.422	0.028	0.043

2.10 *OUTPUT VALUE OF GRAIN CROPS AND INDUSTRIAL CROPS*
(at current prices) (1,000,000,000 yuan)

	1980	1985	1986	1987
Output Value of Crop Farming	137.815	227.980	249.830	283.793
Grain Crops	100.054	142.178	158.132	170.512
Main Products	84.343	122.609	137.339	147.982
By-products	15.711	19.569	20.793	22.530
Industrial Crops	21.637	46.757	44.637	53.107
Main Products	20.397	43.562	41.786	49.831
By-products	1.240	3.195	2.851	3.276
Other Crops	16.124	39.045	47.041	60.174
Percentage				
Output Value of Crop Farming	100.0	100.0	100.0	100.0
Grain Crops	72.6	62.4	63.3	60.1
Main Products	61.2	53.8	55.0	52.1
By-products	11.4	8.6	8.3	7.9
Industrial Crops	15.7	20.5	17.9	18.7
Main Products	14.8	19.1	16.7	17.6
By-products	0.9	1.4	1.2	1.2
Other Crops	11.7	17.1	18.8	21.2

2.11 *OUTPUT VALUE OF GRAIN CROPS AND INDUSTRIAL CROPS BY REGION*

(at current prices) (1,000,000,000 yuan)

Region	Output Value of Crop Farming		Grain Crops		Industrial Crops	
	1986	1987	1986	1987	1986	1987
Total	**2498.30**	**2837.93**	**1581.32**	**1705.12**	**446.37**	**531.07**
Beijing	16.31	19.12	9.41	9.76	0.45	0.49
Tianjin	17.14	20.24	8.94	9.80	1.35	1.42
Hebei	125.24	137.80	74.48	75.28	26.38	31.96
Shanxi	42.24	42.36	28.74	27.94	6.24	6.19
Inner Mongolia	40.28	45.06	26.22	30.20	8.89	8.98
Liaoning	84.47	96.10	57.41	62.91	6.19	5.19
Jilin	70.70	86.12	56.48	68.15	8.46	9.78
Heilongjiang	101.67	99.75	83.26	80.88	9.25	9.38
Shanghai	16.83	17.69	9.90	9.67	2.93	3.32
Jiangsu	211.51	228.11	147.29	150.86	31.06	35.27
Zhejiang	101.00	113.91	59.69	63.78	11.32	11.13
Anhui	155.87	176.15	106.32	114.73	26.67	31.39
Fujian	49.72	60.03	26.61	31.34	8.14	8.42
Jiangxi	69.70	79.76	46.22	53.45	8.80	10.45
Shandong	255.92	299.05	145.93	156.50	66.05	87.56
Henan	183.65	229.74	126.64	146.73	34.71	53.44
Hubei	146.79	160.13	89.84	96.28	35.49	35.71
Hunan	129.63	138.31	80.49	82.76	22.85	23.10
Guangdong	154.28	189.94	69.89	82.99	33.92	39.73
Guangxi	61.24	73.74	32.62	37.23	14.79	16.85
Sichuan	206.50	227.22	134.72	142.24	33.38	37.33
Guizhou	44.37	51.53	26.82	29.02	9.25	11.28
Yunnan	51.79	61.75	29.77	31.64	10.66	15.54
Tibet	3.53	3.64	3.11	3.23	0.13	0.13
Shaanxi	59.45	69.29	41.53	45.72	6.35	7.86
Gansu	37.29	41.48	25.29	26.92	5.85	7.10
Qinghai	6.33	7.03	5.04	5.45	0.89	1.01
Ningxia	10.07	10.40	7.12	6.60	1.04	0.96
Xinjiang	44.78	52.52	21.54	23.06	14.88	20.10

2.12 *PERCENTAGE OF OUTPUT VALUE OF GRAIN CROPS AND INDUSTRIAL CROPS*

(at current prices) (total output value of crop farming = 100)

Region	Grain Crops 1986	Grain Crops 1987	Industrial Crops 1986	Industrial Crops 1987
Nationwide	**63.3**	**60.1**	**17.9**	**18.7**
Beijing	57.7	51.0	2.8	2.6
Tianjin	52.1	48.4	7.9	7.0
Hebei	59.5	54.6	21.0	23.2
Shanxi	68.0	66.0	14.8	14.6
Inner Mongolia	65.1	67.0	22.1	19.9
Liaoning	68.0	65.5	7.3	5.4
Jilin	79.9	79.1	12.0	11.4
Heilongjiang	81.9	81.1	9.1	9.4
Shanghai	58.8	54.6	17.4	18.8
Jiangsu	69.6	66.1	14.7	15.5
Zhejiang	59.1	56.0	11.2	9.8
Anhui	68.2	65.1	17.1	17.8
Fujian	53.5	52.2	16.4	14.0
Jiangxi	66.3	67.0	12.6	13.1
Shandong	57.0	52.3	25.8	29.3
Henan	69.0	63.9	18.9	23.2
Hubei	61.2	60.1	24.2	22.3
Hunan	62.1	59.8	17.6	16.7
Guangdong	45.3	43.7	22.0	20.9
Guangxi	53.3	50.8	24.1	23.0
Sichuan	65.2	62.6	16.2	16.4
Guizhou	60.4	56.3	20.9	21.9
Yunnan	57.5	51.2	20.6	25.2
Tibet	88.1	88.7	3.7	3.6
Shaanxi	69.8	66.0	10.7	11.3
Gansu	67.8	64.3	15.7	17.0
Qinghai	79.6	77.5	14.1	14.4
Ningxia	70.7	63.5	10.3	9.2
Xinjiang	48.1	43.9	33.2	38.3

2.13 *GROSS OUTPUT VALUE OF AGRICULTURE BY BRANCH*

(at current prices)

Branch	Value (1,000,000,000 yuan)		Percentage	
	1986	1987	1986	1987
Gross Output Value of Agriculture	401.301	467.570	100.0	100.0
Output Value of Crop Farming	249.830	283.793	62.2	60.7
Main Products	226.186	257.987	56.4	55.2
Grain Crops	137.339	147.982	34.2	31.6
Industrial Crops	41.786	49.831	10.4	10.7
Vegetables	29.276	37.918	7.3	8.1
Tea, Mulberries and Fruits	13.082	16.778	3.3	3.6
Forage and Green Manure Crops	1.207	1.310	0.3	0.3
Other Crops	3.496	4.168	0.9	0.9
By-products	23.644	25.806	5.9	5.5
Grain Crops	20.793	22.530	5.2	4.8
Industrial Crops	2.851	3.276	0.7	0.7
Output Value of Forestry	20.119	22.198	5.0	4.7
Bamboo and Wood Cutting	7.702	7.747	1.9	1.7
Forest Products	4.856	6.270	1.2	1.3
Wood Growing	7.561	8.181	1.9	1.7
Output Value of Animal Husbandry	87.354	106.578	21.8	22.8
Growing and Increasing Livestock Breeding	56.587	67.474	14.1	14.4
Hogs	46.293	55.391	11.5	11.9
Livestock	7.900	8.615	2.0	1.8
Sheep and Goats	2.394	3.468	0.6	0.7
Fowl Raising	9.085	12.086	2.3	2.6
Products of Livestock and Fowl	18.201	22.950	4.5	4.9
Other Animal Husbandry	3.481	4.068	0.9	0.9
Output Value of Sideline Production	27.562	32.515	6.9	7.0
Collecting	9.406	10.717	2.3	2.3
Hunting	0.217	0.259	0.1	0.1
Household Industry Concurrently Run by Farmers	18.053	21.539	4.5	4.6
Output Value of Fishery	16.436	22.486	4.1	4.8
Seawater Products	7.449	10.878	1.9	2.3
Freshwater Products	8.987	11.608	2.2	2.5

2.14 *MATERIAL CONSUMPTION IN AGRICULTURAL PRODUCTION AND NET OUTPUT VALUE OF AGRICULTURE BY BRANCH*

(at current prices)

Branch	Value (1,000,000,000 yuan)		Percentage	
	1986	1987	1986	1987
Material Consumption	129.296	152.183	100.0	100.0
Crop Farming	69.290	80.492	53.6	52.9
Forestry	4.355	4.745	3.4	3.1
Animal Husbandry	41.738	49.177	32.3	32.3
Sideline Occupation	8.740	10.848	6.7	7.1
Fishery	5.173	6.921	4.0	4.6
Net Output Value of Agriculture	272.005	315.387	100.0	100.0
Crop Farming	180.540	203.301	66.4	64.5
Forestry	15.764	17.453	5.8	5.5
Animal Husbandry	45.616	57.401	16.8	18.2
Sideline Occupation	18.822	21.667	6.9	6.9
Fishery	11.263	15.565	4.1	4.9

2.15 *MATERIAL CONSUMPTION IN AGRICULTURAL PRODUCTION AND NET OUTPUT VALUE OF AGRICULTURE BY REGION* *1987*

(at current prices) (1,000,000,000 yuan)

Region	Material Consumption	Net Output Value of Agriculture	Percentage (grain output value = 100)	
			Material Consumption	Net Output Value
Total	**1521.83**	**3153.87**	**32.5**	**67.5**
Beijing	10.65	23.77	30.9	69.1
Tianjin	13.58	19.35	41.2	58.8
Hebei	65.65	135.01	32.7	67.3
Shanxi	23.79	37.63	38.7	61.3
Inner Mongolia	27.93	59.81	31.8	68.2
Liaoning	61.03	108.19	36.1	63.9
Jilin	40.40	80.41	33.4	66.6
Heilongjiang	49.65	87.35	36.2	63.8
Shanghai	17.56	21.28	45.2	54.8
Jiangsu	141.54	238.71	37.2	62.8
Zhejiang	70.28	157.30	31.0	69.0
Anhui	83.84	171.50	32.8	67.2
Fujian	44.45	88.52	33.4	66.6
Jiangxi	40.96	103.39	28.4	71.6
Shandong	130.23	282.95	31.5	68.5
Henan	109.15	214.47	33.7	66.3
Hubei	65.69	183.99	26.3	73.7
Hunan	69.12	184.27	27.3	72.7
Guangdong	134.97	254.90	34.6	65.4
Guangxi	40.29	97.63	29.2	70.8
Sichuan	124.27	264.67	32.0	68.0
Guizhou	28.06	64.19	30.4	69.6
Yunnan	29.09	82.16	26.1	73.9
Tibet	2.18	8.11	21.2	78.8
Shaanxi	37.09	66.30	35.9	64.1
Gansu	24.85	40.66	37.9	62.1
Qinghai	4.73	11.21	29.7	70.3
Ningxia	4.78	9.98	32.4	67.6
Xinjiang	25.48	56.16	31.2	68.8

2.16 *MATERIAL CONSUMPTION IN AGRICULTURAL PRODUCTION BY BRANCH AND REGION* *1987*

(at current prices) (1,000,000,000 yuan)

Region	Total	Crop Farming	Forestry	Animal Husbandry	Sideline Production	Fishery
Total	**152.183**	**80.492**	**4.745**	**49.177**	**10.848**	**6.921**
Beijing	1.065	0.503	0.016	0.494	0.023	0.029
Tianjin	1.358	0.727	0.016	0.408	0.091	0.116
Hebei	6.565	4.471	0.175	1.414	0.288	0.217
Shanxi	2.379	1.611	0.105	0.579	0.081	0.003
Inner Mongolia	2.793	1.576	0.093	0.930	0.181	0.013
Liaoning	6.103	2.838	0.126	2.137	0.380	0.622
Jilin	4.040	2.722	0.101	1.000	0.178	0.039
Heilongjiang	4.965	3.294	0.227	1.304	0.077	0.063
Shanghai	1.756	0.604	0.015	0.875	0.014	0.248
Jiangsu	14.154	5.643	0.154	5.614	1.770	0.973
Zhejiang	7.082	2.737	0.095	2.219	1.040	0.919
Anhui	8.384	5.243	0.146	2.494	0.390	0.111
Fujian	4.445	1.881	0.257	1.256	0.325	0.726
Jiangxi	4.096	2.060	0.118	1.485	0.369	0.064
Shandong	13.023	8.349	0.241	3.173	0.604	0.656
Henan	10.915	6.661	0.319	2.585	1.309	0.041
Hubei	6.569	3.962	0.208	1.850	0.333	0.216
Hunan	6.912	3.551	0.293	2.723	0.228	0.117
Guangdong	13.497	5.878	0.813	4.110	1.253	1.443
Guangxi	4.029	1.934	0.241	1.550	0.156	0.148
Sichuan	12.427	5.134	0.294	6.280	0.630	0.089
Guizhou	2.806	1.374	0.090	1.087	0.246	0.009
Yunnan	2.909	1.597	0.218	0.859	0.205	0.030
Tibet	0.218	0.116	0.003	0.081	0.018	
Shaanxi	3.709	2.228	0.146	0.956	0.369	0.010
Gansu	2.485	1.533	0.118	0.697	0.135	0.002
Qinghai	0.473	0.267	0.012	0.151	0.042	0.001
Ningxia	0.478	0.336	0.027	0.102	0.008	0.005
Xinjiang	2.548	1.626	0.078	0.692	0.105	0.011

2.17 *NET OUTPUT VALUE OF AGRICULTURE BY BRANCH AND REGION* *1987*

(at current prices) (1,000,000,000 yuan)

Region	Total	Crop Farming	Forestry	Animal Husbandry	Sideline Production	Fishery
Total	**315.387**	**203.301**	**17.453**	**57.401**	**21.667**	**15.565**
Beijing	2.377	1.409	0.064	0.730	0.098	0.076
Tianjin	1.935	1.297	0.021	0.314	0.132	0.171
Hebei	1.301	9.309	0.508	2.949	0.523	0.212
Shanxi	3.763	2.625	0.232	0.657	0.238	0.011
Inner Mongolia	5.981	2.930	0.270	1.972	0.757	0.052
Liaoning	10.819	6.772	0.360	1.821	0.846	1.020
Jilin	8.041	5.890	0.192	1.340	0.530	0.089
Heilongjiang	8.735	6.681	0.442	0.978	0.443	0.191
Shanghai	2.128	1.165	0.019	0.673	0.040	0.231
Jiangsu	23.871	17.168	0.448	3.131	1.259	1.865
Zhejiang	15.730	8.654	1.066	2.654	1.684	1.672
Anhui	17.150	12.372	0.942	2.439	0.778	0.619
Fujian	8.852	4.122	1.100	1.515	0.884	1.231
Jiangxi	10.339	5.916	0.969	1.948	1.047	0.459
Shandong	28.295	21.556	0.970	3.240	0.869	1.660
Henan	21.447	16.313	1.005	2.526	1.453	0.150
Hubei	18.399	12.051	0.789	3.636	0.720	1.230
Hunan	18.427	10.280	1.521	4.517	1.168	0.941
Guangdong	25.490	13.116	2.269	4.422	2.955	2.728
Guangxi	9.763	5.400	0.713	2.402	0.902	0.346
Sichuan	26.467	17.588	1.479	5.568	1.385	0.447
Guizhou	6.416	3.779	0.460	1.332	0.800	0.048
Yunnan	8.216	4.578	0.667	2.083	0.823	0.065
Tibet	0.811	0.248	0.012	0.481	0.070	
Shaanxi	6.630	4.701	0.467	0.925	0.510	0.027
Gansu	4.066	2.651	0.227	0.888	0.296	0.004
Qinghai	1.121	0.436	0.054	0.533	0.097	0.001
Ningxia	0.998	0.704	0.017	0.220	0.043	0.014
Xinjiang	5.616	3.590	0.170	1.507	0.317	0.032

2.18 *MATERIAL CONSUMPTION IN AGRICULTURAL PRODUCTION AS PERCENTAGE OF GROSS OUTPUT VALUE BY BRANCH AND REGION* *1987*

(gross output value of each branch in a region = 100)

Region	Crop Farming	Forestry	Animal Husbandry	Sideline Production	Fishery
Nationwide	**28.4**	**21.4**	**46.1**	**33.4**	**30.8**
Beijing	26.3	20.0	40.4	19.0	27.6
Tianjin	35.9	43.2	56.5	40.8	40.4
Hebei	32.4	25.6	32.4	35.5	50.6
Shanxi	38.0	31.2	46.8	25.4	21.4
Inner Mongolia	35.0	25.6	32.0	19.3	20.0
Liaoning	29.5	25.9	54.0	31.0	37.9
Jilin	31.6	34.5	42.7	25.1	60.5
Heilongjiang	33.0	33.9	57.1	14.8	24.8
Shanghai	34.1	44.1	56.5	25.9	51.8
Jiangsu	14.7	25.6	64.2	58.4	34.3
Zhejiang	24.0	8.2	46.3	38.2	35.5
Anhui	29.8	13.4	50.6	33.4	15.2
Fujian	31.3	18.9	45.3	26.9	37.1
Jiangxi	25.8	10.9	43.3	26.1	12.2
Shandong	27.9	19.9	49.5	41.0	28.3
Henan	29.0	24.1	50.6	47.4	21.5
Hubei	24.7	20.9	33.7	31.6	15.2
Hunan	25.7	16.2	37.6	16.3	11.1
Guangdong	30.9	26.4	48.2	29.8	34.6
Guangxi	26.4	25.3	39.2	14.7	30.0
Sichuan	22.6	16.6	53.0	31.3	16.6
Guizhou	26.7	16.4	44.9	23.5	15.8
Yunnan	25.9	24.6	29.2	19.9	31.6
Tibet	31.9	20.0	14.4	20.5	
Shaanxi	32.2	23.8	50.8	42.0	27.0
Gansu	36.6	34.2	44.0	31.3	33.3
Qinghai	38.0	18.2	22.1	30.2	50.0
Ningxia	32.3	61.4	31.7	15.7	26.3
Xinjiang	31.6	31.5	31.5	24.9	25.6

2.19 *NET OUTPUT VALUE AS PERCENTAGE OF GROSS OUTPUT VALUE OF AGRICULTURE BY BRANCH AND REGION* *1987*

(gross output value of each branch in a region = 100)

Region	Crop Farming	Forestry	Animal Husbandry	Sideline Production	Fishery
Nationwide	**71.6**	**78.6**	**53.9**	**66.6**	**69.2**
Beijing	73.7	80.0	59.6	81.0	72.4
Tianjin	64.1	56.8	43.5	59.2	59.6
Hebei	67.6	74.4	67.6	64.5	49.4
Shanxi	62.0	68.8	53.2	74.6	78.6
Inner Mongolia	65.0	74.4	68.0	80.7	80.0
Liaoning	70.5	74.1	46.0	69.0	62.1
Jilin	68.4	65.5	57.3	74.9	69.5
Heilongjiang	67.0	66.1	42.9	85.2	75.2
Shanghai	65.9	55.9	43.5	74.1	48.2
Jiangsu	75.3	74.4	35.8	41.6	65.7
Zhejiang	76.0	91.8	53.7	61.8	64.5
Anhui	70.2	86.6	49.4	66.6	84.8
Fujian	68.7	81.1	54.7	73.1	62.9
Jiangxi	74.2	89.1	56.7	73.9	87.8
Shandong	72.1	80.1	50.5	59.0	71.7
Henan	71.0	75.9	49.4	52.6	78.5
Hubei	75.3	79.1	66.3	68.4	84.8
Hunan	74.3	83.8	62.4	83.7	88.9
Guangdong	69.1	73.6	51.8	70.2	65.4
Guangxi	73.6	74.7	60.8	85.3	70.0
Sichuan	77.4	83.4	47.0	68.7	83.4
Guizhou	73.3	83.6	55.1	76.5	84.2
Yunnan	74.1	75.4	70.8	80.1	68.4
Tibet	68.1	80.0	85.6	79.5	
Shaanxi	67.8	76.2	49.2	58.0	73.0
Gansu	63.4	65.8	56.0	68.7	66.7
Qinghai	62.0	81.8	77.9	69.8	50.0
Ningxia	67.7	38.6	68.3	84.3	73.7
Xinjiang	68.4	68.5	68.5	75.1	74.4

2.20 *PERCENTAGE OF MATERIAL CONSUMPTION IN AGRICULTURAL PRODUCTION BY BRANCH AND REGION* *1987*

(material consumption of all branches in a region = 100)

Region	Crop Farming	Forestry	Animal Husbandry	Sideline Production	Fishery
Nationwide	**52.9**	**3.1**	**32.3**	**7.1**	**4.6**
Beijing	47.2	1.5	46.4	2.2	2.7
Tianjin	53.5	1.2	30.1	6.7	8.5
Hebei	68.1	2.7	21.5	4.4	3.3
Shanxi	67.7	4.4	24.4	3.4	0.1
Inner Mongolia	56.4	3.3	33.3	6.5	0.5
Liaoning	46.5	2.1	35.0	6.2	10.2
Jilin	67.4	2.5	24.7	4.4	1.0
Heilongjiang	66.3	4.6	26.3	1.5	1.3
Shanghai	34.4	0.9	49.8	0.8	14.1
Jiangsu	39.9	1.1	39.6	12.5	6.9
Zhejiang	38.6	1.3	32.4	14.7	13.0
Anhui	62.5	1.7	29.8	4.7	1.3
Fujian	42.3	5.8	28.3	7.3	16.3
Jiangxi	50.3	2.9	36.2	9.0	1.6
Shandong	64.1	1.9	24.4	4.6	5.0
Henan	61.0	2.9	23.7	12.0	0.4
Hubei	60.3	3.2	28.1	5.1	3.3
Hunan	51.4	4.2	39.4	3.3	1.7
Guangdong	43.5	6.0	30.5	9.3	10.7
Guangxi	48.0	6.0	38.4	3.9	3.7
Sichuan	41.3	2.4	50.5	5.1	0.7
Guizhou	49.0	3.2	38.7	8.8	0.3
Yunnan	54.9	7.5	29.5	7.1	1.0
Tibet	53.2	1.4	37.1	8.3	
Shaanxi	60.1	3.9	25.8	9.9	0.3
Gansu	61.7	4.8	28.0	5.4	0.1
Qinghai	56.5	2.5	31.9	8.9	0.2
Ningxia	70.3	5.7	21.3	1.7	1.0
Xinjiang	65.2	3.1	27.2	4.1	0.4

2.21 *PERCENTAGE OF NET OUTPUT VALUE OF AGRICULTURE BY BRANCH AND REGION* *1987*

(net output value of all branches in a region = 100)

Region	Crop Farming	Forestry	Animal Husbandry	Sideline Production	Fishery
Nationwide	**64.5**	**5.5**	**18.2**	**6.9**	**4.9**
Beijing	59.3	2.7	30.7	4.1	3.2
Tianjin	67.0	1.1	16.2	8.8	8.9
Hebei	68.9	3.8	21.8	3.9	1.6
Shanxi	69.7	6.2	17.5	6.3	0.3
Inner Mongolia	49.0	4.5	33.0	12.6	0.9
Liaoning	62.6	3.3	16.9	7.8	9.4
Jilin	73.2	2.4	16.7	6.6	1.1
Heilongjiang	76.5	5.0	11.2	5.1	2.2
Shanghai	54.7	0.9	31.6	1.9	10.9
Jiangsu	71.9	1.9	13.1	5.3	7.8
Zhejiang	55.0	6.8	16.9	10.7	10.6
Anhui	72.2	5.5	14.2	4.5	3.6
Fujian	46.6	12.4	17.1	10.0	13.9
Jiangxi	57.2	9.4	18.9	10.1	4.4
Shandong	76.2	3.4	11.4	3.1	5.9
Henan	76.0	4.7	11.8	6.8	0.7
Hubei	65.5	4.3	19.8	3.9	6.5
Hunan	55.8	8.3	24.5	6.3	5.1
Guangdong	51.5	8.9	17.3	11.6	10.7
Guangxi	55.3	7.3	24.6	9.2	3.6
Sichuan	66.5	5.6	21.0	5.2	1.7
Guizhou	58.9	7.2	20.7	12.5	0.7
Yunnan	55.7	8.1	25.4	10.0	0.8
Tibet	30.6	1.5	59.3	8.6	
Shaanxi	70.9	7.0	14.0	7.7	0.4
Gansu	65.2	5.6	21.8	7.3	0.1
Qinghai	38.9	4.8	47.5	8.7	0.1
Ningxia	70.5	1.7	22.1	4.3	1.4
Xinjiang	63.9	3.0	26.8	5.7	0.6

Section III

OUTPUT OF MAJOR FARM CROPS, LIVESTOCK, AND TOWNSHIP AND VILLAGE ENTERPRISES' INDUSTRIAL PRODUCTS

3.1 *SOWN AREA OF FARM CROPS*

(1,000 mu*)

	1980	1985	1986	1987	1987 as Percentage of 1986
Total Sown Area of Farm Crops	**2195690**	**2154390**	**2163060**	**2174350**	**100.5**
Grain Crops	1758510	1632680	1663990	1669020	100.3
Rice	508180	481050	483990	482890	99.8
Wheat	438420	438270	444240	431970	97.2
Tubers	152300	128580	130270	133010	102.1
Corn	305290	265410	286860	303180	105.7
Sorghum	40390	29050	28130	27960	99.4
Millet	58080	49780	44700	40320	90.2
Soybeans	108400	115770	124420	126670	101.8
Industrial Crops	238820	335690	304280	310870	102.2
Cotton	73800	77100	64590	72660	112.5
Oil-bearing Crops	118930	177000	171220	167710	97.9
Peanuts	35090	49780	48800	45330	92.9
Rapeseeds	42660	67410	73740	79010	107.2
Sesame	11640	15780	15100	13040	86.4
Sunflower Seeds	12670	22110	15600	13310	85.3
Hemp Crops	10000	18460	11430	14500	126.8
Jute and Ambary Hemp	4710	14870	5170	4080	78.9
Sugar Crops	13830	22880	22050	20350	92.3
Sugarcane	7190	14470	14250	12880	90.4
Beetroots	6640	8410	7810	7470	95.7
Tobacco	7680	19690	16880	16920	100.3
Flue-cured Tobacco	5950	16160	13420	13700	102.1
Crude Drugs	2010	3890	2690	2380	88.3
Other Industrial Crops	12560	16650	15410	16340	106.1
Other Farm Crops	198360	186040	194790	194460	99.8

Note:
*** 1 mu = 1/15 hectare.**

3.2 *PERCENTAGE OF SOWN AREA OF FARM CROPS*

	1980	1985	1986	1987
Total Sown Area of Farm Crops	**100.0**	**100.0**	**100.0**	**100.0**
Grain Crops	80.1	75.8	76.9	76.8
Rice	23.1	22.3	22.4	22.2
Wheat	20.0	20.3	20.5	19.9
Tubers	6.9	6.0	6.0	6.1
Corn	13.9	12.3	13.3	13.9
Sorghum	1.8	1.3	1.3	1.3
Millet	2.6	2.3	2.1	1.9
Soybeans	4.9	5.4	5.8	5.8
Industrial Crops	10.9	15.6	14.1	14.3
Cotton	3.4	3.6	3.0	3.3
Oil-bearing Crops	5.4	8.2	7.9	7.7
Peanuts	1.6	2.3	2.3	2.1
Rapeseeds	1.9	3.1	3.4	3.6
Sesame	0.5	0.7	0.7	0.6
Sunflower Seeds	0.6	1.0	0.7	0.6
Hemp Crops	0.5	0.9	0.5	0.7
Jute and Ambary Hemp	0.2	0.7	0.2	0.2
Sugar Crops	0.6	1.1	1.0	0.9
Sugarcane	0.3	0.7	0.7	0.6
Beetroots	0.3	0.4	0.4	0.3
Tobacco	0.3	0.9	0.8	0.8
Flue-cured Tobacco	0.3	0.7	0.6	0.6
Crude Drugs	0.1	0.2	0.1	0.1
Other Industrial Crops	0.6	0.8	0.7	0.8
Other Farm Crops	9.0	8.6	9.0	8.9

3.3 *SOWN AREA OF FARM CROPS BY REGION*

(1,000 mu*)

Region	Total Sown Area of Farm Crops			Grain Crops: Subtotal			Grain Crops: Rice		
	1980	1986	1987	*1980*	*1986*	*1987*	*1980*	*1986*	*1987*
Total	**2195693**	**2163060**	**2174348**	**1758514**	**1663989**	**1669020**	**508177**	**483992**	**482892**
Beijing	9861	9075	8965	8230	7490	7421	783	602	577
Tianjin	10035	8732	8604	8453	6861	6865	963	530	609
Hebei	135209	131592	130352	112308	102409	100318	2179	1848	1879
Shanxi	63999	59281	59887	52631	47179	48480	183	123	110
Inner Mongolia	71960	68344	67105	58235	53718	53347	223	407	413
Liaoning	58722	54955	54309	48317	45554	46962	5785	7512	8000
Jilin	60855	60552	60553	52864	52043	52286	3790	5270	5522
Heilongjiang	130857	126946	127730	109769	109856	111179	3156	7604	8709
Shanghai	11640	10185	10054	7408	6703	6632	4569	4278	4143
Jiangsu	131205	127709	127505	98089	97416	97250	41677	36333	35992
Zhejiang	69227	65614	65614	51265	48531	48531	37709	35331	35640
Anhui	116095	122443	125578	90389	90774	92265	33574	32770	33118
Fujian	38609	36015	38156	32633	28466	29423	25297	22269	22405
Jiangxi	83305	81581	82240	56629	54447	54718	50756	48760	49031
Shandong	158573	165645	163316	127120	126718	123227	2588	1598	1514
Henan	161824	177292	179293	132884	140583	140478	6253	6176	6211
Hubei	112156	110615	110062	80281	76381	77152	40623	38103	38363
Hunan	118642	113047	112121	81770	78156	77264	66185	64914	63827
Guangdong	99188	91662	91963	79801	66951	66289	62456	54096	53316
Guangxi	73163	68217	69173	59357	52959	53092	41465	37789	37559
Sichuan	180212	177796	179224	158181	140863	141218	46247	46681	45472
Guizhou	42676	47013	48696	36277	34134	34544	11618	11037	10820
Yunnan	60120	60361	61160	53900	49994	50468	15419	15740	15298
Tibet	3308	3165	3144	2986	2855	2852	9	13	11
Shaanxi	76085	70165	71919	64655	59663	61263	2438	2343	2341
Gansu	52187	52525	53690	44099	41470	42308	60	59	58
Qinghai	7630	7617	7617	6179	5805	5767			
Ningxia	13444	12352	12511	11135	9896	10238	696	766	793
Xinjiang	44906	42751	43807	32669	27151	26823	1476	1040	1161

Note:
*** 1 mu = 1/15 hectare.**

SOWN AREA OF FARM CROPS BY REGION

(1,000 mu*) (continued)

	Grain Crops								
	Wheat			Corn			Soybeans		
Region	*1980*	*1986*	*1987*	*1980*	*1986*	*1987*	*1980*	*1986*	*1987*
Total	**438418**	**444244**	**431969**	**305292**	**286855**	**303175**	**108395**	**124418**	**126674**
Beijing	2818	2776	2741	2961	3241	3347	120	157	192
Tianjin	2920	2163	2096	2535	2206	2297	351	576	629
Hebei	41403	37386	35253	35114	28493	29749	3918	5546	5745
Shanxi	14927	15701	15153	11135	8501	9267	2078	2987	3339
Inner Mongolia	14359	14056	13817	9792	8820	9902	2570	3962	4129
Liaoning	614	308	408	21243	18877	20117	7093	6154	5929
Jilin	2063	745	561	25228	29848	31833	8347	7336	7292
Heilongjiang	31578	29539	23804	28260	25335	29633	24451	32950	35993
Shanghai	758	1091	1149	145	151	148	21	54	76
Jiangsu	25786	33989	33273	6462	7243	7433	4132	5249	5280
Zhejiang	4884	4524	4284	983	637	619	1054	959	1027
Anhui	28742	29315	29793	2458	3691	4359	9164	10558	10113
Fujian	2212	1243	1509	24	51	218	867	1180	1268
Jiangxi	1820	1302	1255	119	127	116	1719	2070	2029
Shandong	55027	63269	60066	32141	33657	34718	10426	9313	8747
Henan	58903	69574	70313	25202	28282	29047	13771	14588	13648
Hubei	19384	19584	20228	6104	5734	5905	2605	2738	2576
Hunan	3324	2653	2617	2218	1556	1690	1958	2599	2657
Guangdong	3541	612	620	688	627	672	2089	1883	1847
Guangxi	625	193	197	8028	7170	7571	2595	3295	3014
Sichuan	35682	29931	30217	27322	24272	24743	2565	2969	2980
Guizhou	5019	3902	4022	10766	9270	9169	1637	1819	1988
Yunnan	8831	6440	6514	16662	14059	14294	666	954	980
Tibet	883	530	572	23	28	50	15	02	01
Shaanxi	23855	25470	25464	16151	14251	15239	3173	3260	3764
Gansu	20754	22287	21424	4773	3496	3793	470	781	815
Qinghai	3017	3015	3020						
Ningxia	4367	4368	3705	418	695	946	318	350	450
Xinjiang	20322	18274	17894	8337	6537	6300	222	129	166

Note:
*** 1 mu = 1/15 hectare.**

SOWN AREA OF FARM CROPS BY REGION

(1,000 mu*) (continued)

	Iudustrial Crops								
	Subtotal			Cotton			Peanuts		
Region	*1980*	*1986*	*1987*	*1980*	*1986*	*1987*	*1980*	*1986*	*1987*
Total	**238815**	**304277**	**310865**	**73804**	**64592**	**72663**	**35086**	**48802**	**45332**
Beijing	490	365	294	32	44	43	291	218	188
Tianjin	648	965	847	125	276	240	112	174	159
Hebei	16108	21310	22452	8231	10612	12373	3556	5104	4650
Shanxi	7376	8159	7582	3365	1409	1484	54	375	328
Inner Mongolia	9166	10733	9650					3	3
Liaoning	5882	5075	2989	577	269	69	1463	2424	1299
Jilin	4641	5539	5208				122	98	64
Heilongjiang	10206	10247	10148				40	16	10
Shanghai	2424	1775	1613	1556	485	312	2	1	
Jiangsu	15082	18327	18772	9460	7450	8167	1257	2044	1870
Zhejiang	6154	6867	6302	1607	1208	1061	133	117	126
Anhui	14923	22690	24638	4851	3088	3363	2195	2111	1942
Fujian	3104	3536	3569				1209	1344	1374
Jiangxi	7191	9024	9602	1627	922	933	715	1205	1346
Shandong	24592	31295	32923	11054	15150	18333	9360	12755	11486
Henan	23051	28014	30116	9400	9294	10762	3112	5685	6138
Hubei	14664	19729	19429	8875	6199	6453	611	1058	981
Hunan	8767	11506	13000	2694	1291	966	673	990	1011
Guangdong	13307	16108	16017				6070	6218	5917
Guangxi	8401	9572	10201	41	20	15	2123	2764	2606
Sichuan	14725	22963	23039	3778	1766	1727	1311	2521	2371
Guizhou	4279	9067	9968	32	38	28	187	471	457
Yunnan	3670	6744	6757	70	35	31	350	499	464
Tibet	175	140	136				1		
Shaanxi	6402	5705	5751	3627	814	886	131	602	538
Gansu	3557	5331	5455	84	77	72	1	1	1
Qinghai	1183	1511	1543						
Ningxia	1366	1608	1328						
Xinjiang	7281	10372	11536	2718	4145	5345	7	4	3

Note:
*** 1 mu = 1/15 hectare.**

SOWN AREA OF FARM CROPS BY REGION

(1,000 mu*) (continued)

Region	Rapeseeds 1980	Rapeseeds 1986	Rapeseeds 1987	Sesame 1980	Sesame 1986	Sesame 1987	Iudustrial Crops: Jute and Ambary Hemp 1980	Jute and Ambary Hemp 1986	Jute and Ambary Hemp 1987
Total	**42661**	**73737**	**79011**	**11642**	**15099**	**13041**	**4711**	**5174**	**4082**
Beijing	33	3	2	46	28	22			
Tianjin	4			81	139	108	16	14	9
Hebei	236	344	400	785	1568	1358	171	152	114
Shanxi	105	295	239	83	305	287	2		
Inner Mongolia	1177	1007	937		176	68			
Liaoning	173			184	344	107	38	3	2
Jilin				21	3	1		7	
Heilongjiang	60	456	804	2	5	3	1		
Shanghai	781	1172	1203						
Jiangsu	2543	7135	7439	69	169	122	173	158	100
Zhejiang	3461	4220	3957	90	76	72	461	459	389
Anhui	4468	11519	14285	1804	2861	2415	551	1191	922
Fujian	682	246	394	54	10	8	56	17	10
Jiangxi	3265	4095	4543	880	917	858	96	145	116
Shandong	154	48	189	411	325	241	962	361	195
Henan	3330	3906	4364	4198	4207	4140	670	1002	928
Hubei	2636	6558	6468	1703	3118	2425	183	468	417
Hunan	3807	5965	6226	163	164	107	114	116	38
Guangdong	324	296	282	288	142	173	426	149	103
Guangxi	88	134	131	249	194	168	414	180	127
Sichuan	6462	12702	12521	314	152	127	346	746	602
Guizhou	2845	5537	6173	13	15	12	28	11	8
Yunnan	1182	1384	1378	23	11	10		2	1
Tibet	174	140	136						
Shaanxi	1355	2250	2286	155	154	202	3		1
Gansu	557	1135	1228		1				719.3
Qinghai	1126	1446	1475						
Ningxia	21	49	1						
Xinjiang	1612	1695	1900	26	15	7			

Note:
*** 1 mu = 1/15 hectare.**

SOWN AREA OF FARM CROPS BY REGION

(1,000 mu*) (continued)

Region	Sugarcane 1980	Sugarcane 1986	Sugarcane 1987	Beetroots 1980	Beetroots 1986	Beetroots 1987	Industrial Crops: Flue-cured Tobacco 1980	Flue-cured Tobacco 1986	Flue-cured Tobacco 1987
Total	**7193**	**14249**	**12884**	**6641**	**7805**	**7466**	**5951**	**13415**	**13701**
Beijing									
Tianjin									
Hebei				151	124	106	16	34	29
Shanxi				145	195	135	3	11	12
Inner Mongolia				839	1124	1119	2	8	7
Liaoning				166	193	241	131	108	126
Jilin				916	639	830	90	112	130
Heilongjiang				3649	4595	3944	125	632	762
Shanghai			5						
Jiangsu	5	96	85	87	24	34	48	42	26
Zhejiang	161	324	281						
Anhui	5	52	48	3			233	410	373
Fujian	704	1030	873	1			162	303	326
Jiangxi	286	583	550				17	26	48
Shandong				140	59	48	1060	1161	1089
Henan	25	92	78	16	1		1415	2928	2915
Hubei	22	155	135	2			145	607	496
Hunan	218	433	337				405	884	884
Guangdong	2638	5788	4933				168	182	218
Guangxi	1676	3508	3335				286	107	150
Sichuan	698	788	755	12	30	30	220	738	710
Guizhou	58	77	79				585	2025	2332
Yunnan	684	1319	1386	2	5	4	790	2629	2624
Tibet									
Shaanxi	13	5	4	36	49	38	47	450	423
Gansu				69	236	273	3	18	21
Qinghai				1	2	4			
Ningxia				42	153	136			
Xinjiang				364	376	524			

Note:
*** 1 mu = 1/15 hectare.**

SOWN AREA OF FARM CROPS BY REGION

(1,000 mu*) (continued)

	Other Farm Crops		
Region	1980	1986	1987
Total	**198364**	**194794**	**194463**
Beijing	1141	1220	1250
Tianjin	934	906	892
Hebei	6793	7873	7582
Shanxi	3992	3943	3825
Inner Mongolia	4559	3893	4108
Liaoning	4523	4326	4358
Jilin	3350	2970	3059
Heilongjiang	10882	6843	6403
Shanghai	1808	1707	1809
Jiangsu	18034	11966	11483
Zhejiang	11808	11066	10781
Anhui	10783	8979	8675
Fujian	2872	4013	5164
Jiangxi	19485	1811	17920
Shandong	6861	7632	7166
Henan	5889	865	8699
Hubei	17211	14505	13481
Hunan	28105	235	21857
Guangdong	6080	8603	9657
Guangxi	5405	56	5880
Sichuan	7306	13970	14967
Guizhou	2120	3812	4184
Yunnan	2550	3623	3935
Tibet	147	170	156
Shaanxi	5028	4797	4544
Gansu	4531	5724	5927
Qinghai	268	301	307
Ningxia	943	848	945
Xinjiang	4956	5228	5448

Note:
*** 1 mu = 1/15 hectare.**

3.4 *PERCENTAGE OF SOWN AREA OF FARM CROPS BY REGION*

(total sown area of farm crops = 100)

	Grain Crops			Industrial Crops			Other Farm Crops		
Region	1980	1986	1987	1980	1986	1987	1980	1986	1987
Nationwide	**80.1**	**76.9**	**76.8**	**10.9**	**14.1**	**14.3**	**9.0**	**9.0**	**8.9**
Beijing	83.4	82.5	82.8	5.0	4.0	3.3	11.6	13.4	13.9
Tianjin	84.2	78.6	79.8	6.5	11.1	9.8	9.3	10.4	10.4
Hebei	83.1	77.8	77.0	11.9	16.2	17.2	5.0	6.0	5.8
Shanxi	82.2	79.6	81.0	11.5	13.8	12.7	6.3	6.7	6.4
Inner Mongolia	80.9	78.6	79.5	12.8	15.7	14.4	6.3	5.7	6.1
Liaoning	82.3	82.9	86.5	10.0	9.2	5.5	7.7	7.9	8.0
Jilin	86.9	85.9	86.3	7.6	9.1	8.6	5.5	4.9	5.1
Heilongjiang	83.9	86.5	87.0	7.8	8.1	7.9	8.3	5.4	5.0
Shanghai	63.7	65.8	66.0	20.8	17.4	16.0	15.5	16.8	18.0
Jiangsu	74.8	76.3	76.3	11.5	14.4	14.7	13.7	9.4	9.0
Zhejiang	74.0	72.6	74.0	8.9	10.5	9.6	17.1	16.9	16.4
Anhui	77.9	74.1	73.5	12.8	18.5	19.6	9.3	7.3	6.9
Fujian	84.5	79.0	77.1	8.1	9.8	9.4	7.4	11.1	13.5
Jiangxi	68.0	66.7	66.5	8.6	11.1	11.7	23.4	22.2	21.8
Shandong	80.2	76.5	75.5	15.5	18.9	20.2	4.3	4.6	4.4
Henan	82.1	79.3	78.4	14.3	15.8	16.8	3.6	4.9	4.9
Hubei	71.6	69.1	70.1	13.1	17.8	17.7	15.3	13.1	12.2
Hunan	68.9	69.1	68.9	7.4	10.2	11.6	23.7	20.7	19.5
Guangdong	80.5	73.0	72.1	13.4	17.6	17.4	6.1	9.4	10.5
Guangxi	81.1	77.6	76.8	11.5	14.0	14.7	7.4	8.3	8.5
Sichuan	87.8	79.2	78.8	8.2	12.9	12.9	4.0	7.9	8.4
Guizhou	85.0	72.6	70.9	10.0	19.3	20.5	5.0	8.1	8.6
Yunnan	89.7	82.8	82.5	6.1	11.2	11.0	4.2	6.0	6.4
Tibet	90.3	90.2	90.7	5.3	4.4	4.3	4.4	5.4	5.0
Shaanxi	85.0	85.0	85.7	8.4	8.1	8.0	6.6	6.8	6.3
Gansu	84.5	79.0	78.8	6.8	10.1	10.2	8.7	10.9	11.1
Qinghai	81.0	76.2	75.7	15.5	19.8	20.3	3.5	4.0	4.0
Ningxia	82.8	80.1	81.8	10.2	13.0	10.6	7.0	6.9	7.6
Xinjiang	72.8	63.5	61.2	16.2	24.3	26.3	11.0	12.2	12.4

3.5 *SOWN AREA OF FARM CROPS BY ECONOMIC ZONE**

(1,000 mu**)

	East Economic Zone	Middle Economic Zone	West Economic Zone
Total Sown Area of Farm Crops	**768011**	**924569**	**481768**
Grain Crops	586010	707169	375841
Rice	201634	205304	75954
Wheat	141596	177541	112832
Tubers	42608	45020	45386
Corn	106889	121752	74534
Sorghum	12750	12138	3067
Millet	14932	21433	3958
Soybeans	33754	81776	11144
Industrial Crops	115979	129373	65513
Cotton	40613	23961	8089
Oil-bearing Crops	50334	77498	39875
Peanuts	29675	11823	3834
Rapeseeds	13997	37916	27098
Sesame	2379	10304	358
Sunflower Seeds	2054	8914	2338
Hemp Crops	2085	9976	2439
Jute and Ambary Hemp	1049	2421	612
Sugar Crops	9941	7176	3233
Sugarcane	9512	1148	2224
Beetroots	429	6028	1009
Tobacco	2605	6695	7623
Flue-cured Tobacco	1964	5627	6110
Crude Drugs	878	759	741
Other Industrial Crops	9523	3308	3513
Other Farm Crops	66022	88027	40414

Note:
*** The east economic zone includes Beijing, Tianjin, Hebei, Liaoning, Shanghai, Jiangsu, Zhejiang, Fujian, Shandong, Guangdong and Guangxi. The middle economic zone includes Shanxi, Inner Mongolia, Jilin, Heilongjiang, Anhui, Jiangxi, Henan, Hubei and Hunan. The west economic zone includes Sichuan, Guizhou, Yunnan, Tibet, Shaanxi, Gansu, Qinghai, Ningxia and Xinjiang.**

**** 1 mu = 1/15 hectare.**

3.6 *OUTPUT OF MAJOR FARM CROPS*

(1,000 tons)

	1980	1985	1986	1987	1987 as Percentage of 1986
Grain Crops	320555	379108	391512	404733	103.4
Rice	139905	168569	172224	174416	101.3
Wheat	55205	85805	90040	87768	97.5
Tubers	28725	26036	25337	28223	111.4
Corn	62600	63826	70856	79822	112.7
Sorghum	6775	5609	5384	5428	100.8
Millet	5445	5977	4540	4538	100.0
Soybeans	7940	10500	11614	12184	104.9
Industrial Crops	2707	4147	3540	4245	119.9
Cotton	7691	15784	14738	15278	103.7
Oil-bearing Crops	3600	6664	5882	6171	104.9
Peanuts	2384	5607	5881	6605	112.3
Rapeseeds	259	691	618	526	85.0
Sesame	270	535	485	444	91.6
Sunflower Seeds	910	1732	1544	1241	80.4
Hemp Crops	1436	4448	1927	2084	108.1
Jute and Ambary Hemp	1098	4119	1420	1137	80.1
Ramie	38	82	227	567	250.5
Hemp	76	55	55	44	80.6
Flax	183	158	208	320	153.7
Sugar Crops	29113	60468	58525	55504	94.8
Sugarcane	22807	51549	50219	47363	94.3
Beetroots	6305	8919	8306	8140	98.0
Tobacco	845	2425	1707	1943	113.8
Flue-cured Tobacco	717	2075	1374	1636	119.0

3.7 *OUTPUT OF MAJOR GRAIN CROPS BY REGION*

(1,000 tns)

	Total of Grain						Rice		
	Subtotal			Summer Grain					
Region	*1980*	*1986*	*1987*	*1980*	*1986*	*1987*	1980	1986	1987
Total	**320555**	**391512**	**404733**	**59280**	**93291**	**92348**	**139905**	**172224**	**174416**
Beijing	1860	2165	2270	455	713	759	295	244	240
Tianjin	1380	1576	1677	280	461	476	310	215	239
Hebei	15225	19655	19200	3880	8305	7274	830	756	771
Shanxi	6855	7324	7125	1255	3114	2396	70	51	40
Inner Mongolia	3965	5285	6070				40	83	77
Liaoning	12215	12222	12763	80	87	107	2355	3207	3372
Jilin	8595	13977	16758				1075	1751	2230
Heilongjiang	14625	17763	17376				795	2208	2257
Shanghai	1870	2369	2326	565	547	503	1165	1746	1749
Jiangsu	24185	33396	32577	8735	11767	11542	12285	17027	16518
Zhejiang	14355	16051	15890	1500	1559	1611	11760	13684	13368
Anhui	14540	23719	24287	3610	6869	7580	7730	12223	11892
Fujian	8020	7515	8393	275	209	294	6715	6550	7158
Jiangxi	12400	14538	15628	95	109	95	11880	14069	15090
Shandong	23840	32500	33937	7707	15645	14773	740	630	574
Henan	21485	25457	29484	9215	15950	16583	1780	2063	1977
Hubei	15365	23045	23207	3415	4635	5035	10380	16236	15950
Hunan	21245	26315	25937	365	446	443	19425	24663	24142
Guangdong	18085	17178	18482	645	502	577	16230	15437	16514
Guangxi	11905	11181	12102	65	34	39	10070	9866	10690
Sichuan	34365	39238	39213	6960	8124	8169	15490	20032	19797
Guizhou	6480	6723	6732	620	737	679	3250	3412	3419
Yunnan	8655	8700	9348	1265	755	1339	3875	4400	4580
Tibet	500	454	467					3	2
Shaanxi	7570	9655	9879	2640	4804	4527	755	932	947
Gansu	4925	5510	5294	2945	3756	3471	20	19	22
Qinghai	955	984	1041						
Ningxia	1200	1540	1390	550	760	502	330	421	439
Xinjiang	3885	5477	5880	2165	3403	3574	255	316	362

OUTPUT OF MAJOR GRAIN CROPS CROPS BY REGION

(1,000 tns) (continued)

Region	Wheat			Tuber				
	1980	1986	1987	Subtotal			Potatoes	
				1980	*1986*	*1987*	*1986*	*1987*
Total	**55205**	**90040**	**87768**	**28725**	**25337**	**28223**	**5300**	**5335**
Beijing	405	710	755	25	29	30	3	3
Tianjin	275	461	475	25	26	25		3
Hebei	3840	8268	7235	1250	1251	1362	126	167
Shanxi	1185	3054	2340	525	480	542	367	402
Inner Mongolia	825	1308	1257	300	365	337	363	336
Liaoning	55	40	57	105	153	135	48	50
Jilin	165	67	63	200	271	301	260	284
Heilongjiang	3945	3559	2998	510	475	672	475	672
Shanghai	205	302	277	5				
Jiangsu	5640	9383	8995	1375	1330	1319		
Zhejiang	795	787	641	780	602	659	45	22
Anhui	3405	6566	7179	2125	2772	2672		
Fujian	225	153	211	965	661	824		
Jiangxi	90	92	76	275	206	269		
Shandong	7660	15624	14741	5555	4003	4784		
Henan	8905	15679	16260	3525	1782	2329		
Hubei	2665	3815	4211	875	1027	1041	437	406
Hunan	245	297	283	1075	770	886	60	66
Guangdong	240	68	77	1365	1425	1632	39	43
Guangxi	25	12	12	170	234	266		
Sichuan	5205	6501	6584	5365	4890	5623	1070	1051
Guizhou	350	322	315	505	706	705	426	392
Yunnan	785	435	746	535	647	613	562	518
Tibet	180	95	107		5	2		
Shaanxi	2300	4441	4177	685	603	622	394	347
Gansu	2400	3307	3020	440	458	413	458	413
Qinghai	5	6	6	75	92	88	92	88
Ningxia	495	703	463	65	45	35	45	35
Xinjiang	2130	3382	3537	25	30	37	30	37

OUTPUT OF MAJOR GRAIN CROPS BY REGION

(1,000 tns) (continued)

	Corn			Sorghum			Millet		
Region	1980	1986	1987	1980	1986	1987	1980	1986	1987
Total	**62600**	**70856**	**79822**	**6775**	**5384**	**5428**	**5445**	**4540**	**4538**
Beijing	890	1079	1140	30	19	25	25	21	18
Tianjin	575	642	697	115	111	120	20	33	27
Hebei	6630	6862	7162	890	547	524	980	1088	1218
Shanxi	2630	1913	2178	765	541	609	960	632	698
Inner Mongolia	1390	1927	2733	230	237	324	395	383	521
Liaoning	6535	6073	6715	2265	1684	1590	235	279	257
Jilin	5070	10164	12316	675	437	458	563	300	262
Heilongjiang	5205	6320	6461	630	551	480	1035	601	402
Shanghai	40	59	51						
Jiangsu	1390	2417	2411	20	55	41			
Zhejiang	155	111	118						
Anhui	385	790	1002	100	120	142	15	2	1
Fujian		4	22		6	6			
Jiangxi	10	10	11		2	3		2	2
Shandong	8255	10165	11700	315	289	292	315	626	578
Henan	5880	4370	6770	145	132	169	415	226	303
Hubei	860	1156	1179	20	28	31	10	22	16
Hunan	215	209	221	15	12	13			
Guangdong	65	74	79		1	1	5	1	1
Guangxi	1110	895	981		1	1	5	2	2
Sichuan	6120	5785	5211	175	362	353			
Guizhou	2115	1950	1970	10	22	23	10	7	6
Yunnan	2630	2578	2498	10	5	5			
Tibet	5	5	7						
Shaanxi	2750	2729	3250	140	111	98	285	216	155
Gansu	890	790	895	90	55	59	155	84	64
Qinghai									
Ningxia	85	173	291	30	7	11	15	14	5
Xinjiang	1265	1606	1751	105	49	50	5	1	2

OUTPUT OF MAJOR GRAIN CROPS BY REGION

(1,000 tns) (continued)

Region	Soybeans 1980	1986	1987
Total	**7940**	**11614**	**12184**
Beijing	15	23	31
Tianjin	30	59	67
Hebei	295	412	459
Shanxi	130	176	211
Inner Mongolia	125	410	367
Liaoning	535	635	492
Jilin	605	837	968
Heilongjiang	2205	3780	3835
Shanghai	5	11	14
Jiangsu	350	719	662
Zhejiang	120	117	130
Anhui	495	819	882
Fujian	70	93	99
Jiangxi	115	125	143
Shandong	840	947	1030
Henan	920	749	1104
Hubei	115	290	276
Hunan	135	244	249
Guangdong	115	127	129
Guangxi	100	140	122
Sichuan	205	346	324
Guizhou	80	140	121
Yunnan	70	95	84
Tibet			
Shaanxi	180	210	250
Gansu	50	68	77
Qinghai			
Ningxia	15	24	34
Xinjiang	20	18	24

3.8 *OUTPUT OF MAJOR INDUSTRIAL CROPS BY REGION*

(1,000 tns)

Region	Cotton			Oil-bearing Crops					
				Subtotal			Peanuts		
	1980	1986	1987	*1980*	*1986*	*1987*	*1980*	*1986*	*1987*
Total	**2707**	**3540**	**4245**	**7691**	**14738**	**15278**	**3600**	**5882**	**6171**
Beijing	1	2	3	31	31	33	26	27	29
Tianjin	2	13	13	28	59	52	9	22	22
Hebei	247	511	626	451	618	689	358	476	534
Shanxi	78	64	78	134	352	308	5	42	42
Inner Mongolia				252	660	540			
Liaoning	21	12	3	283	316	192	137	222	130
Jilin				266	388	353	10	9	6
Heilongjiang				263	190	126	3	2	1
Shanghai	76	22	15	96	149	162			
Jiangsu	418	401	444	386	1168	1211	123	365	337
Zhejiang	83	76	65	289	429	397	13	12	15
Anhui	122	163	186	498	1316	1511	188	281	260
Fujian				135	172	175	112	162	163
Jiangxi	43	55	59	138	316	357	51	136	158
Shandong	537	941	1244	1430	2076	2343	1404	2047	2298
Henan	406	399	570	462	990	1366	248	537	763
Hubei	316	439	439	206	819	755	59	151	146
Hunan	96	83	56	193	472	531	43	93	94
Guangdong				532	657	587	520	644	577
Guangxi	1			137	237	186	219	228	178
Sichuan	95	97	102	719	1590	1615	121	270	271
Guizhou	1	1	1	156	419	463	13	45	38
Yunnan	1			65	110	135	18	34	29
Tibet				11	12	12			
Shaanxi	81	42	56	110	301	315	12	76	78
Gansu	3	4	5	140	299	294			
Qinghai				71	104	104			
Ningxia				36	62	44			
Xinjiang	79	216	280	176	426	423	1	1	1

OUTPUT OF MAJOR INDUSTRIAL CROPS BY REGION

(1,000 tns) (continued)

	Oil-bearing crops								
	Rapeseeds			Sesame			Sunflower Seeds		
Region	*1980*	*1986*	*1987*	*1980*	*1986*	*1987*	*1980*	*1986*	*1987*
Total	**2384**	**5881**	**6605**	**259**	**618**	**526**	**910**	**1544**	**1241**
Beijing	1			1	1	1	2		
Tianjin				3	5	5	14	29	24
Hebei	9	7	13	32	45	45	27	65	68
Shanxi	3	22	15	2	15	13	31	125	103
Inner Mongolia	18	23	22		3	2	165	484	386
Liaoning	4			4	9	3	131	76	54
Jilin				1			210	317	294
Heilongjiang	2	12	42				235	164	65
Shanghai	96	149	162						
Jiangsu	203	799	863	1	11	8			
Zhejiang	272	413	373	3	4	4			
Anhui	272	907	1153	34	126	93			
Fujian	20	9	11	2					
Jiangxi	72	157	172	15	24	28			
Shandong	7	4	25	17	19	15	2		
Henan	134	316	453	80	137	149			1
Hubei	116	471	476	31	191	131			
Hunan	144	368	430	4	8	5	1	1	1
Guangdong	7	8	5	5	4	5			
Guangxi	2	5	4	5	3	3			
Sichuan	582	1310	1335	14	5	5	2	4	3
Guizhou	135	367	419				6	5	5
Yunnan	42	67	100	1			2	6	4
Tibet	11	12	12						
Shaanxi	77	180		3	6	11		14	10
Gansu	33	81	90				27	39	30
Qinghai	68	100	100						
Ningxia	1	1					8	11	10
Xinjiang	56	102	130	1	1		46	209	183

OUTPUT OF MAJOR INDUSTRIAL CROPS BY REGION

(1,000 tns) (continued)

	Hemp								
	Subtotal			Jute and Ambary Hemp			Ramie		
Region	*1980*	*1986*	*1987*	*1980*	*1986*	*1987*	*1980*	*1986*	*1987*
Total	**1436**	**1927**	**2084**	**1098**	**1420**	**1137**	**38**	**227**	**567**
Beijing	1								
Tianjin	1	3	1	1	2	1			
Hebei	18	33	23	10	28	19			
Shanxi	6	4	2						
Inner Mongolia	4	2	1						
Liaoning	11	2	2	2					
Jilin	16	7	12						
Heilongjiang	190	207	312						
Shanghai									
Jiangsu	39	58	53	27	46	28		7	22
Zhejiang	151	200	170	150	196	162	1	4	8
Anhui	175	352	311	163	323	271	2	13	28
Fujian	16	5	4	16	5	2		1	1
Jiangxi	23	50	62	22	37	28	1	13	33
Shandong	164	87	52	143	76	41			
Henan	159	210	226	148	200	213		1	5
Hubei	71	243	286	61	189	175	10	52	110
Hunan	54	142	265	42	48	12	13	94	253
Guangdong	99	38	32	99	36	22		2	10
Guangxi	103	52	41	103	47	31	1	5	11
Sichuan	120	219	215	108	185	132	9	32	82
Guizhou	5	4	4	4	2		1	2	3
Yunnan	2	2	2						
Tibet									
Shaanxi	3	2	2	1					1
Gansu	5	4	3						
Qinghai									
Ningxia	1								
Xinjiang	1	1	2						

OUTPUT OF MAJOR INDUSTRIAL CROPS BY REGION

(1,000 tns) (continued)

	Hemp			Sugarcane			Beetroots		
			Hemp	1980	1986	1987	1980	1986	1987
Region	*1980*	*1986*	*1987*						
Total	**76**	**55**	**44**	**22807**	**50219**	**4736**	**6305**	**8306**	**8140**
Beijing									
Tianjin							94	79	58
Hebei	5	3	2				117	272	193
Shanxi	6	4	2				812	1590	1678
Inner Mongolia	3	2	1						
Liaoning	2	1	1				127	218	284
Jilin	5	3	2				1177	598	690
Heilongjiang	14	3	2				3160	3898	3304
Shanghai						2			
Jiangsu	2	4	2	11	306	283	41	18	14
Zhejiang	1	1	1	588	1322	1088			
Anhui	8	13	11	9	130	115	1		
Fujian				3512	4729	4135			
Jiangxi				857	1720	1908			
Shandong	14	8	8				225		38
Henan	4	4	4	54	195	198	16	59	
Hubei				45	524	417	1		
Hunan				734	1662	1230			
Guangdong				9227	20443	18120			
Guangxi				4019	11214	11674			
Sichuan	2	1	1	1783	2470	2404	4	19	10
Guizhou				111	192	195		1	1
Yunnan	2	2	2	1844	5295	5585	1	4	3
Tibet									
Shaanxi	2	1	1	14	17	9	17	32	16
Gansu	5	4	3				63	521	563
Qinghai							1	8	6
Ningxia	1						63	326	317
Xinjiang	1	1	2				385	664	965

OUTPUT OF MAJOR INDUSTRIAL CROPS BY REGION

(1,000 tns) (continued)

	Tobacco					
	Subtotal			Flue-cured Tobacco		
Region	*1980*	*1986*	*1987*	*1980*	*1986*	*1987*
Total	**845**	**1707**	**1943**	**717**	**1374**	**1636**
Beijing						
Tianjin						
Hebei	6	18	16	2	4	3
Shanxi	1	3	3		1	2
Inner Mongolia	2	6	4		1	1
Liaoning	24	27	29	22	10	16
Jilin	15	32	34	13	11	15
Heilongjiang	28	105	104	22	81	88
Shanghai						
Jiangsu	4	6	6	4	5	4
Zhejiang	4	4	5			
Anhui	25	47	55	24	45	53
Fujian	15	26	29	13	24	26
Jiangxi	4	6	10	1	2	4
Shandong	164	167	208	157	155	199
Henan	189	290	403	187	286	399
Hubei	23	90	84	17	53	44
Hunan	45	109	114	37	92	97
Guangdong	27	39	41	10	17	21
Guangxi	24	15	19	21	9	13
Sichuan	53	140	127	21	57	53
Guizhou	67	218	234	56	192	212
Yunnan	111	298	346	104	286	336
Tibet						
Shaanxi	10	50	58	6	41	50
Gansu	5	9	10		3	4
Qinghai						
Ningxia						
Xinjiang	1	2	4			

3.9 *OUTPUT OF FARM CROPS BY ECONOMIC ZONE** *1987*

(1,000 tns)

	East Economic Region	Middle Economic Region	West Economic Region
Grain Crops	159617	165872	79244
Rice	71193	73655	29568
Wheat	33476	34667	19625
Tubers	11036	9049	8138
Corn	31078	32871	15873
Sorghum	2600	2229	590
Millet	2101	2205	232
Soybeans	3235	8035	914
Industrial Crops			
Cotton	2414	1388	443
Oil-bearing Crops	6026	5846	3406
Peanuts	4284	1471	416
Rapeseeds	1460	2762	2384
Sesame	90	420	16
Sunflower Seeds	147	850	245
Hemp Crops	378	1477	229
Jute and Ambary Hemp	306	699	132
Sugar Crops	35696	9734	10074
Sugarcane	35302	3868	8193
Beetroots	394	5866	1881
Tobacco	353	810	779
Flue-cured Tobacco	282	701	653

Note:
*** The east economic zone includes Beijing, Tianjin, Hebei, Liaoning, Shanghai, Jiangsu, Zhejiang, Fujian, Shandong, Guangdong and Guangxi. The middle economic zone includes Shanxi, Inner Mongolia, Jilin, Heilongjiang, Anhui, Jiangxi, Henan, Hubei and Hunan. The west economic zone includes Sichuan, Guizhou, Yunnan, Tibet, Shaanxi, Gansu, Qinghai, Ningxia and Xinjiang.**

3.10 *OUTPUT PER MU* OF MAJOR FARM CROPS*

(kg/mu*)

	1980	1985	1986	1987	1987 as Percentage of 1986
Grain	183	232	235	242	103.0
Rice	276	350	356	361	101.4
Wheat	126	196	203	203	100.0
Corn	205	240	247	263	106.5
Soybeans	73	91	93	96	103.2
Cotton	37	54	55	58	105.5
Oil-bearing Crops	65	89	86	91	107.0
Peanuts	103	134	121	136	112.4
Rapeseed	56	83	80	84	105.0
Sesame	22	44	41	40	97.6
Jute and Ambary Hemp	233	277	274	279	101.8
Sugarcane	3171	3562	3524	3676	104.3
Beetroots	950	1061	1064	1090	102.4
Flue-cured Tobacco	121	128	102	119	116.7

Note:
*** 1 mu = 1/15 hectare.**

3.11 *OUTPUT PER MU* OF MAJOR GRAIN CROPS BY REGION*

(kg/mu*)

Region	Grain 1980	Grain 1986	Grain 1987	Rice 1980	Rice 1986	Rice 1987	Wheat 1980	Wheat 1986	Wheat 1987
Nationwide	**183**	**235**	**242**	**276**	**356**	**361**	**126**	**203**	**203**
Beijing	226	289	306	379	405	417	145	256	275
Tianjin	163	229	244	321	404	392	94	213	227
Hebei	136	192	191	382	409	410	93	221	205
Shanxi	131	155	147	378	417	364	80	195	154
Inner Mongolia	68	98	114	183	204	187	58	93	91
Liaoning	253	268	272	407	426	421	90	129	136
Jilin	163	289	321	284	332	404	82	90	112
Heilongjiang	134	162	165	253	290	259	126	121	126
Shanghai	253	353	351	255	408	422	272	277	241
Jiangsu	247	343	335	295	469	459	219	276	270
Zhejiang	281	338	327	312	337	375	163	174	150
Anhui	161	261	263	230	373	359	119	224	241
Fujian	246	264	285	266	294	319	102	123	140
Jiangxi	219	267	286	234	289	308	48	71	60
Shandong	188	256	275	285	394	379	139	247	245
Henan	162	181	210	285	334	318	151	225	231
Hubei	192	302	301	256	426	416	138	195	208
Hunan	260	337	336	294	380	378	74	112	108
Guangdong	227	257	279	260	285	309	68	111	124
Guangxi	201	211	228	243	261	285	40	62	61
Sichuan	218	279	278	335	429	435	146	217	218
Guizhou	179	197	195	280	309	316	70	82	78
Yunnan	161	174	185	252	280	299	89	68	114
Tibet	169	159	164	248	249	214	205	176	187
Shaanxi	117	162	160	310	398	404	97	174	164
Gansu	112	133	125	334	322	379	116	148	141
Qinghai	155	169	181				187	206	224
Ningxia	108	156	135	473	550	553	133	161	125
Xinjiang	119	202	219	174	304	312	105	185	198

Note:
*** 1 mu = 1/15 hectare.**

OUTPUT PER MU* OF MAJOR GRAIN CROPS BY REGION

(kg/mu*) (continued)

Region	Corn			Soybeans			Cotton		
	1980	1986	1987	1980	1986	1987	1980	1986	1987
Nationwide	**205**	**247**	**263**	**73**	**93**	**96**	**37**	**55**	**58**
Beijing	301	333	341	117	147	160	31	49	60
Tianjin	228	291	303	87	103	106	13	67	53
Hebei	189	241	241	76	74	80	30	48	51
Shanxi	236	225	235	63	59	63	23	46	52
Inner Mongolia	142	218	276	48	103	89			
Liaoning	308	322	334	76	103	83	37	43	48
Jilin	201	341	387	73	114	133			
Heilongjiang	184	250	252	91	115	107			
Shanghai	276	392	343	301	207	179	49	44	50
Jiangsu	215	334	324	85	137	125	44	54	54
Zhejiang	157	174	191	112	123	127	52	63	62
Anhui	157	214	230	54	78	87	25	53	55
Fujian	44	80	102	82	79	78			
Jiangxi	77	82	98	66	60	71	27	59	64
Shandong	257	302	337	81	102	118	49	62	68
Henan	212	155	233	67	51	81	43	43	53
Hubei	142	202	200	45	106	107	36	71	68
Hunan	96	134	131	69	94	94	36	65	57
Guangdong	95	118	118	69	68	70			
Guangxi	139	125	130	39	142	40	17	16	16
Sichuan	224	238	211	81	116	109	25	55	59
Guizhou	197	210	215	49	77	61	16	15	18
Yunnan	158	183	175	105	100	86	17	13	11
Tibet	212	197	138	81	217	219			
Shaanxi	171	192	213	57	64	66	23	51	63
Gansu	187	226	236	107	87	94	32	47	69
Qinghai									
Ningxia	204	249	307	50	70	75			
Xinjiang	152	246	278	89	142	145	29	52	52

Note:
*** 1 mu = 1/15 hectare.**

OUTPUT PER MU* OF MAJOR GRAIN CROPS BY REGION

(kg/mu*) (continued)

Region	Oil-bearing Crops 1980	Oil-bearing Crops 1986	Oil-bearing Crops 1987	Peanuts 1980	Peanuts 1986	Peanuts 1987	Rapeseeds 1980	Rapeseeds 1986	Rapeseeds 1987
Nationwide	**65**	**86**	**91**	**103**	**121**	**136**	**56**	**80**	**84**
Beijing	75	104	267	90	122	155	24	11	16
Tianjin	62	94	97	78	125	141	21		15
Hebei	66	63	73	101	93	115	37	21	31
Shanxi	39	56	53	93	112	128	27	75	62
Inner Mongolia	33	73	66			86	16	22	22
Liaoning	62	75	85	94	92	100	23		33
Jilin	95	95	97	80	88	96			
Heilongjiang	72	70	50	76	116	75	25	27	52
Shanghai	123	127	135	94			121	127	135
Jiangsu	86	125	128	99	179	180	80	111	116
Zhejiang	79	97	95	100	105	121	79	98	95
Anhui	58	79	81	86	133	134	61	79	81
Fujian	69	106	97	93	121	119	30	36	27
Jiangxi	29	51	53	71	113	117	22	38	38
Shandong	144	157	196	150	161	200	46	91	133
Henan	44	72	93	80	94	124	40	81	104
Hubei	42	76	76	96	143	149	44	72	74
Hunan	41	66	72	64	94	93	38	62	69
Guangdong	80	99	92	86	104	97	22	29	19
Guangxi	55	76	63	61	83	68	23	37	27
Sichuan	88	103	107	93	107	114	90	103	107
Guizhou	48	68	68	70	96	82	48	66	68
Yunnan	39	55	70	52	69	62	36	48	73
Tibet	62	83	110	64		24	62	83	87
Shaanxi	46	75	79	88	127	146	57	80	86
Gansu	48	70	68	50	161	166	59	71	73
Qinghai	60	69	67				61	69	68
Ningxia	28	44	38				28	24	35
Xinjiang	44	85	87	83	180	183	35	60	69

Note:
*** 1 mu = 1/15 hectare.**

OUTPUT PER MU OF MAJOR GRAIN CROPS BY REGION*

(kg/mu*) (continued)

Region	Sesame			Jute and Ambary Hemp			Sugarcane		
	1980	1986	1987	1980	1986	1987	1980	1986	1987
Nationwide	**22**	**41**	**40**	**233**	**274**	**279**	**3171**	**3524**	**3676**
Beijing	31	35	42						
Tianjin	36	38	44	44	162	135			
Hebei	41	29	33	57	183	170			
Shanxi	27	48	45	40	40	13			
Inner Mongolia		16	26						
Liaoning	22	26	29	64	105	88			
Jilin	25	30	67						
Heilongjiang	38	66	26	47	229				
Shanghai									470
Jiangsu	17	64	63	159	290	279	2071	3187	3312
Zhejiang	36	56	57	325	424	416	3638	4080	3871
Anhui	19	44	39	296	271	294	1786	2501	2406
Fujian	41	35	42	286	179	230	4985	4593	4735
Jiangxi	17	26	32	225	253	243	3000	2950	3472
Shandong	41	58	63	149	212	208			
Henan	19	32	36	221	199	230	2157	2124	2545
Hubei	18	61	54	333	405	420	1994	3381	3077
Hunan	24	49	44	366	417	316	3366	3844	3654
Guangdong	18	26	29	233	244	214	3498	3530	3673
Guangxi	18	18	19	248	260	242	2398	3197	3501
Sichuan	44	35	37	312	248	219	2556	3139	3186
Guizhou	32	31	32	135	187	44	1904	2479	2463
Yunnan	37	29	24		100	163	2697	4014	4030
Tibet									
Shaanxi	21	42	52	167		47	1096	3359	2210
Gansu	18	11							
Qinghai									
Ningxia									
Xinjiang	34	52	50						

Note:
*** 1 mu = 1/15 hectare.**

OUTPUT PER MU OF MAJOR GRAIN CROPS BY REGION*

(kg/mu) (continued)

Region	Beetroots 1980	Beetroots 1986	Beetroots 1987	Flue-cured Tobacco 1980	Flue-cured Tobacco 1986	Flue-cured Tobacco 1987
Nationwide	**950**	**1064**	**1090**	**121**	**102**	**119**
Beijing		1313				
Tianjin						
Hebei	627	636	544	99	109	103
Shanxi	806	1399	1429	115	114	128
Inner Mongolia	968	1415	1500	48	102	89
Liaoning	767	1131	1178	171	96	125
Jilin	1285	935	831	143	96	117
Heilongjiang	866	848	838	179	128	115
Shanghai						
Jiangsu	468	725	411	85	118	163
Zhejiang						
Anhui	507	174	245	104	109	141
Fujian	833			79	78	80
Jiangxi				57	63	73
Shandong	1599	1007	807	148	134	182
Henan	1035	326	1260	132	98	137
Hubei	420			116	87	90
Hunan				92	104	109
Guangdong				63	92	98
Guangxi				73	84	84
Sichuan	352	631	346	94	77	74
Guizhou	623	2710	2460	95	95	91
Yunnan	700	702	815	131	109	128
Tibet						
Shaanxi	470	651	408	123	92	117
Gansu	915	2209	2123	100	157	183
Qinghai	970	4456	1548			
Ningxia	1494	2137	2328		40	51
Xinjiang	1059	1766	1842			

Note:
*** 1 mu = 1/15 hectare.**

3.12 *OUTPUT AND LAND USE FOR SILKWORM COCOONS, TEA AND FRUITS*

Item	Unit	1980	1985	1986	1987	1987 as Percentage of 1986
Output						
Silkworm Cocoons	1,000 tns	326	371	369	402	1090
Mulberry Silkworm Cocoons	1,000 tns	250	335	336	353	1052
Tussah Silkworm Cocoons	1,000 tns	76	36	33	49	1484
Tea	1,000 tns	304	432	461	508	1103
Crude Black Tea	1,000 tns	71	87	124	125	1011
Crude Green Tea	1,000 tns	178	238	257	301	1172
Fruits	1,000 tns	6793	11639	13477	16679	1238
Apples	1,000 tns	2363	3614	3337	4264	1278
Citrus Fruits	1,000 tns	713	1808	2548	3224	1265
Pears	1,000 tns	1466	2137	2348	2489	1060
Grapes	1,000 tns	110	361	442	641	1451
Bananas	1,000 tns	61	631	1251	2029	1622
Pineapples	1,000 tns	75	183	303	412	1360
Red Dates	1,000 tns	372	432	545	572	1049
Persimmons	1,000 tns	560	680	656	761	1160
Longan	1,000 tns	44	104	73	82	1124
Litchi	1,000 tns	69	101	152	116	764
Land Use						
Mulberry gardens	1,000 mu*	4305	6195	5412	5065	936
Tussah Hillside Fields	1,000 mu*	12832	13732	13151	13060	993
Tea Plantations	1,000 mu*	15612	15673	15359	15661	1020
Orchards	1,000 mu*	6741	41044	55074	67623	1228
Apple	1,000 mu*	11144	12981	17607	21614	1228
Citrus Fruit	1,000 mu*	3902	7604	10082	12957	1285
Pear	1,000 mu*	4490	5069	5918	6624	1119
Grape	1,000 mu*	474	1300	1721	2141	1244
Banana	1,000 mu*	79	710	1074	2290	2132

Note:
*** 1 mu = 1/15 hectare.**

3.13 *OUTPUT OF SILKWORM COCOONS BY REGION*

(1,000 tns)

Region	Mulberry Silkworm Cocoons 1980	Mulberry Silkworm Cocoons 1986	Mulberry Silkworm Cocoons 1987	Tussah Silkworm Cocoons 1980	Tussah Silkworm Cocoons 1986	Tussah Silkworm Cocoons 1987
Total	**250**	**336**	**353**	**76**	**33**	**49**
Beijing						
Tianjin						
Hebei	1					
Shanxi	2	3	3			
Inner Mongolia					1	1
Liaoning				57	25	39
Jilin				1		
Heilongjiang				2	1	1
Shanghai						
Jiangsu	38	80	83			
Zhejiang	65	89	98			
Anhui	5	10	11			
Fujian						
Jiangxi			1			
Shandong	11	11	11	6	2	2
Henan	1			7	4	6
Hubei	6	4	4	1		
Hunan	2	3	2			
Guangdong	22	21	15			
Guangxi	2	4	3			
Sichuan	92	103	113			
Guizhou						
Yunnan	1	2	2			
Tibet						
Shaanxi	3	5	5			
Gansu						
Qinghai						
Ningxia						
Xinjiang	1	1	1			

3.14 *OUTPUT OF TEA BY REGION*
(1,000 tns)

Region	Subtotal			Crude Black Tea		
	1980	1986	1987	1980	1986	1987
Total	**304**	**461**	**508**	**178**	**257**	**301**
Beijing						
Tianjin						
Hebei						
Shanxi						
Inner Mongolia						
Liaoning						
Jilin						
Heilongjiang						
Shanghai						
Jiangsu	5	11	12	2	5	8
Zhejiang	75	104	116	69	93	102
Anhui	32	47	52	26	39	43
Fujian	26	44	50	16	22	25
Jiangxi	10	16	17	8	11	13
Shandong	1	1	1	1	1	1
Henan	1	3	2	1	3	2
Hubei	17	23	26	8	10	13
Hunan	61	73	79	12	17	22
Guangdong	12	26	29	5	9	10
Guangxi	7	12	14	3	4	7
Sichuan	9	52	54	11	16	23
Guizhou	7	12	13	4	5	6
Yunnan	18	34	39	10	19	23
Tibet						
Shaanxi	1	3	4	1	3	
Gansu						
Qinghai						
Ningxia						
Xinjiang						

3.15 *OUTPUT OF FRUITS BY REGION*

(1,000 tns)

Region	Subtotal			Apples			Citrus Fruits		
	1980	1986	1987	1980	1986	1987	1980	1986	1987
Total	**6793**	**13477**	**16679**	**2393**	**3337**	**4264**	**713**	**2548**	**3224**
Beijing	149	175	215	46	49	63			
Tianjin	34	67	92	8	25	33			
Hebei	801	1699	2002	178	391	579			
Shanxi	273	429	447	86	136	156			
Inner Mongolia	31	59	65	10	19	19			
Liaoning	783	804	933	610	547	637			
Jilin	45	59	100	15	4	5			
Heilongjiang	28	24	31	3	9	11			
Shanghai	37	44	47					6	10
Jiangsu	206	366	418	48	97	94	6	21	33
Zhejiang	225	521	709	3	1	01	91	362	549
Anhui	100	184	220	18	30	47		3	5
Fujian	127	347	457				35	136	189
Jiangxi	56	161	173				29	112	126
Shandong	1515	1981	2432	918	1269	1570			
Henan	436	612	778	155	276	438			
Hubei	114	238	357	3	6	15	16	105	172
Hunan	107	521	541				51	402	435
Guangdong	322	2009	2788				117	552	723
Guangxi	209	697	939				93	222	234
Sichuan	432	884	1047	43	49	68	261	600	711
Guizhou	50	139	152	1	2	5	5	13	16
Yunnan	119	275	316	11	21	30	4	9	11
Tibet	4	4	5	3	4	4			
Shaanxi	280	377	488	89	152	212	3	5	8
Gansu	128	248	272	59	110	128			
Qinghai	7	19	21	4	12	13			
Ningxia	21	36	44	13	26	33			
Xinjiang	156	498	590	38	102	100			

OUTPUT OF FRUITS BY REGION

(1,000 tns) (continued)

Region	Pears			Grapes			Red Dates		
	1980	1986	1987	1980	1986	1987	1980	1986	1987
Total	**1466**	**2348**	**2489**	**110**	**442**	**641**	**372**	**545**	**572**
Beijing	31	45	49	5	11	13	2	2	1
Tianjin	7	11	16	1	6	8	2	4	4
Hebei	360	874	904	8	31	44	124	193	191
Shanxi	56	78	68	4	7	8	28	72	76
Inner Mongolia	4	10	13	1	2	3			
Liaoning	110	172	178	6	24	35			
Jilin	15	30	46	1	4	12			
Heilongjiang					1	1			
Shanghai	23	13	13		2	5			
Jiangsu	112	161	181	3	13	17	2	2	1
Zhejiang	46	31	28		4	11	4	4	4
Anhui	56	97	103	4	15	24	5	7	6
Fujian	6	8	8		1	1			
Jiangxi	14	16	14		1	1		3	3
Shandong	292	319	343	12	92	141	115	96	124
Henan	53	51	54	9	35	51	52	98	82
Hubei	43	56	77	1	2	2	2	7	8
Hunan	25	24	22			3	6	11	9
Guangdong	5	9	7						
Guangxi	15	16	12				2	3	4
Sichuan	59	81	94						
Guizhou	12	32	35	1	2	3			1
Yunnan	56	99	105		3	3			
Tibet									
Shaanxi	13	14	17	1	16	24	21	34	45
Gansu	36	54	47		1	1	5	7	9
Qinghai	3	5	7						
Ningxia	3	4	4	1	1	1	2	1	1
Xinjiang	11	38	43	51	168	229		1	1

3.16 *AREAS OF MULBERRY GARDENS AND TUSSAH HILLSIDE FIELDS BY REGION*

(1,000 mu*)

Region	Area of Mulberry Gardens			Area of Tussah Hillside Fields		
	1980	1986	1987	1980	1986	1987
Total	**4305**	**5412**	**5065**	**12832**	**13151**	**13060**
Beijing	6	3	3			
Tianjin						
Hebei	101	62	143	144	179	181
Shanxi	86	90	74	17	6	4
Inner Mongolia	1	2	1	384	327	288
Liaoning	8	4	3	7515	7360	7496
Jilin	4			25	25	250
Heilongjiang	5	5		411	1132	985
Shanghai	2	3	3			
Jiangsu	760	1534	1409			
Zhejiang	1257	1282	1243			
Anhui	250	341	327	3		
Fujian	5	5	5			
Jiangxi	27	29	26			
Shandong	282	175	172	1287	920	1059
Henan	70	42	34	2316	2563	2438
Hubei	307	142	112	327	308	285
Hunan	121	53	39			
Guangdong	212	267	175			
Guangxi	27	41	31	2		
Sichuan	464	704	694	49	23	19
Guizhou	15	29	28	82	23	23
Yunnan	30	68	55			
Tibet						
Shaanxi	247	489	443	40	35	9
Gansu	1	18	17	4	22	23
Qinghai						
Ningxia						
Xinjiang	17	24	27			

Note:
*** 1 mu = 1/15 hectare.**

3.17 *AREAS OF TEA PLANTATIONS AND ORCHARDS BY REGION*

(1,000 mu*)

Region	Areas of Tea Plantations			Orchards		
	1980	1986	1987	1980	1986	1987
Total	**15612**	**15359**	**15661**	**26741**	**55074**	**67623**
Beijing				178	467	559
Tianjin				150	336	416
Hebei				3075	7056	8499
Shanxi				1023	2058	2460
Inner Mongolia				416	343	392
Liaoning				3672	5092	5827
Jilin				328	357	456
Heilongjiang				259	255	291
Shanghai				49	116	138
Jiangsu	179	212	201	489	1054	1574
Zhejiang	2540	2591	2559	898	2490	3031
Anhui	1496	1741	1744	395	753	992
Fujian	1648	1798	1838	1246	2752	3418
Jiangxi	940	897	897	450	794	939
Shandong	67	29	26	3808	7941	9515
Henan	163	230	218	2148	3567	4132
Hubei	1191	1001	1020	797	1188	1410
Hunan	2367	1638	1596	1266	1707	2153
Guangdong	631	711	737	601	6592	8809
Guangxi	375	307	328	685	1288	1733
Sichuan	1711	1579	1664	1255	2620	2893
Guizhou	543	418	410	98	221	210
Yunnan	1395	1821	2003	470	791	849
Tibet	1	2	18	12	10	9
Shaanxi	360	377	395	1564	2478	3282
Gansu	5	7	7	513	1033	1638
Qinghai				37	69	98
Ningxia				124	176	230
Xinjiang				735	1470	1730

Note:
*** 1 mu = 1/15 hectare.**

3.18 *OUTPUT OF MAJOR FOREST PRODUCTS*

	Unit	1980	1985	1986	1987	1987 as Percentage of 1986
Timber in Rural Areas	1,000 cu.m	30419	31729	29667	25153	83.9
Rubber	1,000 tns	113	188	210	238	113.3
Lacquer	1,000 tns	2	2	3	3	100.0
Tung Oil Seeds	1,000 tns	303	379	346	342	98.8
Tea-oil Seeds	1,000 tns	490	619	438	518	118.2
Chinese Tallow Seeds	1,000 tns	93	71	70	68	97.1
Gallnut	1,000 tns	2	3	4	5	125.0
Palm Fiber	1,000 tns	23	36	33	36	109.1
Lac	1,000 tns		4	2	3	150.0
Pine Resin	1,000 tns	421	344	416	523	125.7
Dry Bamboo Shoots	1,000 tns	13	46	68	62	91.2
Walnuts	1,000 tns	119	122	136	147	108.1
Chestnuts	1,000 tns	67	83	95	115	121.1

3.19 *OUTPUT OF MAJOR FOREST PRODUCTS BY REGION*

Region	Timber Cut in Rural Areas (1,000 cu.m)			Rubber (1,000 tns)			Tung Oil Seeds (tn)		
	1980	1986	1987	1980	1986	1987	1980	1986	1987
Total	**30419**	**29667**	**25153**	**113**	**209**	**238**	**303350**	**346227**	**341742**
Beijing	69	49	37						
Tianjin	46	41	37						
Hebei	519	566	587						
Shanxi	168	144	149						
Inner Mongolia	85	78	74						
Liaoning	279	364	389						
Jilin	147	76	148						
Heilongjiang	1	30	30						
Shanghai	6	14	16						
Jiangsu	188	412	612				100	185	60
Zhejiang	2724	1626	1695				3550	5091	3175
Anhui	691	1379	1407				4350	3617	3530
Fujian	3317	3895	3340		1	1	2750	3660	3438
Jiangxi	2802	2551	1965				3800	7647	5507
Shandong	1007	1630	1355						
Henan	990	2045	1576				9450	12275	12070
Hubei	903	1198	885				38250	35123	31459
Hunan	5191	2609	2573				33650	46024	56106
Guangdong	4981	2419	1419	92	167	190	950	766	720
Guangxi	2148	3580	2044	2	2	3	21200	24499	24338
Sichuan	874	993	1070				112850	116807	109138
Guizhou	1358	1398	1191				42400	60518	63781
Yunnan	1270	1809	1654	19	38	44	12250	13784	14165
Tibet	72	25	125						
Shaanxi	285	304	289				177000	158520	139970
Gansu	84	204	181				1000	3160	2580
Qinghai	40	43	45						
Ningxia	22	51	63						
Xinjiang	152	134	197						

OUTPUT OF MAJOR FOREST PRODUCTS BY REGION

(tn) (continued)

Region	Tea-oil Seeds 1980	Tea-oil Seeds 1986	Tea-oil Seeds 1987	Walnuts 1980	Walnuts 1986	Walnuts 1987	Chestnuts 1980	Chestnuts 1986	Chestnuts 1987
Total	**490350**	**437746**	**518398**	**118900**	**136335**	**147241**	**67300**	**95375**	**114539**
Beijing				6600	570	3710	1900	4111	4310
Tianjin				300	515	522	100	165	214
Hebei				1190	13023	13409	350	31604	28095
Shanxi				25600	22915	21348	50	81	53
Inner Mongolia						4			
Liaoning				800	2358	1293	2950	4670	8732
Jilin						24			
Heilongjiang									
Shanghai									
Jiangsu				200	14	6	1600	2277	2543
Zhejiang	100	88	79	1950	5580	6653	3300	3863	6717
Anhui	26900	16029	26069		417	463	2300	4126	7337
Fujian	3350	3393	5074			1	350	973	1326
Jiangxi	17500	25185	30080		8	2	800	1066	1816
Shandong	125200	00864	134232		3314	3582	8850	12874	13143
Henan	1250	1869	3020	2000	9088	7113	3500	5007	8373
Hubei	6650	9603	10809	5000	1673	1673	6950	8287	9638
Hunan	21900	84846	200011	550	731	980	3000	2716	5400
Guangdong	13200	11457	24044				400	528	620
Guangxi	58350	70530	71821	250	150	161	2250	3078	3390
Sichuan	9100	4454	3654	9250	9079	10847	500	730	920
Guizhou	6600	5734	5963	1750	4288	5604	1000	2425	2885
Yunnan	2950	2885	3350	350	24071	32256	1450	3471	4379
Tibet				25700		929			
Shaanxi	200	210	191	5800	19990	19930	2700	3211	4524
Gansu				50	9960	12525		112	91
Qinghai					79	22			
Ningxia				1500	31	32			
Xinjiang					2549	4154			

3.20 *OUTPUT OF MAJOR LIVESTOCK PRODUCTS*

	Unit	1980	1985	1986	1987	1987 as Percentage of 1986
Output of Pork, Beef and Mutton	1,000 tns	12054	17607	19171	19860	103.6
Pork	1,000 tns	11341	16547	17960	18349	102.2
Average Pork Output Per Pig	kg/head	57.1	69.3	69.8	70.1	100.4
Beef	1,000 tons	269	467	589	792	134.5
Average Beef Output Per Cattle	kg/head	30.9	102.3	106.1	107.0	100.8
Mutton	1,000 tns	445	593	622	719	115.6
Average Mutton Output Per Sheep or Goat	kg/head	10.5	11.7	11.9	11.9	100.0
Cow Milk	1,000 tns	1141	2499	2899	3301	113.9
Sheep and Goat Milk	1,000 tns	226	395	430	487	113.3
Sheep Wool	1,000 tns	176	178	185	209	112.8
Fine Wool	1,000 tns	72	86	90	100	111.5
Semi-fine Wool	1,000 tns	35	32	32	37	115.6
Goat Hair	1,000 tns	12	11	12	13	109.7
Cashmere	1,000 tns	4	3	3	4	115.3
Honey	1,000 tns	96	155	172	204	118.6
Fresh Eggs	1,000 tns		4316	5550	5902	106.3
Slaughtered Fatling Hogs	1,000 heads	19861	23875	25722	26177	101.8
Proportion to Hogs at Year Beginning	percentage	62.1	77.8	77.6	77.6	
Cattle Buffaloes Sold and Slaughtered	1,000 heads	3320	4570	5550	7400	133.4
Sheep and Goats Sold and Slaugthered	1,000 heads	42420	50810	52270	60530	115.8
Proportion to Sheep and Goats at Year Beginning	percentage	23.2	32.1	33.5	36.4	

3.21 *OUTPUT OF MAJOR LIVESTOCK PRODUCTS BY REGION*

(1,000 tns)

Region	Pork, Beef and Mutton: Subtotal 1980	Subtotal 1986	Subtotal 1987	Pork 1980	Pork 1986	Pork 1987	Beef 1980	Beef 1986	Beef 1987
Total	**12054**	**19171**	**19860**	**11341**	**17960**	**18349**	**269**	**589**	**792**
Beijing	131	131	129	129	126	123		2	3
Tianjin	61	68	65	60	62	57		2	3
Hebei	421	918	953	404	849	865	4	28	39
Shanxi	173	208	206	162	180	169	2	11	18
Inner Mongolia	238	374	407	116	236	241	46	51	71
Liaoning	429	588	573	423	570	550	5	12	16
Jilin	246	345	343	236	317	308	8	23	30
Heilongjiang	371	331	321	348	311	291	16	15	24
Shanghai	166	179	188	164	179	186			1
Jiangsu	1069	1399	1349	1038	1358	1294	4	8	12
Zhejiang	698	811	762	688	800	750	5	5	5
Anhui	518	768	769	494	710	692	6	39	55
Fujian	242	481	520	237	473	511	3	4	5
Jiangxi	371	729	781	362	723	773	8	5	7
Shandong	901	1307	1264	862	1201	1115	9	52	80
Henan	530	742	803	494	650	664	7	55	89
Hubei	554	1100	1146	541	1089	1131	5	5	7
Hunan	924	1559	1638	914	1548	1626	5	8	9
Guangdong	677	1188	1271	668	1161	1240	8	25	28
Guangxi	402	636	711	397	621	691	3	13	18
Sichuan	1715	3155	3360	1643	3080	3278	36	45	52
Guizhou	267	550	597	255	535	579	5	9	12
Yunnan	309	567	596	292	539	562	10	17	23
Tibet	48	75	88	2	3	3	21	37	41
Shaanxi	232	319	319	223	298	291	2	10	16
Gansu	140	293	308	123	248	251	5	20	26
Qinghai	84	113	133	20	32	40	25	36	45
Ningxia	19	40	47	15	28	31		2	3
Xinjiang	119	195	213	33	33	37	21	50	54

OUTPUT OF MAJOR LIVESTOCK PRODUCTS BY REGION

(1,000 tns) (continued)

Region	Pork, Beef and Mutton			Cow Milk			Sheep and Goat Milk		
			Mutton	1980	1986	1987	1980	1986	1987
	1980	*1986*	*1987*						
Total	**445**	**622**	**719**	**1141**	**2899**	**3301**	**226**	**430**	**487**
Beijing	1	3	3	68	146	155		1	1
Tianjin	1	4	5	22	47	53		1	1
Hebei	13	41	49	27	84	102	19	31	34
Shanxi	10	17	19	23	106	126	13	18	18
Inner Mongolia	77	87	95	67	245	268	3	10	8
Liaoning	2	6	7	97	103	109	10	7	7
Jilin	2	5	5	25	77	82	6	3	3
Heilongjiang	7	5	6	124	538	663	15	25	18
Shanghai	1		1	73	154	169			
Jiangsu	27	33	43	27	82	87		1	
Zhejiang	5	6	7	35	121	133	2	1	1
Anhui	18	19	22	7	22	24			
Fujian	3	4	4	14	46	50			
Jiangxi		1	1	9	19	22			
Shandong	31	56	69	13	40	50	55	130	146
Henan	29	37	50	8	26	29	14	29	35
Hubei	8	6	8	24	40	41			
Hunan	5	3	3	7	10	11			
Guangdong	1	2	3	23	46	47			
Guangxi	2	2	2	5	7	8			
Sichuan	37	30	30	132	243	243	1	3	5
Guizhou	7	6	6	5	7	9			
Yunnan	6	11	11	15	48	57		2	2
Tibet	24	35	44	70	139	141	28	34	44
Shaanxi	6	11	12	17	70	91	45	103	124
Gansu	12	25	31	25	58	66	1	1	2
Qinghai	40	45	48	116	155	175	4	4	7
Ningxia	4	10	13	4	16	23		1	1
Xinjiang	65	112	122	58	204	267	9	25	29

OUTPUT OF MAJOR LIVESTOCK PRODUCTS BY REGION

(1,000 tns) (continued)

	Sheep Wool					
	Subtotal			Fine Wool		
Region	*1980*	*1986*	*1987*	*1980*	*1986*	*1987*
Total	**176**	**185**	**209**	**69**	**90**	**100**
Beijing						
Tianjin						
Hebei	5	8	10	3	5	5
Shanxi	3	3	4	1	1	1
Inner Mongolia	39	48	53	13	23	26
Liaoning	3	6	7	1	3	4
Jilin	5	5	5	2	4	5
Heilongjiang	10	7	7	4	3	3
Shanghai						
Jiangsu	3	2	1			
Zhejiang	4	3	2	3	2	3
Anhui	4	1	1	1		
Fujian						
Jiangxi						
Shandong	11	10	14	4	5	6
Henan	12	4	5	8	4	4
Hubei						
Hunan						
Guangdong						
Guangxi						
Sichuan	3	2	3			
Guizhou		1	1			
Yunnan	1	2	2			
Tibet	10	8	9			
Shaanxi	3	3	3	1	2	2
Gansu	9	12	13	1	4	5
Qinghai	17	14	20			
Ningxia	3	4	4			
Xinjiang	32	42	45	26	34	36

OUTPUT OF MAJOR LIVESTOCK PRODUCTS BY REGION

(1,000 tns) (continued)

	Honey			Fresh Eggs	
Region	1980	1986	1987	1986	1987
Total	**96**	**172**	**204**	**5550**	**5902**
Beijing	1	1	2	147	168
Tianjin				106	112
Hebei	3	5	6	358	369
Shanxi	2	3	3	123	118
Inner Mongolia	1	3	3	92	94
Liaoning	2	3	3	305	311
Jilin	2	2	2	181	174
Heilongjiang	5	4	5	186	205
Shanghai	1		1	100	113
Jiangsu	3	10	14	657	688
Zhejiang	24	63	72	165	175
Anhui	3	6	9	271	279
Fujian	4	7	6	89	94
Jiangxi	3	6	7	129	129
Shandong	3	5	6	697	791
Henan	5	8	10	373	435
Hubei	5	8	10	428	437
Hunan	3	4	4	235	226
Guangdong	3	5	5	135	140
Guangxi	2	1	2	43	38
Sichuan	9	14	17	357	392
Guizhou	1	2	2	48	48
Yunnan	3	3	4	67	73
Tibet			1	1	12
Shaanxi	4	4	5	122	133
Gansu	2	3	3	60	68
Qinghai				10	8
Ningxia	1	1		14	15
Xinjiang	1	1	2	51	57

3.22 *NUMBER OF LIVESTOCK AT YEAR-END*

(1,000 heads)

	1980	1985	1986	1987	1987 as Percentage of 1986
Large Domestic Animals	95246	113818	118961	121911	102.5
Draught Animals	50886	66464	69050	71131	103.0
Cattle and Buffaloes	71676	86820	91667	94651	103.3
Cattle	52515	65259	69384	71589	103.2
Cow of Fine and Improved Breed	641	1627	1846	2164	117.2
Buffaloes	18520	19934	20437	20898	102.3
Horses	11042	11081	10988	10691	97.3
Donkeys	7748	10415	10689	10846	101.5
Mules	4166	4972	5113	5248	102.6
Camels	614	530	504	475	94.2
Hogs	305431	331396	337191	327733	97.2
Sheep and Goats	187311	155884	166229	180342	108.5
Goats	80684	61674	67220	77687	115.6
Milk Goats		2334	2330	3001	128.8
Sheep	10627	94210	99009	102655	103.7
Fine-wool Sheep	24668	23936	25741	28064	109.0
Semi-fine Wool Sheep	11761	12016	11429	12754	111.6

3.23 NUMBER OF LIVESTOCK AT YEAR-END BY REGION

(1,000 heads)

	Large Domestic Animals								
	Subtotal			Draught Animals			Cattle and Buffloes		
Region	1980	1986	1987	1980	1986	1987	1980	1986	1987
Total	**95246**	**118961**	**121911**	**50880**	**69050**	**71131**	**71676**	**91667**	**94651**
Beijing	299	264	282	193	86	87	96	100	118
Tianjin	211	263	274	149	213	226	44	68	73
Hebei	3411	4752	4923	2529	3628	3695	1207	1725	1812
Shanxi	2240	2701	2717	1624	2044	2012	1093	1531	1570
Inner Mongolia	6813	7513	7308	1754	2612	2517	3537	4056	3931
Liaoning	2791	3139	3153	1773	2195	2546	1306	1402	1407
Jilin	2368	2849	2745	1436	1882	1831	1124	1602	1541
Heilongjiang	2578	3140	3146	1490	1919	1833	1034	1886	1962
Shanghai	60	68	71	28	14	13	60	68	71
Jiangsu	1122	875	857	874	682	630	985	695	670
Zhejiang	830	758	747	581	526	507	830	758	747
Anhui	2915	4862	5054	2413	3644	3760	2409	4377	4614
Fujian	994	1212	1236	716	878	898	991	1210	1234
Jiangxi	2093	2679	2845	1581	2108	2216	2093	2679	2845
Shandong	3435	4801	5387	2843	3794	4173	2178	2925	3446
Henan	5420	9574	10008	4238	7081	7384	3396	6977	7507
Hubei	3200	3391	3471	2199	2538	2563	3109	3332	3410
Hunan	3251	3662	3802	2324	2772	2930	3240	3647	3786
Guangdong	3949	5379	5525	2700	3942	4058	3949	5379	5525
Guangxi	4294	6181	6510	2733	4223	4422	4110	5955	6272
Sichuan	9541	10108	10265	3783	4269	4342	9173	9602	9728
Guizhou	4288	5720	5976	2851	3860	4053	3795	5101	5340
Yunnan	6789	9045	9233	3043	4632	4771	5704	7564	7697
Tibet	5017	5558	5633	815	1049	1143	4659	5138	5191
Shaanxi	2473	2700	2836	1634	1879	1931	1759	2009	2169
Gansu	3924	5389	5561	2239	3274	3355	2225	3068	3187
Qinghai	5539	6213	6025	398	663	590	4868	5445	5296
Ningxia	575	787	778	390	588	561	196	273	279
Xinjiang	4826	5378	5543	1549	2055	2084	2506	3095	3223

NUMBER OF LIVESTOCK AT YEAR-END BY REGION

(1,000 heads) (continued)

	Large Domestic Animals								
	Horses			Donkeys			Mules		
	1980	*1986*	*1987*	*1980*	*1986*	*1987*	*1980*	*1986*	*1987*
Total	**11042**	**10988**	**1069**	**7748**	**10689**	**10846**	**4166**	**5113**	**5248**
Beijing	76	39	36	53	49	53	74	76	75
Tianjin	65	38	36	43	86	97	59	71	68
Hebei	780	692	649	783	1540	1642	639	795	820
Shanxi	211	159	139	467	493	486	469	518	522
Inner Mongolia	1810	1824	1760	768	884	878	330	475	497
Liaoning	619	561	537	469	753	779	397	423	430
Jilin	850	868	833	154	146	138	240	233	233
Heilongjiang	1436	1133	1065	46	65	64	62	56	55
Shanghai									
Jiangsu	48	27	24	77	131	140	12	22	23
Zhejiang									
Anhui	180	139	116	274	279	262	52	67	62
Fujian	1	1	1	1			1	1	1
Jiangxi									
Shandong	370	366	345	629	1128	1195	258	382	401
Henan	522	510	473	943	1425	1372	559	662	656
Hubei	31	24	26	54	32	32	6	3	3
Hunan	4	8	9	4	5	5	3	2	2
Guangdong									
Guangxi	177	220	232	1			6	6	6
Sichuan	317	440	465	29	43	47	22	23	25
Guizhou	488	691	627				5	8	8
Yunnan	714	932	950	143	200	233	228	329	353
Tibet	244	296	308	104	113	122	10	11	12
Shaanxi	123	71	62	352	430	418	239	190	187
Gansu	433	495	480	886	1329	1363	313	455	489
Qinghai	419	466	440	150	165	136	75	115	129
Ningxia	55	45	38	229	295	289	90	167	165
Xinjiang	1069	1023	1040	1089	1078	1094	17	23	26

NUMBER OF LIVESTOCK AT YEAR-END BY REGION

(1,000 heads) (continued)

Region	Hogs			Sheep and Goats					
				Subtotal			Goat		
	1980	1986	1987	*1980*	*1986*	*1987*	*1980*	*1986*	*1987*
Total	**305431**	**337191**	**327737**	**187311**	**166229**	**180342**	**80684**	**67220**	**77687**
Beijing	2325	1456	1204	560	531	630	468	374	435
Tianjin	1002	768	505	363	543	564	250	317	327
Hebei	12934	14074	13636	8148	8159	9457	4614	4218	4912
Shanxi	5312	3665	2913	9099	4418	5101	5357	1829	2140
Inner Mongolia	5182	4810	4555	25534	25022	25447	7064	6699	6983
Liaoning	10575	10317	9304	1947	2155	2337	366	395	470
Jilin	5929	4812	4161	1709	1429	1519	135	67	63
Heilongjiang	7167	5648	4384	3030	2104	2185	326	251	235
Shanghai	2609	2093	1751	411	230	230	241	178	150
Jiangsu	20894	19257	17433	5458	5020	6403	4366	4534	5964
Zhejiang	14038	14033	13224	3240	1722	1760	1000	618	708
Anhui	11141	12235	11674	3833	2589	3217	2950	2389	3034
Fujian	6870	8513	8597	718	604	594	718	604	594
Jiangxi	10180	13441	13876	108	99	107	102	99	107
Shandong	21125	16689	15470	10413	9853	14041	6823	7071	10129
Henan	14742	15394	14047	11477	7777	9985	7648	6605	8760
Hubei	15893	19897	19255	1690	1365	1641	1577	1336	1606
Hunan	20338	25969	26478	849	580	634	846	577	626
Guangdong	19146	22627	22211	356	411	426	356	411	426
Guangxi	10341	15638	15646	803	636	667	801	636	667
Sichuan	51463	60635	62027	10886	8585	8848	7010	5193	5490
Guizhou	8957	12140	12572	2018	1474	1598	1725	1128	1211
Yunnan	13130	17126	18213	7468	6851	6995	5613	5191	5329
Tibet	196	144	156	18253	16873	17474	5601	5652	5797
Shaanxi	7605	7792	6918	6659	3962	4636	4784	2743	3330
Gansu	4239	5747	5295	11875	9761	10188	3312	1838	1903
Qinghai	683	880	894	16128	14945	14265	1658	1549	1494
Ningxia	559	658	599	3224	3442	3490	1084	822	857
Xinjiang	846	733	735	21054	25089	25903	3889	3896	3940

NUMBER OF LIVESTOCK AT YEAR-END BY REGION

(1,000 heads) (continued)

	Sheep and Goats		
			Sheep
Region	*1980*	*1986*	*1987*
Total	**106627**	**99009**	**102655**
Beijing	92	157	195
Tianjin	113	226	237
Hebei	3534	3941	4545
Shanxi	3742	2589	2961
Inner Mongolia	18470	18323	18464
Liaoning	1581	1760	1867
Jilin	1574	1362	1456
Heilongjiang	2704	1853	1950
Shanghai	170	52	80
Jiangsu	1092	486	439
Zhejiang	2240	1104	1052
Anhui	883	200	183
Fujian			
Jiangxi	6		
Shandong	3590	2782	3912
Henan	3829	1172	1225
Hubei	113	29	35
Hunan	3	3	8
Guangdong			
Guangxi	2		
Sichuan	3876	3392	3358
Guizhou	293	346	387
Yunnan	1855	1660	1666
Tibet	12652	11221	11677
Shaanxi	1875	1219	1306
Gansu	8563	7923	8285
Qinghai	14470	13396	12771
Ningxia	2140	2620	2633
Xinjiang	17165	21193	21963

3.24 *OUTPUT OF LIVESTOCK PRODUCTS AND LIVESTOCK RAISED BY ECONOMIC ZONE** *1987*

	Unit	East Economic Zone	Middle Economic Zone	West Economic Zone
Output of Livestock Products				
Pork, Beef and Mutton	1,000 tns	7785	6414	5661
Cow Milk	1,000 tns	963	1266	1072
Sheep and Goat Milk	1,000 tns	191	82	214
Sheep Wool	tn	34954.3	75101.3	98853.3
Goat Hair	tn	3886.5	3360.5	5364.3
Cashmere	tn	516.7	1842.2	1643.7
Honey	1,000 tns	117	53	34
Fresh Eggs	1,000 tns	2999	2097	806
Livestock Raising				
Large Domestic Animals (year-end)	1,000 heads	28965	41096	51850
Draught Animals	1,000 heads	21255	27046	22830
Hogs (year-end)	1,000 heads	118981	101343	107409
Sheep and Goats (year-end)	1,000 heads	37109	49836	93397
Goats	1,000 heads	24782	23554	29351
Sheep	1,000 heads	12327	26282	64046

Note:
***The east economic zone includes Beijing, Tianjin, Hebei, Liaoning, Shanghai, Jiangsu, Zhejiang, Fujian, Shandong, Guangdong and Guangxi. The middle economic zone includes Shanxi, Inner Mongolia, Jilin, Heilongjiang, Anhui, Jiangxi, Henan, Hubei and Hunan. The west economic zone includes Sichuan, Guizhou, Yunnan, Tibet, Shaanxi, Gansu, Qinghai, Ningxia and Xinjiang.**

3.25 OUTPUT OF AQUATIC PRODUCTS AND CULTIVATED WATER AREAS

	Unit	1980	1985	1986	1987	1987 as Percentage of 1986
Total Output of Aquatic Products	1,000 tns	4497	7052	8236	9553	116.0
Fresh Water Aquatic Products	1,000 tns	1240	2854	3482	4072	116.9
Breeding and Culturing	1,000 tns	900	2378	2944	3472	117.9
Fish	1,000 tns	1164	2765	3364	3938	117.1
Shrimps, Prawns and Crabs	1,000 tns	51	55	62	81	130.6
Shell Fishes	1,000 tns	25	34	56	53	94.6
Saltwater Aquatic Products	1,000 tns	3257	4198	4754	5481	115.3
Fish	1,000 tns	444	712	858	1100	128.2
Shrimps, Prawns and Crabs	1,000 tns	2341	2745	3094	3516	113.6
Shell Fish	1,000 tns	421	706	769	840	109.2
Algae	1,000 tns	234	473	658	889	135.1
Output of Major Saltwater Aquatic Products	1,000 tns	262	273	233	236	101.3
Large Croaker	1,000 tns	864	26	17	17	100.0
Small Croaker	1,000 tns	360	31	20	20	100.0
Hair Tail	1,000 tns	4733	451	406	393	96.8
Scad and Mackerel	1,000 tns	2478	327	370	511	138.1
Black Carp	1,000 tns	380	3	6	13	216.7
Prawns	1,000 tns	334	73	29	34	117.2
Kelp	1,000 tns	2529	254	203	179	88.2
Cultivated Aquatic Product Areas	1,000 mu*	44903	58537	61679	63387	102.8
State-Run Units	1,000 mu*	16867	18735	19195	19396	101.0
Freshwater Areas	1,000 mu*	42909	54381	56802	57847	101.8
Saltwater Areas	1,000 mu*	1994	4156	4877	5540	113.6

3.26 OUTPUT OF AQUATIC PRODUCTS BY REGION

(1,000 tns)

	Output of Aquatic Products								
	Total			Freshwater Aquatic Products			Saltwater Aquatic Products		
Region	*1980*	*1986*	*1987*	*1980*	*1986*	*1987*	*1980*	*1986*	*1987*
Total	**4497.0**	**8235.6**	**9553.5**	**1239.9**	**3481.9**	**4071.9**	**3257.1**	**4753.7**	**5481.6**
Beijing	4.0	22.2	30.2	4.0	22.0	30.0		0.1	0.2
Tianjin	32.1	67.3	81.3	7.4	35.8	48.5	24.7	31.5	32.9
Hebei	97.7	155.1	179.3	11.1	32.1	38.7	86.6	123.0	140.6
Shanxi	0.8	4.0	5.4	0.8	4.0	5.4			
Inner Mongolia	11.3	20.7	23.1	11.3	20.7	23.1			
Liaoning	420.7	669.5	806.0	8.5	37.6	46.8	412.2	631.9	759.2
Jilin	8.4	38.3	45.1	8.4	38.3	45.1			
Heilongjiang	20.2	84.3	101.5	20.2	84.3	101.5			
Shanghai	204.5	237.1	263.8	18.9	74.7	87.7	185.6	162.4	176.1
Jiangsu	427.1	804.8	921.9	205.6	540.9	642.1	221.5	263.8	279.8
Zhejiang	817.4	1172.1	1249.8	67.1	198.5	221.5	750.3	973.6	1028.4
Anhui	72.8	207.4	240.7	72.8	207.4	240.7			
Fujian	471.3	809.9	982.0	16.8	61.3	71.3	454.5	748.6	910.7
Jiangxi	75.5	192.8	225.9	75.5	192.8	225.9			
Shandong	619.6	914.4	1106.6	48.7	108.3	123.5	570.9	806.1	983.1
Henan	29.1	66.1	76.2	29.1	66.1	76.2			
Hubei	135.7	466.6	582.7	135.7	466.6	582.7			
Hunan	159.1	381.7	443.8	159.1	381.7	443.8			
Guangdong	692.2	1465.0	1666.0	220.6	595.4	665.0	471.6	869.7	1001.0
Guangxi	111.3	211.8	240.3	32.1	80.4	88.9	79.2	131.3	151.4
Sichuan	52.4	158.4	171.7	52.4	158.4	171.7			
Guizhou	5.4	14.0	18.2	5.4	14.0	18.2			
Yunnan	15.2	31.2	38.1	15.2	31.2	38.1			
Tibet	0.1	0.2		0.1	0.2				
Shaanxi	2.5	8.9	11.9	2.5	8.9	11.9			
Gansu	0.2	1.2	1.9	0.2	1.0	1.9			
Qinghai	3.2	4.6	2.3	3.2	4.6	2.3			
Ningxia	0.3	3.2	5.0	0.3	3.2	5.0			
Xinjiang	6.9	11.3	14.5	6.9	11.3	14.5			
China National Aquatic Products Corporation	11.6	18.1					11.6	18.1	

OUTPUT OF AQUATIC PRODUCTS BY REGION

(1,000 tns) (continued)

Region	Output of Aquatic Products: Volume of Fine Ocean Products 1980	1986	1987
Total	**1414.4**	**1446.3**	**1959.8**
Beijing			
Tianjin	12.4	8.4	11.1
Hebei	25.5	40.4	47.8
Shanxi			
Inner Mongolia			
Liaoning	92.4	102.0	132.8
Jilin			
Heilongjiang			
Shanghai	101.2	72.3	79.8
Jiangsu	122.1	78.4	92.0
Zhejiang	572.4	409.2	564.8
Anhui			
Fujian	165.8	243.1	381.6
Jiangxi			
Shandong	186.5	195.5	251.3
Henan			
Hubei			
Hunan			
Guangdong	111.7	253.2	320.0
Guangxi	24.4	43.8	78.5
Sichuan			
Guizhou			
Yunnan			
Tibet			
Shaanxi			
Gansu			
Qinghai			
Ningxia			
Xinjiang			

3.27 AREAS FOR BREEDING AND CULTIVATING AQUATIC PRODUCTS BY REGION

(1,000 mu*)

	Total Breeding and Cultivating Areas								
	Subtotal			Freshwater Areas			Saltwater Areas		
Region	1980	1986	1987	1980	1986	1987	1980	1986	1987
Total	**44903.3**	**61679**	**63387**	**429094**	**56802**	**57847**	**19939**	**4877**	**5540**
Beijing	242.7	310	329	2427	309	324		1	5
Tianjin	61.8	327	375	541	281	312	77	46	63
Hebei	1041.1	1036	1066	9288	861	843	1123	175	223
Shanxi	236.0	288	270	2360	288	270			
Inner Mongolia	1483.0	1266	1274	14830	1266	1274			
Liaoning	1571.8	2420	2479	10676	1526	1534	5042	894	945
Jilin	2237.0	2536	2614	22370	2536	2614			
Heilongjiang	1550.7	3472	3580	15507	3472	3580			
Shanghai	324.1	477	494	3237	464	474	4	13	20
Jiangsu	4258.8	6532	6746	39754	5587	5767	2834	945	979
Zhejiang	2317.0	3212	3229	21915	2795	2781	1255	417	448
Anhui	4360.7	5461	5549	43607	5461	5549			
Fujian	841.1	1452	1621	5232	770	819	3179	682	802
Jiangxi	2606.9	3803	3817	26069	3803	3817			
Shandong	2032.1	2431	2576	17471	1864	1867	2850	567	709
Henan	2213.4	2382	2393	22134	2382	2393			
Hubei	4130.3	6534	6634	41303	6534	6634			
Hunan	4086.2	5070	5126	40862	5070	5126			
Guangdong	3409.5	5237	5474	30763	4142	4177	3332	1095	1297
Guangxi	1325.4	1903	1866	13011	1861	1817	243	42	49
Sichuan	2227.3	2561	2576	22273	2561	2576			
Guizhou	89.0	124	304	890	124	304			
Yunnan	700.9	922	990	7009	922	990			
Tibet									
Shaanxi	342.3	406	417	3423	406	417			
Gansu	216.6	281	290	2166	281	290			
Qinghai	79.0	65	70	790	65	70			
Ningxia	32.1	148	162	321	140	162			
Xinjiang	886.5	1023	1066	8865	1023	1066			

Note:
*** 1 mu = 1/15 hectare.**

3.28 *COMPARISON OF PEAK YEAR FOR OUTPUT OF MAJOR AGRICULTURAL PRODUCTS PRE-1949 AND POST-1949*

(1,000 tns)

Item	Output of 1987	The Peak Year since 1949		The Peak Year before 1949		1987 as Percentage of the Peak Year since 1949	1987 as Percentage of the Peak Year before 1949
		Year	Output	Year	Output		
Grain	404730	1984	407310	1936	150000	99	270
Rice	174420	1984	178260	1936	57350	98	304
Wheat	87770	1986	90040	1936	23300	97	377
Tubers	28220	1958	32730	1936	6350	86	444
Corn	79820	1984	73410	1936	10100	109	790
Sorghum	5430	1974	11380	1936	11950	48	45
Millet	4540	1952	11530	1936	10600	39	43
Soybeans	12180	1986	11610	1936	11300	105	108
Cotton	4250	1984	6260	1936	850	68	500
Peanuts	6170	1985	6660	1933	3170	93	195
Rapeseed	6610	1986	5880	1934	1910	112	346
Sesame	530	1985	690	1933	990	77	54
Jute and Ambary Hemp	1140	1985	4120	1945	110	28	1036
Ramie	570	1986	230	1939	120	248	475
Mulberry Silkworm Cocoons	350	1986	340	1931	220	103	159
Tussah Silkworm Cocoons	50	1980	80	1921	90	63	56
Tea	510	1986	460	1932	230	111	222
Sugarcane	47360	1985	51550	1940	5650	92	838
Beetroots	8140	1983	9180	1939	330	89	2467
Flue-cured Tobacco	1640	1985	2080	1948	180	79	911
Fruits	16680	1986	13480			124	
Apples	4260	1985	3610	1936	120	118	3550
Citrus Fruits	3220	1986	2550	1936	400	126	805
Bananas	2030	1986	1250	1937	100	162	2030
Pears	2500	1986	2350			106	
Grapes	640	1986	440			145	
Large Domestic Animals	121910	1986	118960	1935	71510	102	170
Cattle	71590	1986	69380	1935	35280	103	203
Buffalo	20900	1988	20440	1935	12990	102	161
Horses	10690	1977	11450	1935	6490	93	165
Donkeys	10850	1954	12700	1935	12150	85	89
Mules	5250	1986	5110	1935	4600	103	114
Hogs	327730	1986	337190	1934	78530	97	417
Sheep and Goats	180340	1981	187730	1937	62520	96	288
Sheep	102660	1981	109470	1937	39660	94	259
Goats	77690	1980	80680	1937	22860	96	340
Aquatic Products	9550	1986	8240	1936	1500	116	637

3.29 *OUTPUT OF MAJOR INDUSTRIAL PRODUCTS OF TOWNSHIP AND VILLAGE ENTERPRISES*

Item	Unit	1980	1986	1987	1987 as Percentage of 1986
Silk Textiles	1,000 m	107300	698750	630200	90.2
Machine-made Paper and Paper-board	1,000 tns	805	2619	3325	126.9
Grain Processing	1,000 tns	50170	94420	92230	97.7
Edible Vegetable Oil	1,000 tns	849.4	1207	1368	113.3
Crude Sugar	1,000 tns	118.6	105	81	77.1
Crude Salt	1,000 tns	1554.3	1790	1743	97.5
Coal	1,000,000 tns	107	232	239	103.0
Electricity	1,000,000 kwh	3396	8166	9170	112.2
Pyrite Ore	1,000 tns	1284.6	1810	2720	150.3
Phosphate Rock	1,000 tns	2794	4080	8330	204.2
Nitrogenous Fertilizers	1,000 tns	28	432	45.5	105.3
Phosphate Fertilizers	1,000 tns	861	638	1263	198.0
Iron Farm Tools	1,000,000 pcs	310	270	260	96.3
Wooden Farm Tools	1,000,000 pcs	53900	78380	61890	71.0
Bamboo Farm Tools	1,000,000 pcs	49270	32000	36130	112.9
Cement	1,000 tns	6700	36670	44980	122.7
Bricks	1,000 000 pcs	110430	280280	330200	117.8
Lime	1,000 tns	32240	70500	81890	116.2

3.30 OUTPUT OF MAJOR INDUSTRIAL PRODUCTS OF TOWNSHIP AND VILLAGE ENTERPRISES BY REGION

Region	Silk Textiles (1,000 m)			Machine-made Paper and Paper-board (1,000 tns)			Grain Processing(1,000 tns)		
	1980	1986	1987	1980	1986	1987	1980	1986	1987
Total	**107300**	**698750**	**630200**	**805**	**2620**	**3325**	**50170**	**94420**	**92230**
Beijing	2780	3990	4820	14	93	95	20	50	240
Tianjin				3	37	51	10	100	680
Hebei		2120	3220	66	228	300	3710	7780	12160
Shanxi	480	440	840	26	87	123	1480	3190	1190
Inner Mongolia				1	6	7	180	130	380
Liaoning	1850	11910	11980	21	88	109	740	1240	2880
Jilin				8	28	39	250	240	970
Heilongjiang				6	16	17	840	1320	1470
Shanghai	10550	47110	39880	10	96	122	390	190	100
Jiangsu	23990	184380	208570	28	167	251	4180	11710	18940
Zhejiang	47710	211720	234100	59	237	309	2770	2510	2420
Anhui	90	67060	3550	9	54	77	3180	16240	8180
Fujian		2200	3530	40	82	97	960	968	2520
Jiangxi		950	2490	7	30	27	2860	3350	3030
Shandong	5770	16050	16260	53	230	312	3970	7800	7610
Henan	4660	17280	18890	8	517	592	3800	2210	2710
Hubei		2010	4500	12	59	78	2230	6030	6500
Hunan	200	1570	1270	31	84	99	4920	4060	4250
Guangdong	7370	124140	66060	17	97	149	4970	3300	2410
Guangxi	280	160	240	30	45	56	370	480	1170
Sichuan	1560	5460	8970	56	171	197	6360	7310	7140
Guizhou				1	5	5	400	240	2250
Yunnan		150	380	8	16	19	470	2170	360
Tibet									
Shaanxi	10	40	620	27	112	140	580	1400	1120
Gansu				10	17	29	250	710	410
Qinghai					1		80	510	60
Ningxia		10	30	5	6	19	30	50	70
Xinjiang						7	260	400	1010

OUTPUT OF MAJOR INDUSTRIAL PRODUCTS OF TOWNSHIP AND VILLAGE ENTERPRISES BY REGION

(continued)

Region	Edible Vegetable Oil (1,000 tns)			Sugar (1,000 tns)			Coal (1,000 tns)		
	1980	1986	1987	1980	1986	1987	1980	1986	1987
Total	**849**	**1207**	**1368**	**119**	**105**	**81**	**107110**	**231510**	**238910**
Beijing							1530	2810	2800
Tianjin		1	1						
Hebei	25	51	66		22	5	5610	9530	8720
Shanxi	11	17	17		1		30900	87330	89360
Inner Mongolia	12	8	11				2940	5690	6450
Liaoning	10	51	56				2180	3740	3770
Jilin	10	22	23				2050	3620	3160
Heilongjiang	28	60	58				2870	7480	8110
Shanghai		13	11						
Jiangsu	40	27	90		3		430	1900	2470
Zhejiang	5	26	23	6	11	4	90	130	140
Anhui	110	123	166		1	1	480	2450	2160
Fujian	7	7	9	15	13	7	960	2630	2710
Jiangxi	74	58	56	3	2	2	4140	7140	7390
Shandong	130	212	238				5870	9730	10530
Henan	30	39	44				9330	18380	19360
Hubei	58	89	82				1330	5020	4030
Hunan	56	93	101	2	1	1	9280	12020	12380
Guangdong	39	46	43	53	37	28	1090	1960	2220
Guangxi	2	4	2	7		1	1070	1310	1630
Sichuan	172	214	223	22	20	23	10430	19140	20940
Guizhou	8	6	5	1			4170	8310	7940
Yunnan	2	2	3	10	10	8	4170	6290	7230
Tibet									
Shaanxi	9	11	12				2590	6590	7090
Gansu	2	8	12				1080	2540	2530
Qinghai	1	2	2				140	410	450
Ningxia	1		1				250	910	940
Xinjiang	7	15	14		1	1	2130	4440	4400

OUTPUT OF MAJOR INDUSTRIAL PRODUCTS OF TOWNSHIP AND VILLAGE ENTERPRISES BY REGION

(continued)

Region	Salt (1,000 tns)			Electricity (1,000,000 kwh)			Nitrogenous Fertilizers (1,000 tns)		
	1980	1986	1987	1980	1986	1987	1980	1986	1987
Total	**1554**	**1790**	**1743**	**3400**	**8170**	**9170**	**276720**	**432040**	**454680**
Beijing				20	20	30			
Tianjin	2	2	1				990		860
Hebei	20		81	50	60	30		1360	1100
Shanxi	2		1	40	40	50			
Inner Mongolia	11	3	3	10					
Liaoning								17830	20
Jilin	45	77	48	20	40	50	7310		
Heilongjiang				20	80	90			
Shanghai				10	40	50	5050		
Jiangsu	132	194	216		440	570	38010	142750	79380
Zhejiang	114	319	169	230	530	640	3400	16970	13060
Anhui				20	40	60		27020	
Fujian								1000	
Jiangxi	1	31	32	150	310	360	670		
Shandong	446	311	313	100	80	60			
Henan				160	290	90	138730	146740	234110
Hubei	4	3	3	170	280	550	70		2720
Hunan				380	620	650			19670
Guangdong	117	111	213	550	1770	1970	2760		
Guangxi	8	3	3	110	210	280			
Sichuan	72	110	153	550	1490	1580	77080	77470	89280
Guizhou				100	200	200			
Yunnan	2		1	150	420	430			
Tibet									
Shaanxi	2	2	6	20	60	60	2650		
Gansu	8	9	14	10	30	40		500	
Qinghai		8	8		10	10			
Ningxia	1								
Xinjiang	5	10	9	30	60	60		400	14480

OUTPUT OF MAJOR INDUSTRIAL PRODUCTS OF TOWNSHIP AND VILLAGE ENTERPRISES BY REGION

(1,000 tns) (continued)

Region	Phosphate Fertilizers			Phosphate Rock			Pyrite Ore		
	1980	1986	1987	1980	1986	1987	1980	1986	1987
Total	**861**	**638**	**1263**	**2790**	**4080**	**8330**	**1290**	**1810**	**2720**
Beijing									
Tianjin	3	1	5						
Hebei	79	20	89				30	70	60
Shanxi	28	1	3				320	500	790
Inner Mongolia							30		20
Liaoning	93	25	46	50			140	70	230
Jilin	10		6		10				
Heilongjiang								10	
Shanghai	16	17	19						
Jiangsu	109	53	75	60		30	20	40	30
Zhejiang	17	48	71	10	20	200	10	40	10
Anhui	27	80		30	40	200	80	130	380
Fujian	3	2	7				10	30	
Jiangxi	13	9	40	50	120	210	10	30	30
Shandong	15	34	155	10			30	20	
Henan	26	51	29				20	50	120
Hubei	122	198	369	850	1440	4100	70	160	120
Hunan	21		44	160		380	80	60	140
Guangdong	3	2	3	10		10	130	180	250
Guangxi	15			10	10	10	60	30	30
Sichuan	111	29	57	110	430	740	180	200	270
Guizhou	3	9	24	690	890	900	50	150	160
Yunnan	11	23	112	720	1100	1490			
Tibet									
Shaanxi	53	24	71	30	20	60	30	30	60
Gansu	16	10	35				10	10	10
Qinghai	1							10	
Ningxia	8	2	1						
Xinjiang			2						

OUTPUT OF MAJOR INDUSTRIAL PRODUCTS OF TOWNSHIP AND VILLAGE ENTERPRISES BY REGION

(continued)

Region	Iron Farm Tools (1,000)			Wooden Farm Tools (1,000)			Cement (1,000 tns)		
	1980	1986	1987	1980	1986	1987	1980	1986	1987
Total	**306360**	**268340**	**262120**	**53900**	**78380**	**61890**	**6700**	**36670**	**44980**
Beijing	430	530	1850	200	170	7980	120	400	530
Tianjin	1630	3570	3870	10	10		30	90	100
Hebei	41090	22350	18220	4990	13490	6640	230	1610	2180
Shanxi	5950	2250	2050	1430	630	400	310	1090	1150
Inner Mongolia	3370	1990	2000	1140	470	590	70	190	200
Liaoning	5290	1860	5230	360	940	340	450	2030	2120
Jilin	6230	11570	11700	2070	2750	2450	40	150	200
Heilongjiang	4170	5430	6420	310	460	220	40	70	90
Shanghai	100	210	450	20	60	20	70	230	260
Jiangsu	28670	18280	19380	3180	2170	3000	1470	5210	6600
Zhejiang	7420	8620	9660	1060	1490	600	820	4890	6540
Anhui	15890	14770	14470	4890	11250	6430	120	1530	2060
Fujian	5330	6250		2540	2560	3130	20	450	690
Jiangxi	10080	9120	13890	4660	5410	6870	230	640	630
Shandong	30540	58320	49590	4040	6690	6480		4060	5130
Henan	25610	28910	20810	6110	18000	3620	610	1990	2310
Hubei	17680	11260	8830	2710	4520	4090	190	1890	1460
Hunan	27060	16100	25230	6140	1680	3070	730	2200	2700
Guangdong	11450	10900	11670	2440	1050	2470	220	2530	3280
Guangxi	8760	5280	6800	590	390	430	70	300	410
Sichuan	25120	15350	16260	1980	1590	1230	460	2500	3180
Guizhou	3950	2430	2450	110	160	50	60	390	410
Yunnan	6690	2450	3080	130	60	50	80	550	790
Tibet									
Shaanxi	8710	4820	4310	2200	1220	1150	140	920	1070
Gansu	2360	1950	3410	310	380	430	120	680	740
Qinghai	370	80	100	40	10		10	50	100
Ningxia	310	410	110	50	120	60			
Xinjiang	2100	280	280	190	50	70	10	30	50

OUTPUT OF MAJOR INDUSTRIAL PRODUCTS OF TOWNSHIP AND VILLAGE ENTERPRISES BY REGION

(continued)

Region	Lime (1,000 tns)		
	1980	1986	1987
Total	**32240**	**70500**	**81890**
Beijing	1650	2800	1910
Tianjin	60	60	
Hebei	2250	15920	6770
Shanxi	2030	1690	1770
Inner Mongolia	240	160	160
Liaoning	1210	1430	1440
Jilin	280	590	770
Heilongjiang	150	8120	1890
Shanghai	380	360	450
Jiangsu	1650	3630	4120
Zhejiang	1770	2720	3740
Anhui	660	1100	2440
Fujian	520	830	19680
Jiangxi	1570	1540	2150
Shandong	4410	6870	9330
Henan	2280	4500	7630
Hubei	1170	5990	3890
Hunan	2950	3210	3900
Guangdong	2560	1710	2320
Guangxi	620	650	820
Sichuan	1990	2650	1900
Guizhou	60	270	60
Yunnan	220	730	60
Tibet			
Shaanxi	1250	1290	2450
Gansu	220	320	2210
Qinghai	40	80	20
Ningxia	70	70	
Xinjiang	20	1210	10

Section IV

RURAL COMMERCE

4.1 *PURCHASING VOLUME OF MAJOR FARM AND SIDELINE PRODUCTS**

	Unit	1980	1985	1986	1987	1987 as Percentage of 1986
Total Value of Farm and Sideline Products Purchased	1,000,000 yuan	84220	16800	19900	23692	119.1
Grain	1,000 tons	61290	107628	115162	120920	105.0
Edible Vegetable Oil	1,000 tons	1910	4098	4270	4411	103.3
Fatling Hogs	1,000 tons	142500	160208	173505	180445	104.0
Beef Cattle	1,000 tons	2216	4638	5320	6650	125.0
Mutton Sheep and Goats	1,000 heads	16802	28393	29387	32649	111.1
Fowl	1,000	266030	671042	747244	821968	110.0
Fresh Eggs	1,000 tons	991	1922	2066	2324	112.5
Aquatic Products	1,000 tons	2393	3342	3696	4269	115.5
Dried and Fresh Vegetables	1,000,000 yuan	3890	10100	13120	16210	123.6
Dried and Fresh Fruits	1,000,000 yuan	1950	6460	8550	11750	137.4
Tea	1,000 tons	262	395	418	489	117.0
Honey	1,000 tons	95	105	164	223	136.0
Cotton	1,000 tons	2610	4319	3794	4071	107.3
Short Staple Cotton	1,000 tons	214	325	313	266	85.0
Jute and Ambary Hemp	1,000 tons	544	1203	1105	829	75.0
Hemp	1,000 tons	54	27	37	28	75.7
Ramie	1,000 tons	38	72	157	301	191.7
Sugarcane	1,000 tons	15840	36875	34663	34975	100.9
Beetroots	1,000 tons	5541	8064	7516	7651	101.8
Flue-cured Tobacco	1,000 tons	698	1779	1232	1398	113.5
Sun-cured Tobacco	1,000 tons	73	94	114	105	92.1
Crude Chinese Drugs	1,000,000 yuan	930	3290	4060	6890	169.7
Mulberry Silkworm Cocoons	1,000 tons	243	361	356	350	
Tussah Silkworm Cocoons	1,000 tons	72	24	22	36	98.3
Mao Bamboo	1,000 pcs	83150	105200	858350	77252	163.6
Palm Fiber	1,000 tons	17	26	22	20	90.0
Raw Lacquer	1,000 tons	2	2	3	3	90.9
Reed Mats	1,000 pcs	59710	42210	35160	30240	86.0
Sheep Wool	1,000 tons	161	219	218	207	95.0
Goats Hair	1,000 tons	8	5	7	5	71.4
Cashmere	1,000 tons	3	4	8	4	50.0
Cattle Hides	1,000 pcs	4300	5810	5880	6650	113.1
Sheep Fur	1,000 pcs	14700	18020	17890	17030	95.2
Goat Fur	1,000 pcs	39010	43260	28300	26490	93.6
Pig Bristles	1,000 pcs	208	268	322	388	120.5
Pig Casings	1,000 pcs	107220	91900	151850	123450	81.3
Tung Oil	1,000 tons	105	112	101	73	72.3

Note:
*** Grain refers to trade grain. Vegetable Oil includes soybean oil, rice bran oil and maize plumule oil as well as oil-bearing crops equivalent to oil. Aquatic products include fresh and dried. Jute and ambary hemp are primarily processed.**

4.2 VOLUME OF MAJOR FARM AND SIDELINE PRODUCTS PURCHASED BY STATE-OWNED UNITS AND SUPPLY AND MARKETING COOPERATIVE COMMERCIAL DEPARTMENTS

Item	Unit	1980	1985	1986	1987*	1987 as Percentage of 1986
Grain	1,000 tns	57070	90616	96148	102023	106.1
Edible Vegetable Oil	1,000 tns	1850	3777	3697	3760	101.7
Fatling Hogs	1,000 heads	133927	83736	90369	104220	115.3
Mutton Sheep and Goats	1,000 heads	11518	7279	6265	8463	135.1
Fresh Eggs	1,000 tns	762	637	612	862	140.8
Aquatic Products	1,000 tns	2055	1304	1370	1984	144.8
Tea	1,000 tns	256	306	342	321	93.9
Cotton	1,000 tns	2609	4224	3321	3898	117.4
Jute and Ambary Hemp	1,000 tns	542	1128	1017	685	67.4
Flue-cured Tobacco	1,000 tns	695	1748	1210	1262	104.3
Mulberry Silkworm Cocoons	1,000 tns	243	291	284	289	101.8
Tussah Silkworm Cocoons	1,000 tns	70	22	18	32	177.8
Sheep Wools	1,000 tns	160	155	142	135	95.1
Cattle Hides	1,000 tns	4150	4590	4240	4262	100.5

Note:
*** The 1987 figures for grain, edible vegetable oil, hogs, fresh eggs and aquatic products by all kinds of commercial units.**

4.3 VOLUME OF MAJOR FARM AND SIDELINE PRODUCTS PURCHASED BY STATE-OWNED UNITS AND SUPPLY AND MARKETING COOPERATIVE COMMERCIAL DEPARTMENTS BY REGION

Region	Grain (1,000 tn)			Edible Vegetable Oil (1,000 tn)			Fatling Hogs (1,000 head)		
	1980	1986	1987	1980	1986	1987	1980	1986	1987
Beijing	252	704	738	7	13	14	2282.9	1726.6	1547.7
Tianjin	177	321	476	5	7	7	922.0	518.6	382.2
Hebei	2325	5239	5139	81	196	197	5483.5	3190.5	4488.9
Shanxi	1095	2200	1951	20	70	71	2288.4	849.9	1127.0
Inner Mongolia	744	1682	1674	57	119	73	1201.9	259.6	355.1
Liaoning	3664	5141	6680	98	120	127	3924.2	2004.8	2463.5
Jilin	2271	6535	9553	75	113	121	1698.1	1019.2	1602.9
Heilongjiang	5256	7263	7542	143	138	129	3016.9	1165.8	2211.7
Shanghai	258	516	630	50	75	73	3379.7	2883.8	3016.8
Jiangsu	4627	8119	8115	92	234	253	19317.6	13480.0	10292.3
Zhejiang	2179	2828	2803	83	104	92	12382.9	5613.6	6517.8
Anhui	3207	6705	7198	133	323	387	4684.4	2765.0	3431.3
Fujian	1214	1387	1616	21	38	47	2266.6	1147.3	2318.6
Jiangxi	2353	3587	3433	39	52	60	3825.5	2005.1	3033.4
Shandong	3388	7141	7302	262	388	433	8981.0	9420.8	6860.2
Henan	3786	7754	8364	123	343	413	6335.2	3730.7	4329.1
Hubei	2892	5980	7181	54	234	187	6372.0	2984.6	5291.7
Hunan	2979	4249	3426	71	75	86	10062.0	5768.9	8660.2
Guangdong	3294	3413	3779	79	167	161	6939.5	5515.4	9153.9
Guangxi	1507	1714	1854	26	38	15	2304.9	1040.9	3229.7
Sichuan	5053	6202	6140	206	414	449	18819.7	17803.1	18205.9
Guizhou	694	742	708	42	103	123	1015.2	923.3	1421.1
Yunnan	946	1191	1327	16	25	34	2340.4	1298.1	1370.7
Tibet	52								
Shaanxi	852	2151	1835	20	60	58	2356.8	1807.6	1451.5
Gansu	634	1185	1140	19	44	39	1276.0	1206.2	1025.7
Qinghai	109	150	175	15	17	17	120.1	104.2	199.2
Ningxia	189	421	348	6	11	8	193.6	89.4	99.5
Xinjiang	1075	1630	1690	28	99	86	135.8	45.5	132.5

VOLUME OF MAJOR FARM AND SIDELINE PRODUCTS PURCHASED BY STATE-OWNED UNITS AND SUPPLY AND MARKETING COOPERATIVE COMMERCIAL DEPARTMENTS BY REGION

(continued)

	Cotton (tn)			Fresh Eggs (tn)			Aquatic Products (tn)		
Region	1980	1986	1987	1980	1986	1987	1980	1986	1987
Beijing		221	654	24206	44199	78676	1978	2474	6167
Tianjin	895	11130	8415	6374	51033	68275	15037	17640	51083
Hebei	243344	509806	399251	37402	28343	46205	31347	12003	19887
Shanxi	71347	60087	73619	18096	7265	11016	243	2463	3698
Inner Mongolia		234	1053	13322	4861	6290	3295	670	553
Liaoning	19333	7394	3527	11112	11005	18347	225737	169809	210010
Jilin		143	571	5936	2297	6898	1575	6947	17650
Heilongjiang		203		14211	6700	24741	6030	9448	27650
Shanghai	74377	21589	14140	46380	72518	95761	267502	195005	248029
Jiangsu	403938	352068	405774	69189	83277	72215	166523	111762	94112
Zhejiang	78910	67935	59051	38745	32527	50443	374349	262884	385595
Anhui	112169	152040	174841	49908	24342	41885	11382	8043	28849
Fujian	2		7	14967	8248	17599	180048	106354	173861
Jiangxi	42559	50480	55649	11940	1778	5767	10134	9532	14334
Shandong	520758	820574	1158611	48401	24135	32165	359025	125297	148833
Henan	382870	436956	507943	66291	44834	68102	1630	2536	9958
Hubei	312155	415838	406924	129654	62740	75101	26390	22042	47956
Hunan	94471	66599	47640	83410	47877	40533	13094	12186	14917
Guangdong			22	18587	8992	32634	304041	240059	410116
Guangxi	44	218	653	4790	256	7254	48281	36643	43389
Sichuan	91742	84377	82321	13121	16018	19657	1578	5813	7687
Guizhou	12	637	350	4097	1824	5173	225	596	876
Yunnan	935	186	44	4357	8659	8504	2673	5682	7126
Tibet									
Shaanxi	78042	786004	50918	14009	11305	16342	713	642	1038
Gansu	2505	3480	4271	9624	3603	6154	168	392	983
Qinghai		496		1026	533	1442	1407	675	1567
Ningxia			37	2100	558	234	54	45	102
Xinjiang	77628	210165	242106	283	1907	4551	543	1897	5096

4.4 *URBAN AND RURAL FREE MARKETS*

Item	1980	1985	1986	1987	1987 as Percentage of 1986
Number of Trade Markets	40809	61337	67610	69683	103.1
Urban	2919	8013	9701	10908	112.4
Rural	37890	53324	57909	58775	101.5
Transaction (1,000,000 yuan)	23500	7050	9068	11579	127.7
Urban	2400	1810	2447	3471	142.0
Rural	21100	5240	6621	8108	122.5
Grain and Oil	3443	496	712	847	119.0
Meat, Fowl and Eggs	4205	1401	2468	3203	129.8
Aquatic Products	932	332	644	854	132.6
Vegetables	215	488	969	1311	135.3
Dried and Fresh Fruits	746	255	593	831	140.1
Agricultural Producer Goods	707	139	152	158	103.9
Large Domestic Animals	2653	326	311	326	104.8
Fowl		485	510	558	109.4
Industrial Products		534	1680	2280	135.7

4.5 *RETAIL SALES BY FARMERS TO NON-AGRICULTURAL RESIDENTS IN VOLUME AND VALUE*

Item	Unit	1980		1986		1987	
		Volume	Value (1,000,000 yuan)	Volume	Value (1,000,000 yuan)	Volume	Value (1,000,000 yuan)
Total Value			**6900**		**37500**		**46100**
Food		310	6050	630	35100	661	43560
Grain	1,000 tn	5	1800	34	3280	39	4100
Edible Vegetable Oil	1,000 tn	705	140	4430	1130	4785	1410
Fatling Hogs	1,000 head	45	700	204	7950	265	10240
Beef Cattle	1,000 head	350	60	1472	480	1481	750
Mutton Sheep and Goats	1,000 head	11200	120	48372	490	51613	580
Fowl	1,000 head	18	280	122	1990	125	2250
Fresh Eggs	1,000 tn	27	500	145	3660	159	4480
Aquatic Products	1,000 tn	13	600		4570		6130
Dried and Fresh Vegetables		5	110		60000		6700
Dried and Fresh Fruit		3	380	91	3070	108	3680
Apples	1,000 tn	1	70	63	1090	76	1390
Citrus Fruit	1,000 tn	56	30	15	880	16	1220
Tea	1,000 tn		30	4	150	5	170
Honey	1,000 tn			58	10	54	10
Sugar Cane	1,000 tn				140		140
Articles for Daily Use			450		1550		1750
Fuels			400		850		790

4.6 *MAJOR EXPORT VOLUME OF FARM AND SIDELINE PRODUCTS AND PROCESSED GOODS*

(customs statistics)

Item	Unit	1985	1986	1987	1987 as Percentage of 1986
Live Hogs	1,000 heads	2960	3100	3020	97.4
Live Poultry	1,000	34510	42430	41150	97.0
Fresh or Frozen Beef	tn	31625	25704	33589	130.7
Fresh or Frozen Pork	tn	111061	104670	99964	95.5
Frozen Chicken	tn	12571	27971	16768	59.9
Frozen Rabbit Meat	tn	24211	13974	20545	147.0
Fresh Eggs	1,000,000	1018	1063	1109	104.3
Aquatic Products	tn	119595	166756	218210	130.9
Grain	1,000 tns	9330	9420	7370	78.2
Rice	1,000 tns	1010	950	1020	107.4
Soybeans	1,000 tns	1140	1370	1710	124.8
Cotton	tn		558089	754576	135.2
Vegetables	tn	512008	644038	670199	104.1
Fruits	tn	214112	223859	245398	109.6
Bitter Apricot Kernel	tn	6649	9269	7934	85.6
Walnuts in Shell	tn	11844	13786	9777	70.9
Walnut Meats	tn	8212	8212	11293	137.5
Chestnuts	tn	30991	38817	35966	92.7
Sugar	tn	184025	266474	452494	169.8
Natural Honey	tn	54790	80589	66831	82.9
Tea	tn	136787	172085	174279	101.3
Dried Chillies	tn	40368	31610	33232	105.1
Canned Food	tn	389874	445177	513525	115.4

MAJOR EXPORT VOLUME OF FARM AND SIDELINE PRODUCTS AND PROCESSED GOODS

(customs statistics) (continued)

Item	Unit	1985	1986	1987	1987 as Percentage of 1986
Canned Pork	tn	98589	88664	93757	105.7
Canned Vegetables	tn	233768	287134	301404	105.0
Canned Fruits	tn	40697	47896	87351	182.4
Other Canned Food	tn	16820	21483	31003	144.3
Flue-cured Tobacco	tn	17777	15387	17019	110.6
Goat Skin	1,000 pcs	17790	14180	9370	66.1
Furskin	1,000 pcs	4460	5120	3840	75.0
Raw Silk	tn	10893	9394	9242	98.4
Cashmere	tn	2069	1503	1814	120.7
Rabbit Hair	tn	4450	3556	4778	134.4
Hog Bristles	tn	9018	9368	11070	118.2
Sheep Casings	tn	962	631	719	113.9
Goat Casings	tn	516	412	571	138.6
Salted Pig Casings	tn	10746	12939	12123	93.7
Chicken, Duck and Goose Feathers		8001	9684	19527	201.6
Medicinal Materials	tn	53990	65018	90413	139.1
Edible Oil Seeds	tn	409604	509789	528947	103.8
Peanuts and Shelled Peanuts	tn	163365	262419	267988	102.1
Edible Vegetable Oil	tn	161618	165723	55659	33.4
Tung Oil	tn	11458	19912	30570	153.5
Resin	tn	156567	163920	205102	125.1
Skin Plates	tn	2820	2740	2320	84.7

4.7 OVERALL PURCHASING PRICE INDEXES OF FARM AND SIDELINE PRODUCTS BY CATEGORY OF COMMODITIES*

Item	1980	1985	1986	1987
1950 = 100				
Comprehensive Index	284.4	362.9	386.1	432.4
Grain	364.6	522.2	573.9	619.8
Industrial Crops	247.6	277.3	287.3	296.8
Poultry and Livestock Products	259.2	343.0	353.3	416.5
Other Farm and Sideline Products	324.2	458.6	493.9	
1978 = 100				
Comprehensive Index	130.8	166.8	177.5	198.8
Grain	140.8	201.7	221.7	239.4
Industrial Crops	136.9	153.2	158.7	163.9
Poultry and Livestock Products	127.7	168.9	174.0	205.2
Other Farm and Sideline Products	115.8	163.8	176.4	
1980= 100				
Comprehensive Index	100.0	127.6	135.8	152.1
Grain	100.0	143.2	157.4	170.0
Industrial Crops	100.0	112.0	116.0	119.8
Poultry and Livestock Products	100.0	132.3	136.3	160.7
Other Farm and Sideline Products	100.0	141.3	152.2	

Note:
*** Purchasing price indexes of farm and sideline products includes list prices, negotiated prices and free market prices.**

OVERALL PURCHASING PRICE INDEXES OF FARM AND SIDELINE PRODUCTS BY CATEGORY OF COMMODITIES

(the preceding year = 100) (continued)

Item	1980	1985	1986	1987
Comprehensive Index	107.1	108.6	106.4	112.0
Grain	107.9	101.8	109.9	108.0
Industrial Crops	110.9	101.5	103.6	103.3
Edible Vegetable Oil and Oil-bearing Crops	112.4	104.3	104.6	106.0
Cotton	116.7	97.7	99.5	104.7
Hemp Crops	106.4	109.5	117.8	74.1
Tobacco Crops	104.3	102.4	100.2	105.9
Sugar Crops	102.5	102.1	104.8	110.5
Tea	100.0	113.5	114.3	112.6
Bamboo and Timber	115.8	155.5	114.9	112.6
Paints for Industrial Purposes	110.6	101.6	99.8	
Poultry and Livestock Products	103.5	124.1	103.0	117.9
Livestock for Slaughtering	102.8	122.6	104.5	119.0
Poultry and Eggs	100.5	115.1	112.1	123.7
Hides and Skins	112.7	139.4	117.0	112.6
Bristles	104.7	169.0	82.1	113.4
Silkworm cocoons and Silk	100.4	105.5	107.4	124.7
Dried and Fresh Fruits	105.5	124.7	108.8	109.2
Fresh Melons and Fruits	105.9	131.6	105.0	105.3
Dried Fruits	103.5	113.5	113.7	118.0
Dried and Fresh Vegetables	107.0	122.2	104.8	119.5
Fresh Vegetables	107.3	150.4	101.2	126.2
Dried Vegetables and Condiments	106.6	114.1	113.9	113.5
Crude Drugs	101.3	122.7	77.9	111.8
Native Products	103.7	108.1	112.9	115.5
Aquatic Products	108.0	151.3	110.4	122.8

4.8 *FREE MARKET PRICE INDEXES BY CATEGORY OF COMMODITIES*

(1978 = 100)

Item	1980	1985	1986	1987
Comprehensive Index	97.4	131.0	141.1	163.4
Comsumer Goods	96.8	128.7	139.1	161.8
Grain	84.8	75.8	91.4	107.9
Edible Vegetable Oil	91.5	82.8	90.1	99.6
Meat, Poultry and Eggs	95.5	131.5	140.2	167.4
Aquatic Products	111.3	212.4	227.3	274.6
Dried Vegetables	97.7	110.3	129.9	147.3
Fresh Vegetables	102.8	155.5	166.1	198.3
Dried and Fresh Fruits	103.4	173.0	192.4	211.8
Goods for Daily Use	95.5	131.6	152.0	172.8
Firewood and Grass	105.2	153.5	178.2	207.4
Agricultural Producer Goods	99.7	150.8	157.0	174.4

FREE MARKET PRICE INDEXES BY CATEGORY OF COMMODITIES

(current period list price = 100) (continued)

Item	1980	1985	1986	1987
Comprehensive Index	147.6	135.0	116.7	121.3
Comsumer Goods	147.7	132.3	116.7	121.3
Grain	230.5	184.0	178.1	191.5
Edible Vegetable Oil	217.7	182.4	170.4	164.2
Meat, Poultry and Eggs	122.4	122.1	106.5	107.4
Aquatic Products	155.0	143.2	130.3	131.5
Dried Vegetables	148.4	129.5	126.5	118.3
Fresh Vegetables	164.9	126.2	175.4	117.6
Goods for Daily Use	115.6	112.1	97.4	105.3
Firewood and Grass	145.4	148.3	100.2	102.0
Agricultural Producer Goods	133.5	158.7	109.7	109.9

4.9 *PARITY PRICE RATIO OF MAJOR FARM AND INDUSTRIAL PRODUCTS*

Farm Products (100 kg)	Industrial Products	1980	1985	1986	1987
Wheat	Salt (kg)	117	146	153	157
	Granulated Sugar (kg)	21	27	29	30
	Plain White Cloth (m)	35	35	37	37
	Matches (100 boxes)	160	150	150	155
	Kerosene (kg)	47	59	62	64
Rice	Salt (kg)	98	117	116	134
	Granulated Sugar (kg)	17	22	22	26
	Plain White Cloth (m)	29	28	28	31
	Matches (100 boxes)	140	120	120	133
	Kerosene (kg)	39	47	47	55
Corn	Salt (kg)	81	99	111	121
	Granulated Sugar (kg)	15	18	21	23
	Plain White Cloth (m)	25	24	27	28
	Matches (100 boxes)	110	100	110	120
	Kerosene (kg)	32	40	45	50
Soybeans	Salt (kg)	172	221	257	273
	Granulated Sugar (kg)	30	41	48	52
	Plain White Cloth (m)	51	53	62	64
	Matches (100 boxes)	230	230	260	270
	Kerosene (kg)	67	89	105	112
Peanuts	Salt (kg)	244	330	333	366
	Granulated Sugar (kg)	45	61	63	70
	Plain White Cloth (m)	74	79	81	86
	Matches (100 boxes)	340	340	330	361
	Kerosene (kg)	96	133	136	149
Rapeseeds	Salt (kg)	248	318	318	326
	Granulated Sugar (kg)	45	58	60	63
	Plain White Cloth (m)	77	76	77	76
	Matches (100 boxes)	360	330	320	321
	Kerosene (kg)	102	128	130	133
Sesame	Salt (kg)	415	545	533	561
	Granulated Sugar (kg)	74	100	100	108
	Plain White Cloth (m)	129	131	130	131
	Matches (100 boxes)	580	560	530	554
	Kerosene (kg)	162	220	217	229

PARITY PRICE RATIO OF MAJOR FARM AND INDUSTRIAL PRODUCTS
(continued)

Farm Products (100 kg)	Industrial Products	1980	1985	1986	1987
Ginned Cotton	Salt (kg)	1033	1184	1110	1173
	Granulated Sugar (kg)	187	217	209	225
	Plain White Cloth (m)	322	284	270	275
	Matches (100 boxes)	1480	1230	1100	1158
	Kerosene (kg)	425	477	453	479
Flue-cured Tobacco	Salt (kg)	512	515	5758	649
	Granulated Sugar (kg)	96	95	124	125
	Plain White Cloth (m)	160	124	160	152
	Matches (100 boxes)	750	530	650	641
	Kerosene (kg)	200	208	269	265
Crude Tea	Salt (kg)	904	1182	1181	1721
	Granulated Sugar (kg)	176	217	223	330
	Plain White Cloth (m)	285	283	287	403
	Matches (100 boxes)	1170	1220	1170	1698
	Kerosene (kg)	356	476	482	702
Sugar Cane	Salt (kg)	16	20.8	23.2	24.4
	Granulated Sugar (kg)	3	3.8	4.4	4.7
	Plain White Cloth (m)	4.7	5.0	5.6	5.7
	Matches (100 boxes)	20	20	20	24.1
	Kerosene (kg)	6	8.4	9.5	10.0
Beetroots	Salt (kg)	31	29.9	30.4	35.9
	Granulated Sugar (kg)	5	5.5	5.7	6.9
	Plain White Cloth (m)	8.7	7.2	7.4	8.4
	Matches (100 boxes)	40	30	30	35.5
	Kerosene (kg)	12.0	12.0	12.4	14.7

PARITY PRICE RATIO OF MAJOR FARM AND INDUSTRIAL PRODUCTS

(continued)

Farm Products (100 kg)	Industrial Products	1980	1985	1986	1987
Mulberry Silkworm Cocoons	Salt (kg)	1046	1237	1187	1613
	Granulated Sugar (kg)	188	227	224	309
	Plain White Cloth (m)	321	296	289	377
	Matches (100 boxes)	1500	1280	1180	1592
	Kerosene (kg)	416	498	484	658
Sheep Wool	Salt (kg)	1240	1771	2027	2147
	Granulated Sugar (kg)	211	325	382	412
	Plain White Cloth (m)	358	424	493	502
	Matches (100 boxes)	1700	1830	2010	2119
	Kerosene (kg)	483	713	827	876
Fatling Hogs	Salt (kg)	450	593	576	728
	Granulated Sugar (kg)	84	109	109	140
	Plain White Cloth (m)	137	142	140	170
	Matches (100 boxes)	650	610	570	718
	Kerosene (kg)	179	239	235	297
Chicken Eggs	Salt (kg)	604	762	857	1062
	Granulated Sugar (kg)	108	140	162	204
	Plain White Cloth (m)	186	183	208	248
	Matches (100 boxes)	880	790	850	1048
	Kerosene (kg)	244	307	350	433

4.10 *MIXED AVERAGE PURCHASING PRICES OF MAJOR FARM AND SIDELINE PRODUCTS**

(yuan)

Item	Unit	1980	1985	1986	1987
Grain**	1,000 kg	360.6	416.12	465.87	508.53
Edible Vegetable Oil	1,000 kg	2640.8	2701.2	2846.0	3077.8
Fresh Eggs	100 kg	171.4	226.6	242.4	304.2
Aquatic Products	tn	770.0	2046	2269	3046
Fresh Vegetables	100 kg	10.4	19.8	22.5	27.9
Tea	100 kg	315.6	414.2	341.6	545.4
Sugarcane	tn	50.3	66.6	74.1	77.5
Beetroots	tn	85.2	88.7	89.3	108.2
Honey	100 kg	200.8	187.4	206.5	214.4
Apples	tn	344.0	754.2	845.6	866.8
Citrus Fruits	tn	445	1077	1055	1114
Ginned Cotton	100 kg	317.4	321.8	321.6	356.3
Flue-cured Tobacco	100 kg	140.2	181.8	196.1	248.5
Jute and Ambary Hemp	100 kg	108.2	69.1	92.3	102.5
Hemp	100 gk	180.0	172.1	234.7	167.5
Ramie	100 kg	234.2	797.5	1212.3	560.9
Tussah Silkworm Cocoons	100 kg	130.0	127.4	157.0	202.6
Mulberry Silkworm Cocoons	100 kg	340.8	364.0	365.0	461.7
Cattle Hides	piece	24.2	65.7	43.8	52.0
Sheep Skins	piece	4.5	9.4	16.6	25.4
Goat Skins	piece	4.1	12.2	16.5	15.5
Sheep Wool	100 kg	344.0	504.3	600.8	628.5
Goat Hair	100 kg	240.0	253.5	542.8	469.0
Cashmere	100kg	1110	2994	5080	7018
Mao Bamboo	100 pcs	95.4	187.4	194.2	211.6
Palm Fiber	100 kg	98.0	128.9	118.5	122.1
Raw Lacquer	100 kg	1260	1296	1419	1581
Timber	cubic meter	56.0	60.5	344.3	244.8
Non-Edible Vegetable Oil	1,000 tns	569.8	2939.4	2633.6	3347.6
Tung Oil	1,000 tns	2215.6	3203.8	3105.8	3384.7

Note:
*** Mixed average price refers to average price of a certain commodity with all specifications, grades and qualities.**

**** Grain refers to trade grain. Aquatic products refer to both fresh and dried aquatic products.**

4.11 RURAL RETAIL SALES AND RURAL RESIDENTS CONSUMPTION OF INDUSTRIAL GOODS

Item	Unit	1980	1985	1986	1987	1987 as Percentage of 1986
Total Rural Retail Sales	1,000,000,000 yuan	118.97	251.70	285.60	335.00	117.3
Consumer Goods	1,000,000,000 yuan	84.37	201.34	228.00	264.50	116.0
Agricultural Producer Goods	1,000 000,000 yuan	34.60	50.36	57.60	70.50	122.4
Rural Residents Consumption of Industrial Goods						
Sugar	1,000 tns	2145	3498	3947	4408	111.7
Cigarettes	1,000 cases	9632	17315	18700	19673	105.2
Salt	1,000 tns	6620	7433	8107	8162	100.7
Cloth	1,000,000 m		8.84	8.55	8.81	103.0
Woolen Fabrics	1,000 m	54060	160564	149164	146018	97.9
Silk and Stockings	1,000 m	198590	602094	599899	592183	98.7
Socks and Stockings	1,000 pairs		728564	723951	726424	100.3
Knitted Underwear	1,000 pcs	657360	1034620	1037500	1057170	101.9
Bed Sheets	1,000		54797	71384	74811	104.8
Knitting Wool	1,000 kg		42452	48205	61314	127.2
Shoes	1,000 pairs	665000	1024010	1063630	1100620	103.5
Matches	1,000 cases	15890	20720	21359	21827	102.2
Soap	1,000 cases	17980	32808	37536	35610	97.0
Detergent	1,000 tns	178	575	684	753	110.1
Thermos Bottles	1,000	48310	97143	99629	97599	98.0
Enamel Mugs	1,000	61500	76315	70129	58208	83.0
Enamel Basins	1,000	59610	69110	70472	61341	87.0
Sewing Machines	1,000	3500	6680	7148	5859	82.0
Wrist Watches	1,000	10140	46110	42870	40653	94.8
Bicycles	1,000	6460	20883	23228	23449	101.0
Electric Fans	1,000		9783	10558	12160	115.2
Washing Machines	1,000		2623	3930	4094	104.2
Refrigerators	1,000		629	951	1209	127.1
Television Sets	1,000		10745	11242	11810	105.1
Tape Recorders	1,000		5932	7383	9046	122.5
Radios	1,000	1634	17004	1382	10401	75.3
Cameras	1,000		725	786	849	108.0
Coal	1,000 tns	6374	111740	110000		

4.12 *SALES OF AGRICULTURAL PRODUCER GOODS BY STATE-OWNED UNITS AND SUPPLY AND MARKETING COOPERATIVE DEPARTMENTS*

Item	Unit	1980	1985	1986	1987	1987 as Percentage of 1986
Chemical Fertilizers	1,000 tns	55311	62318	75716	80552	106.4
Nitrogenous	1,000 tns	39881	43846	54566	54740	100.3
Phosphate	1,000 tns	13993	9506	14363	16087	112.0
Potash	1,000 tns	341	905	746	1411	189.1
Compound	1,000 tns	1096	7749	6042	8315	137.6
Chemical Pesticides	1,000 tns	1527	653	659	774	117.5
Tractors	1,000	74	32	25	44	176.0
	1,000 kw	2581	1119	1101	1496	135.9
Walking Tractors	1,000	217	283	289	390	134.9
	1,000 kw	1852	2353	2470	3109	125.9
Small Four Wheel Tractors	1,000		243	300	457	152.3
	1,000 kw		2259	3139	4218	134.4
Large Combine Harvesters	1,000	38420	4810	4920	11270	229.1
Tractor-towed Ploughs	1,000	52	26	28	36	128.6
Tractor-towed Harrow	1,000	28	5	5	6	120.0
Tractor-towed Sowing Machines	1,000	21	8	9	19	211.1
Agricultural Power-generating Equipment	1,000	754	902	935	1222	130.7
	1,000 kw	6398	7234	8105	9578	118.2
Diesel Engines	1,000	443	550	577	810	140.4
	1,000 kw	3887	5075	5312	7226	136.0
Pumps	1,000	509	557	735	903	122.9
Tires for Handcarts	1,000	7027	5710	5132	5086	99.1
Plastic Covering for Agriculture	1,000 tn		213	236	287	121.6
Soil Covering	1,000 tn		46	55	78	141.8
Middle and Small Farm Tools	1,000	547700	305080	282330	269260	95.4
Small Metal Farm Tools	1,000		137750	130260	128900	99.0
Wooden Farm Tools	1,000		44990	38510	36600	95.0
Sprayers	1,000	4908	7165	7657	9140	119.4
Powder Sprayers	1,000	508	135	151	172	113.9

Section V

RURAL ECONOMIC EFFICIENCY

5.1 *MAJOR RURAL ECONOMIC EFFICIENCY INDICATORS*

(at current prices)

Item	Unit	1980	1986	1987	1987 as Percentage of 1986
Labor Productivity in Output Value					
Rural Total Output Value of Society per Rural Laborer	yuan	869.6	1971.6	2400.4	121.8
Gross Output Value of Rural Agriculture per Agricultural Laborer	yuan	668.1	1286.3	1486.0	115.5
Gross Output Value of Industry per Industrial Laborer	yuan	2800.7	8097.5	10207.0	126.1
Gross Output Value of Construction per Construction Laborer	yuan	6359.4	4854.5	5279.8	108.8
Gross Output Value of Transportation per Transportation Laborer	yuan	5237.8	5220.2	6260.0	119.9
Gross Output Value of Commerce* per Commerce Laborer	yuan	8837.5	6498.4	7258.6	111.7
Labor Productivity in Output Volume					
Grain Per Laborer	kg	1102.8	1254.9	1286.3	102.5
Cotton per Laborer	kg	9.3	11.3	13.5	119.5
Oil-bearing Crops per Laborer	kg	26.5	47.2	48.6	103.0
Sugar Crops per Laborer	kg	100.2	187.6	176.4	94.0
Pork, Beef and Mutton per Laborer	kg	41.5	61.5	63.1	102.6
Aquatic Products per Laborer	kg	15.5	26.4	30.4	115.2
Output Value of Crop per Mu of Farmland**	yuan	92.5	173.1	197.4	114.0
Output Volume per Mu of Sown Area**					
Grain	kg	183	235	242	103.0
Cotton	kg	37	55	58	105.5
Oil-bearing Crops	kg	65	86	91	105.8
Jute and Ambary Hemp	kg	233	274	279	101.8
Sugar Crops	kg	2105	2654	2727	102.8
Sugarcane	kg	3171	3524	3676	104.3
Sugarbeets	kg	950	1064	1090	102.4
Flue-cured Tobacco	kg	121	102	119	116.7
Percentage of Non-self-consumed Farm and Sideline Products		49.6	58.0	58.2	
Purchases of Farm and Sideline Products	1,000,000,000 yuan	84.22	199.00	236.92	119.1
Percentage of Gross Agricultural Output Value at Current Prices	%	43.8	49.6	50.7	
Purchases of Grain	1,000 tns	72995	115162	120920	105.0
Percentage of Total Output of Grain	%	22.8	33.8	34.4	
Purchases of Cotton	1,000 tns	2681	3794	4071	107.3
Percentage of Total Output of Cotton	%	99.1	107.2	95.9	
Purchases of Edible Vegetable Oil	1,000 tns	1955	4270	4411	103.3
Percentage of Total Output of Edible Vegetable Oil	%	71.2	74.9	74.6	
Purchases of Fatling Hogs	1,000 heads	142500	173505	180445	104.0
Percentage of Total Output of Fatling Hogs	%	71.7	67.5	68.9	
Purchases of Aquatic Products	1,000 tns	2800	3696	4269	115.5
Percentage of Total Output of Aquatic Products		62.3	44.9	44.7	
Percentage of Non-self-consumed Rural Industrial and Agricultural Products		56.9	68.1	69.0	
Percentage Ratio of Total Expenditure to Total Revenue of Rural Economy		39.1	44.9	48.0	
Percentage Ratio of Net Revenue to Gross Revenue of Rural Economy		60.9	55.1	52.0	
Rural Household Net Labor Income Per Capita	yuan	166.4	374.68	418.35	111.7

Note:
* Commerce includes food services.

** 1 mu = 1/15 hectare.

5.2 *RURAL LABOR PRODUCTIVITY BY REGION*

(yuan)

	Total Output Value of Rural Society per Rural Laborer					
	Overall		Gross Output Value of Agriculture per Agricultural Laborer		Gross Output Value of Industry per Industrial Laborer	
Region	*1986*	*1987*	*1986*	*1987*	*1986*	*1987*
Nationwide	**1971.6**	**2400.4**	**1286.3**	**1486.0**	**8097.5**	**10207.0**
Beijing	4992.6	6310.1	2963.7	3716.5	9342.9	12108.2
Tianjin	4765.7	6570.2	2761.0	3467.4	8832.9	12802.3
Hebei	1798.3	2211.9	1051.4	1214.7	8073.3	9947.7
Shanxi	1889.5	2020.1	1024.2	1060.1	7200.5	7721.1
Inner Mongolia	1768.2	2036.8	1563.8	1778.9	5549.6	6356.2
Liaoning	3675.3	4691.4	2234.8	2671.1	12620.6	17135.6
Jilin	3072.4	3768.4	2258.6	2631.0	14687.3	19443.0
Heilongjiang	3473.2	3811.0	2646.3	2644.4	14089.6	17237.5
Shanghai	5784.2	7759.8	2778.6	3549.5	9106.2	11784.4
Jiangsu	2990.6	4612.6	1943.5	2278.1	10069.5	13091.3
Zhejiang	2876.7	3622.0	1504.8	1788.2	7797.3	9716.2
Anhui	1645.2	1946.2	1258.4	1432.8	7005.2	9081.5
Fujian	2140.1	2624.4	1496.7	1818.5	10562.6	13127.9
Jiangxi	1522.2	1728.9	1198.0	1342.1	5121.9	5054.3
Shandong	2247.2	2782.1	1520.7	1739.6	8790.8	11478.4
Henan	1543.5	1972.5	1007.4	1250.2	8970.2	10956.8
Hubei	2095.6	2458.9	1579.3	1778.0	6374.9	8465.8
Hunan	1448.9	1703.5	1109.5	1246.0	4599.9	5788.0
Guangdong	2380.9	3084.3	1720.2	2149.0	7788.3	10134.5
Guangxi	999.1	1121.9	798.5	910.7	6344.0	6935.7
Sichuan	1188.0	1372.4	877.9	989.8	5934.3	7125.7
Guizhou	942.7	1023.0	753.0	852.8	3068.6	2860.8
Yunnan	878.3	995.0	716.8	805.8	4627.1	5370.2
Tibet	1191.6	1244.4	1159.6	1200.2	1411.8	3200.0
Shaanxi	1415.5	1695.6	976.3	1149.9	5243.6	6368.1
Gansu	1078.2	1253.3	962.7	1074.4	5453.1	6244.4
Qinghai	1471.2	1565.5	1263.8	1416.8	4140.8	4628.6
Ningxia	1489.3	1596.9	1218.6	1247.6	9955.6	11884.6
Xinjiang	2136.4	2613.2	1870.1	2323.8	8472.7	9133.3

RURAL LABOR PRODUCTIVITY BY REGION

(yuan) (continued)

	Total Output Value of Rural Society per Rural Laborer					
	Gross Output Value of Construction per Construction Laborer		Gross Output Value of Transportation per Transportation Laborer		Gross Output Value of Commerce per Commercial Laborer	
Region	*1986*	*1987*	*1986*	*1987*	*1986*	*1987*
Nationwide	**4854.5**	**5279.8**	**5220.2**	**6260.0**	**6498.4**	**7258.6**
Beijing	9879.8	9120.7	8973.0	12859.7	9890.1	13800.0
Tianjin	4930.5	6627.7	10160.7	12800.0	7552.6	10381.0
Hebei	3914.8	4083.7	1631.0	3354.3	4941.8	4714.9
Shanxi	3910.3	3838.7	4934.3	5278.6	4237.8	4737.2
Inner Mongolia	6947.4	8013.3	8025.6	8673.9	8076.9	9500.0
Liaoning	4622.1	5491.7	7425.5	8612.7	9343.8	10234.0
Jilin	15229.7	16590.4	9724.8	13730.2	15397.8	17232.1
Heilongjiang	18222.2	20552.2	20091.7	25333.3	15531.9	19980.6
Shanghai	17100.6	28262.5	6164.4	8207.8	25913.0	23531.3
Jiangsu	4790.5	5544.1	4878.2	5433.0	7669.5	8695.5
Zhejiang	6571.2	8943.7	4223.0	4198.6	6922.0	6832.3
Anhui	5238.6	5223.5	4404.4	6537.6	5544.0	6354.9
Fujian	3239.2	3544.5	6483.8	7146.2	6593.1	6686.4
Jiangxi	4310.1	5033.4	4378.0	5209.2	6009.0	6811.0
Shandong	4559.9	4790.9	3639.2	4414.8	5477.2	6117.7
Henan	4236.7	4500.2	6356.3	8517.7	5623.7	6972.4
Hubei	5569.8	5893.8	6296.3	7233.6	7096.4	8141.3
Hunan	4879.9	4911.6	6324.3	6951.7	5793.4	6546.4
Guangdong	4683.3	5569.6	5416.5	6282.9	7225.1	8713.3
Guangxi	6300.0	4289.5	4291.1	3989.9	5791.0	5559.9
Sichuan	3169.4	3036.2	5833.0	6962.3	5456.0	5727.9
Guizhou	8390.5	5010.4	4812.0	4986.7	6503.8	6630.9
Yunnan	3244.2	3395.9	2873.4	3011.1	5134.3	6058.3
Tibet	5111.1	4444.4	5111.1	4200.0	2705.9	3222.2
Shaanxi	3752.7	3830.3	4778.5	5648.4	4866.4	6011.8
Gansu	3986.4	3780.1	3790.1	4435.2	7919.2	6696.3
Qinghai	4571.4	3090.9	3756.1	3083.3	6166.7	4814.8
Ningxia	2724.1	2969.7	7162.8	7833.3	4181.8	4538.5
Xinjiang	12782.6	13611.9	5966.7	6774.2	10037.0	11258.6

5.3 *OUTPUT OF MAJOR FARM PRODUCTS PER LABORER BY REGION*

(kg/person)

Region	Grain		Cotton		Oil-bearing Crops	
	1986	1987	1986	1987	1986	1987
Nationwide	**1254.9**	**1286.3**	**11.3**	**13.5**	**47.2**	**48.6**
Beijing	2280.1	2451.0	2.3	3.2	32.6	35.6
Tianjin	1616.4	1765.8	13.7	13.7	60.1	54.8
Hebei	1185.1	1162.3	30.8	37.9	37.2	41.7
Shanxi	1275.3	1229.7	11.2	13.5	61.2	53.2
Inner Mongolia	1069.8	1230.6			133.7	109.5
Liaoning	1923.1	2104.6	1.8	0.5	49.8	30.3
Jilin	3207.2	3649.6			89.1	76.9
Heilongjiang	3426.8	3354.0			36.7	24.3
Shanghai	1949.8	2125.7	17.7	13.7	123.0	148.1
Jiangsu	1951.0	1951.7	23.4	26.6	68.2	72.6
Zhejiang	1257.7	1245.6	5.9	5.1	33.6	31.1
Anhui	1345.0	1362.8	9.2	10.4	74.6	84.8
Fujian	1050.5	1147.8			24.0	23.9
Jiangxi	1395.7	1453.0	5.2	5.5	30.3	33.2
Shandong	1368.4	1428.8	39.6	52.4	87.4	98.7
Henan	988.3	1139.0	15.5	22.0	38.4	52.8
Hubei	1661.1	1652.6	31.7	31.3	59.0	53.8
Hunan	1311.1	1275.4	4.2	2.8	23.5	26.1
Guangdong	938.5	1018.7			35.9	32.4
Guangxi	752.2	799.1			16.0	12.3
Sichuan	1016.2	997.7	2.5	2.6	41.2	41.1
Guizhou	638.3	622.4	0.1	0.1	39.8	42.8
Yunnan	649.5	676.7			8.2	9.8
Tibet	530.7	544.7			13.6	14.0
Shaanxi	1080.9	1098.8	4.7	6.2	33.7	35.0
Gansu	940.4	868.3	0.6	0.8	51.0	48.2
Qinghai	881.7	925.3			92.9	92.4
Ningxia	1325.3	1174.9			53.5	37.2
Xinjiang	1563.1	1673.7	61.7	79.7	121.7	120.4

OUTPUT OF MAJOR FARM PRODUCTS PER LABORER BY REGION

(kg/person) (continued)

Region	Sugar Crops		Pork, Beef and Mutton		Aquatic Products	
	1986	1987	1986	1987	1986	1987
Nationwide	**187.6**	**176.4**	**61.5**	**63.1**	**26.4**	**30.4**
Beijing	0.5		138.0	139.3	23.4	32.6
Tianjin			69.7	68.4	69.0	85.6
Hebei	4.8	3.5	55.4	57.7	9.3	10.9
Shanxi	47.4	33.3	36.2	35.6	0.7	0.9
Inner Mongolia	321.9	340.2	75.7	82.5	4.2	4.7
Liaoning	34.3	44.8	92.5	90.5	105.3	127.2
Jilin	137.1	150.3	79.2	74.7	8.8	9.8
Heilongjiang	752.0	637.8	63.9	62.0	16.3	19.6
Shanghai		14.6	147.3	171.8	195.1	241.1
Jiangsu	18.9	17.0	81.7	80.8	47.0	55.2
Zhejiang	103.6	85.3	63.5	59.7	91.8	98.0
Anhui	7.4	6.5	43.5	43.2	11.8	13.5
Fujian	661.1	565.5	67.2	71.1	113.2	134.3
Jiangxi	165.2	177.4	70.0	72.6	18.5	21.0
Shandong	2.5	1.6	55.1	53.2	38.5	46.6
Henan	7.6	7.7	28.8	31.0	2.6	2.9
Hubei	37.8	29.7	79.3	81.6	33.6	41.5
Hunan	82.8	60.5	77.7	80.5	19.0	21.8
Guangdong	1116.9	998.8	64.9	70.1	80.0	91.8
Guangxi	754.4	770.9	42.8	47.0	14.2	15.9
Sichuan	64.5	61.4	81.7	85.5	4.1	4.4
Guizhou	18.3	18.1	52.2	55.2	1.3	1.7
Yunnan	395.6	404.5	42.3	43.1	2.3	2.8
Tibet			87.7	102.6	0.2	
Shaanxi	5.5	2.8	35.7	35.5	1.0	1.3
Gansu	89.0	92.3	50.0	50.5	0.2	0.3
Qinghai	6.8	5.3	101.3	118.2	4.1	2.0
Ningxia	280.8	267.9	34.4	39.7	2.8	4.2
Xinjiang	189.4	274.7	55.7	60.6	3.2	4.1

5.4 PURCHASING VALUE OF FARM AND SIDELINE PRODUCTS AS PERCENTAGE OF GROSS OUPUT VALUE OF AGRICULTURE AT CURRENT PRICE BY REGION

Region	Purchasing Value (1,000,000 yuan)			Percentage of Gross Agricultural Value		
	1980	1986	1987	1980	1986	1987
Nationwide	**84220**	**199000**	**236920**	**43.81**	**49.50**	**50.67**
Beijing	713	1901	2067	49.86	67.56	60.05
Tianjin	477	1613	1838	62.11	59.92	55.82
Hebei	3763	9346	9822	38.48	53.59	48.95
Shanxi	1410	2979	3665	36.88	50.65	59.67
Inner Mongolia	1295	3280	3872	42.07	42.46	44.13
Liaoning	3213	7064	9144	43.68	49.74	54.04
Jilin	1752	5441	7314	36.30	55.28	60.54
Heilongjiang	3359	7181	7989	39.24	52.35	58.31
Shanghai	1405	3007	3582	74.97	89.07	92.22
Jiangsu	6726	13325	15102	48.58	40.05	39.72
Zhejiang	4230	9036	10469	45.58	47.05	45.89
Anhui	3531	8862	10752	41.72	39.93	42.11
Fujian	2066	4738	5836	45.43	44.25	43.89
Jiangxi	2076	4850	5890	30.46	38.87	40.80
Shandong	7533	13711	17083	43.44	37.96	41.35
Henan	5579	11216	13701	41.93	43.22	42.34
Hubei	3960	10515	12870	42.07	47.99	51.55
Hunan	4172	9144	10736	37.54	41.06	42.37
Guangdong	5620	15161	18079	47.10	48.15	46.37
Guangxi	2400	4863	5663	38.52	40.97	41.06
Sichuan	6963	13235	15680	38.11	39.04	40.31
Guizhou	1041	2137	2404	28.88	26.94	26.06
Yunnan	1466	4041	4959	31.93	42.09	44.58
Tibet		104			10.48	
Shaanxi	1499	3142	3946	35.44	36.03	30.17
Gansu	764	2041	2500	28.00	36.19	38.16
Qinghai	199	524	585	25.58	37.14	36.70
Ningxia	202	602	658	31.46	42.51	44.58
Xinjiang	1231	3773	4631	39.86	57.58	56.72

5.5 *MAIN INDICATORS OF RURAL ECONOMIC EFFICIENCY BY ECONOMIC ZONE** 1987

Item	Unit	East Economic Region	Middle Economic Region	West Economic Region
Total Output Value of Rural Society per Rural Laborer	yuan	3247.0	2120.0	1349.8
Gross Output Value of Agriculture per Agricultural Laborer	yuan	1804.3	1493.8	1031.5
Major Agricultural Products per Agricultural Laborer				
Grain	kg	1334.3	1517.0	924.7
Cotton	kg	20.2	12.7	5.2
Oil-bearing Crops	kg	50.4	53.5	39.7
Sugar Crops	kg	298.4	89.0	117.6
Pork, Beef and Mutton	kg	65.1	58.7	66.0
Output Value of Farm Crops per Mu* of Farmland	yuan	267.6	168.0	154.6
Net Productive Revenue per Capita of Farmer Household	yuan	504.9	400.2	322.6

Note:
***The east economic zone includes Beijing, Tianjin, Hebei, Liaoning, Shanghai, Jiangsu, Zhejiang, Fujian, Shandong, Guangdong and Guangxi. The middle economic zone includes Shanxi, Inner Mongolia, Jilin, Heilongjiang, Anhui, Jiangxi, Henan, Hubei and Hunan. The west economic zone includes Sichuan, Guizhou, Yunnan, Tibet, Shaanxi, Gansu, Qinghai, Ningxia and Xinjiang.**

*** *1 mu = 1/15 hectare.**

5.6 COST, RETURN AND LABOR PRODUCTIVITY OF CROP PRODUCTION 1986

(yuan)

Item	Average	Rice	Wheat	Corn	Soybean	Cotton	Flue-cured Tobacco
	Average of Grain						
Per Mu							
Output of Main Products (kg)	231.23	386.24	207.77	310.98	99.73	62.75	124.01
Output of By-products (kg)	280.15	331.24	242.79	430.37	108.74	276.96	97.42
Total Output value	109.71	158.35	106.66	124.59	88.67	244.28	259.74
Main Products	96.10	143.55	96.14	111.82	83.96	210.08	255.17
By-products	13.61	14.80	10.52	12.77	4.71	34.20	4.57
Material Cost	32.05	47.13	41.02	34.80	21.66	58.43	75.81
Standard Labor Day Used	14.85	21.60	13.72	16.28	11.49	40.62	48.28
Labor Cost	22.28	32.40	20.58	24.42	17.24	60.93	72.42
Total Production Cost	54.33	79.53	61.60	59.22	38.90	119.36	148.23
Taxes	3.07	4.35	3.08	2.88	2.38	5.65	3.15
Net Output Value	77.66	111.22	65.64	89.79	67.01	185.85	183.93
After-tax Profit	52.32	74.47	41.98	62.49	47.39	119.27	108.36
Ratio of After-tax Profit to Cost	96.30	93.64	68.15	105.52	121.85	99.92	73.10
Per 100 Yuan Output Value							
Material Cost	29.21	29.76	38.46	27.93	24.43	23.92	27.18
Total Production Cost	49.52	50.22	57.75	47.53	43.86	48.86	57.06
Per 100 kg Main Products							
Production Cost	20.58	18.66	26.72	17.10	36.94	163.60	119.52
Production Cost plus Taxes	21.90	19.80	28.20	18.02	39.32	172.60	122.06
Average Purchasing Price	41.56	37.16	46.28	35.96	84.20	334.82	205.76
Per Standard Labor Day							
Output of Main Products (kg)	15.57	17.88	15.15	19.10	8.68	1.55	1.12
Output Value of Main and By-products	7.39	7.33	7.77	7.65	7.72	6.01	5.38
Net Output Value	5.23	5.15	4.78	5.52	5.83	4.58	3.81
Price per 100 kg of Main Products*	38.90	35.14	45.40	32.84	79.26	327.06	204.96
Gross Output Value per Mu*	103.56	150.52	104.83	114.87	83.76	239.20	258.73
Net Output Value per Mu*	71.51	103.39	63.81	80.07	62.10	180.77	182.92
After-tax Profit per Mu*	46.16	66.64	40.15	52.77	42.49	114.19	107.35
Net Output Value per Labor Day*	4.82	4.79	4.65	4.92	5.40	4.45	3.78

Note:
* These indicators are based on list purchasing prices. Other indicators are based on actual purchasing prices, including list prices, above-quota markup prices and negotiated prices

COST, RETURN AND LABOR PRODUCTIVITY OF CROP PRODUCTION 1986

(yuan) (continued)

Item	Average of Oil-bearing Crops: Average	Peanuts	Rapeseeds	Sesame	Ambary Hemp (processed)	Jute (processed)	Sugarcane	Beetroots
Per Mu								
Output of Main Products (kg)	90.79	140.56	80.99	50.83	173.24	149.63	525.33	126.25
Output of By-products (kg)	133.42	151.30	132.96	116.01	277.65	281.88	508.55	250.75
Total Output value	109.75	156.33	80.81	92.10	181.72	166.23	385.68	119.38
Main Products	103.64	148.26	76.29	86.36	162.61	149.83	366.37	113.46
By-products	6.11	8.07	4.52	5.74	19.11	16.40	19.31	5.92
Material Cost	30.42	48.72	26.63	15.94	41.29	42.95	121.10	43.73
Standard Labor Day Used	17.65	23.47	17.80	11.68	36.85	47.80	47.89	14.53
Labor Cost	26.47	35.20	26.70	17.52	55.28	71.70	76.80	24.07
Total Production Cost	56.89	83.93	53.33	33.46	96.57	114.65	197.90	67.80
Taxes	2.65	2.74	2.86	2.36	5.00	2.57	6.97	3.15
Net Output Value	79.33	107.61	54.18	76.16	140.43	123.28	264.58	75.65
After-tax Profit	50.21	69.66	24.62	56.28	80.16	49.01	180.81	48.43
Ratio of After-tax Profit to Cost	88.24	83.01	46.17	168.20	83.01	42.75	91.36	71.43
Per 100 Yuan Output Value								
Material Cost	27.72	31.16	32.95	17.31	22.72	25.84	31.40	36.63
Total Production Cost	51.84	53.68	65.99	36.33	53.14	68.97	51.31	56.79
Per 100 kg Main Products								
Production Cost	59.18	56.62	62.16	61.74	49.88	69.06	3.58	5.12
Production Cost plus Taxes	62.10	58.58	65.70	66.38	52.76	70.78	3.72	5.36
Average Purchasing Price	114.16	105.48	94.20	169.92	93.86	100.14	6.98	8.99
Per Standard Labor Day								
Output of Main Products (kg)	5.15	5.99	4.55	4.35	4.70	3.13	109.70	86.89
Output Value of Main and By-products	6.22	6.66	4.54	7.89	4.93	3.48	8.05	8.22
Net Output Value	4.49	4.59	3.04	6.52	3.81	2.58	5.52	5.21
Price per 100 kg of Main Products*	107.46	97.32	93.59	157.72	93.22	94.60	6.64	9.00
Gross Output Value per Mu*	103.68	144.86	80.29	85.90	180.60	157.95	368.34	119.55
Net Output Value per Mu*	73.26	96.14	53.66	69.96	139.31	115.00	247.24	75.82
After-tax Profit per Mu*	44.14	58.19	24.10	50.08	79.04	40.73	163.47	48.60
Net Output Value per Labor Day*	4.15	4.10	3.01	5.99	3.78	2.41	5.16	5.22

Note:
* These indicators are based on list purchasing prices. Other indicators are based on actual purchasing prices, including list prices, above-quota markup prices and negotiated prices

COST, RETURN AND LABOR PRODUCTIVITY OF CROP PRODUCTION 1986

(yuan) (continued)

Item	Raw Black Tea	Mulberry Silkworm Cocoons	Apples	Mandarin Oranges
Per Mu				
Output of Main Products (kg)	62.86	87.79	1141.66	1329.51
Output of By-products (kg)	1.77	320.29	142.48	19.10
Total Output value	267.95	380.43	906.76	1403.24
Main Products	267.04	358.60	898.22	1398.97
By-products	0.91	21.83	8.54	4.27
Material Cost	65.91	122.51	135.73	246.77
Standard Labor Day Used	57.65	86.99	58.85	90.04
Labor Cost	86.48	147.48	88.28	135.06
Total Production Cost	152.39	270.00	224.01	381.83
Taxes	8.90	7.16	19.22	28.08
Net Output Value	202.04	257.91	771.03	1156.47
After-tax Profit	106.67	103.28	663.54	993.33
Ratio of After-tax Profit to Cost	70.00	42.86	296.21	260.15
Per 100 Yuan Output Value				
Material Cost	24.60	29.62	14.97	18.01
Total Production Cost	56.87	69.03	24.70	26.50
Per 100 kg Main Products				
Production Cost	241.62	277.04	19.44	27.86
Production Cost Plus Taxes	255.78	284.56	21.12	30.16
Average Purchasing Price	424.86	400.22	78.68	105.16
Per Standard Labor Day				
Output of Main Products (kg)	1.09	0.97	19.40	14.77
Output Value of Main and By-products	4.65	4.37	15.41	15.58
Net Output Value	3.50	2.89	13.10	12.84

COST, RETURN AND LABOR PRODUCTIVITY OF CROP PRODUCTION *1986*

(yuan) (continued)

Item	Honey
Per Hive	
Output of Main Products (kg)	37.18
Output of By-products (kg)	
Total Output value	128.20
Main Products	70.49
By-products	57.71
Material Cost	50.78
Standard Labor Day Used	10.36
Labor Cost	15.54
Total Production Cost	66.32
Taxes	
Net Output Value	77.42
After-tax Profit	61.88
Ratio of After-tax Profit to Cost	93.31
Per 100 Yuan Output Value	
Material Cost	39.61
Total Production Cost	51.73
Per 100 kg (100 piece) Main Products	
Production Cost	98.08
Production Cost plus Taxes	98.08
Average Purchasing Price	89.60
Per Standard Labor Day	
Output of Main Products (kg)	3.59
Output Value of Main and By-products	12.37
Net Output Value	7.47

Item	Mao Bamboo	Raw Lacquer
Per 100 kg Product		
Output of Main Products (kg)	100.00	100.00
Output of By-products (kg)		103.81
Total Output value	209.15	1680.72
Main Products	167.71	1652.58
By-products	41.44	28.14
Material Cost	28.52	303.90
Standard Labor Day Used	21.94	256.44
Labor Cost	32.91	512.88
Total Production Cost	28.52	816.78
Taxes	3.83	50.00
Net Output Value	180.63	1376.82
After-tax Profit	176.80	813.94
Ratio of After-tax Profit to Cost	619.92	99.65
Per 100 Yuan Output Value		
Material Cost	13.64	18.08
Total Production Cost	13.64	48.60
Per 100 kg (100 piece) Main Products		
Production Cost	22.88	803.16
Production Cost plus Taxes	26.71	853.16
Average Purchasing Price	167.71	1652.58
Per Standard Labor Day		
Output of Main Products (kg)	4.56	0.39
Output Value of Main and By-products	9.53	6.55
Net Output Value	8.23	5.37

5.7 *COST AND RETURN OF PIG RAISING* *1986*

Item	Unit	Rural Households	Specialized Households
Average Raising Days per Hog	day	267.02	202.21
Average Gross Weight per Hog	kg	109.08	95.70
Average Purchasing Price per 100 kg of Fatling Hog	yuan	194.16	193.75
Average Revenue per Head of Hog	yuan	212.64	185.83
Material Cost per Head of Hog	yuan	173.52	152.50
Purchasing Cost of Piglings	yuan	34.23	36.19
Weight of Pigling	kg	14.78	14.48
Cost of Concentrated Feed	yuan	87.00	88.90
Volume of Concentrated Feed	kg	266.71	268.12
Cost of Green and Coarse Fodder	yuan	32.40	14.32
Volume of Green and Coarse Fodder	kg	608.58	324.33
Cost for Processing Fodder and Fuels	yuan	9.26	3.41
Depreciation Charge of Hog Houses	yuan	2.72	2.78
Cost of Medical Treatment	yuan	2.38	2.31
Loss due to Death	yuan	2.33	2.02
Materials for Hog House Beds and Other Costs	yuan	3.20	2.58
Average Labor Cost per Hog	yuan	33.93	14.58
Work Days	day	20.92	9.23
Average Total Cost per Hog	yuan	207.47	167.08
Average Hog Manure Fertilizer Value per Hog	yuan	17.92	9.33
Average Net Cost per Head of Fatling Hog	yuan	189.56	157.75
Net Cost per 100 kg of Fatling Hog	yuan	173.78	165.19
Income per Head of Fatling Hog	yuan	23.08	28.08
Income per 100 kg of Fatling Hog	yuan	21.15	28.47

Section VI

RURAL FINANCIAL STATISTICS

6.1 *RURAL AGGREGATE FINANCIAL INDICATORS*

Item	1980	1985	1986	1987	1987 as Percentage of 1986
Value (1,000,000,000 yuan)					
Total Revenue	246.45	599.01	688.19	840.80	122.2
Total Non-labor Costs	96.37	253.33	309.07	403.58	130.6
Income	150.08	345.68	379.12	437.22	115.3
Taxes	6.63	18.83	22.55	27.22	120.7
Collective Retained Income	22.17	27.92	29.72	39.31	132.3
Personal Earnings	121.28	298.93	326.85	370.69	113.4
Percentage					
Total Revenue	100.0	100.0	100.0	100.0	
Total Non-labor Costs	39.1	42.3	44.9	48.0	
Income	60.9	57.7	55.1	52.0	
Taxes	2.7	3.1	3.3	3.2	
Collective Retained Income	9.0	4.7	4.3	4.7	
Personal Earnings	49.2	49.9	47.5	44.1	

6.2 *PRINCIPAL FINANCIAL INDICATORS OF TOWNSHIP AND VILLAGE ENTERPRISES*

Item	Unit	1980	1985	1986	1987	1987 as Percentage of 1986
Total Revenue	1,000,000,000 yuan	596.1	182.74	222.36	293.41	131.9
Total Expenditures	1,000,000,000 yuan	452.1	154.75	191.37	256.05	133.8
Production Cost	1,000,000,000 yuan	339.1	126.69	160.68	213.62	132.9
Taxes	1,000,000,000 yuan	25.7	10.86	13.73	16.81	122.4
Income Taxes	1,000,000,000 yuan	7.9	3.27	3.86	4.39	113.7
After-Tax Profit	1,000,000,000 yuan	118.4	17.13	16.10	18.78	116.6
Profit Used Within the Year	1,000,000,000 yuan	94.6	15.44			
Expanding Production	1,000,000,000 yuan	47.0	7.94	8.03	10.00	124.5
Purchasing Agricultural Machinery	1,000,000,000 yuan	9.1				
Capital Construction on Farmland	1,000,000,000 yuan	9.4	0.88	0.69	0.85	123.2
Supporting Poor Brigades	1,000,000,000 yuan	4.2				
Collective Welfare Activities	1,000,000,000 yuan	6.8	1.97	1.45	1.80	124.1
Total Wage Bill	1,000,000,000 yuan	119.4	30.14	35.55	42.77	120.3
Principal Financial Ratios						
After-tax Profit/Original Value of Fixed Assets	%	45	23	17	15	88.2
After-tax Profit/Total Capital	%	24	12	8	7	87.5
Before-tax Profit/Total Capital	%	29	19	16	13	81.3
After-tax Profit/Total Revenue	%	20	9	7	6	85.7
Total Revenue/Original Value of Fixed Assets	%	244	243	234	239	102.1
Total Revenue/Circulating Capital	%	30	32	35	39	111.4

6.3 PRINCIPAL FINANCIAL INDICATORS OF TOWNSHIP AND VILLAGE ENTERPRISES BY REGION

(1,000,000 yuan)

Region	Total Revenue		Total Expenditures			Taxes		
	1986	1987	1980	1986	1987	1980	1986	1987
Total	**222355.27**	**293412.44**	**45208.97**	**191367.80**	**256046.49**	**2565.63**	**13733.94**	**16807.75**
Beijing	6121.44	7892.36	853.50	4994.86	6453.07	82.42	467.84	603.44
Tianjin	4056.52	5505.37	695.56	3282.11	4528.93	82.74	407.99	483.84
Hebei	9850.41	13288.18	2210.75	7708.68	10650.54	196.22	572.28	664.32
Shanxi	4748.31	5591.78	1003.48	3682.94	4472.33	41.40	356.31	418.85
Inner Mongolia	1008.72	1227.77	352.81	864.48	1065.47	15.32	37.93	54.73
Liaoning	12372.02	15752.63	2110.77	10338.64	13310.74	144.56	968.47	1100.89
Jilin	2759.73	3749.31	659.92	2367.17	3202.92	26.75	156.22	217.18
Heilongjiang	2877.50	3722.32	854.46	2522.00	3275.03	35.13	141.09	173.61
Shanghai	11548.54	13539.97	2048.19	9263.70	11063.53	258.53	1053.40	1078.53
Jiangsu	41447.72	55755.51	8578.30	37193.96	50760.57	560.77	2663.37	3285.12
Zhejiang	24125.76	32467.18	3627.21	20871.70	28639.49	190.53	1890.78	2324.79
Anhui	5421.01	6914.72	989.88	4729.24	6099.04	28.91	257.13	325.40
Fujian	5588.67	7088.76	1309.33	4883.64	6194.94	47.91	274.20	346.44
Jiangxi	3817.15	4413.67	1182.51	3383.22	3919.49	55.07	204.19	244.86
Shandong	25328.71	33585.90	4011.78	21221.02	28773.22	165.41	1344.94	1659.38
Henan	7399.15	10321.19	2163.55	6204.49	8821.57	97.09	354.36	425.23
Hubei	8348.41	10523.55	1774.53	7410.20	9527.67	92.58	377.38	454.18
Hunan	8590.31	11183.97	2517.88	7599.87	9953.70	97.87	417.50	538.38
Guangdong	16795.68	25283.07	3376.75	14853.63	22357.39	157.10	747.53	1069.18
Guangxi	1716.08	2233.43	773.78	1500.47	1974.18	29.76	113.87	140.56
Sichuan	9448.66	12154.23	2075.95	8622.20	11134.52	93.66	485.82	635.31
Guizhou	729.06	844.93	183.67	594.89	698.35	13.70	57.46	74.29
Yunnan	2052.79	2910.64	497.04	1868.76	2635.91	6.32	77.56	120.27
Tibet	19.06			17.15			0.43	
Shaanxi	3566.75	4362.50	700.29	3131.89	3838.24	28.08	168.36	213.20
Gansu	1293.08	1642.95	270.42	1125.18	1432.80	8.03	61.28	84.33
Qinghai	213.01	216.70	58.68	184.68	192.29	1.10	11.14	10.37
Ningxia	317.43	388.73	89.10	272.13	335.79	2.73	16.22	19.97
Xinjiang	791.59	851.12	238.88	675.50	734.77	5.94	38.89	41.20

PRINCIPAL FINANCIAL INDICATORS OF TOWNSHIP AND VILLAGE ENTERPRISES BY REGION

(1,000,000 yuan) (continued)

	After-tax Profit			Wage Bill			
Region	1980	1986	1987	1980	1985	1986	1987
Total	**11837.92**	**16103.43**	**18775.13**	**11941.99**	**30142.79**	**35551.48**	**42768.16**
Beijing	278.28	613.39	769.09	185.31	783.59	926.75	1094.11
Tianjin	183.22	392.26	521.47	173.53	567.03	603.37	722.74
Hebei	1271.67	1489.24	1754.72	471.46	1502.15	1757.56	2099.53
Shanxi	625.58	651.58	697.66	325.33	1049.19	1143.16	1222.47
Inner Mongolia	79.65	96.31	107.57	131.01	207.76	239.17	264.08
Liaoning	572.49	1002.14	1161.51	587.14	1637.44	1844.38	2214.79
Jilin	116.83	231.16	325.88	215.27	438.69	500.18	644.15
Heilongjiang	130.50	211.91	252.63	262.64	524.41	555.64	681.13
Shanghai	607.25	724.14	659.77	371.81	1249.72	1569.46	1583.10
Jiangsu	1807.97	1473.51	1709.82	1657.34	4396.27	5258.87	6680.94
Zhejiang	801.83	1363.28	1232.02	955.35	2735.65	3241.73	3949.27
Anhui	188.41	433.13	490.28	344.78	862.56	1202.16	1191.30
Fujian	250.79	430.83	547.38	494.37	1011.71	1025.17	1380.85
Jiangxi	187.06	231.74	249.32	392.47	638.53	692.94	758.09
Shandong	1710.14	2542.56	2889.22	831.89	3008.25	1414.10	4452.74
Henan	643.58	838.78	1074.39	492.78	1167.78	3764.84	1694.18
Hubei	338.05	560.63	540.43	532.23	1204.39	1337.50	1582.21
Hunan	498.36	568.78	691.89	818.68	1381.22	1551.27	1864.03
Guangdong	631.23	1182.39	1847.11	1040.19	2344.28	2909.32	4227.17
Guangxi	106.90	100.79	117.61	243.91	300.53	324.51	385.32
Sichuan	283.71	310.02	351.41	659.18	1409.23	1801.51	1926.38
Guizhou	41.25	75.85	75.36	95.16	194.57	207.32	219.19
Yunnan	95.16	90.74	154.46	203.31	383.92	446.97	584.14
Tibet		1.48			6.67		
Shaanxi	201.93	261.65	311.06	198.27	534.89	582.83	678.04
Gansu	62.90	103.58	123.22	114.73	310.43	356.21	398.23
Qinghai	19.37	16.44	14.13	19.70	72.51	62.78	56.30
Ningxia	20.12	28.35	30.57	25.99	50.88	56.27	31.32
Xinjiang	83.69	76.77	75.15	98.16	168.54	175.51	182.36

6.4 FINANCIAL INDICATORS OF RURAL ECONOMIC ASSOCIATIONS* BY SECTOR

Item	Original Value of Fixed Assets (1,000,000 yuan)		Total Revenue (1,000,000 yuan)		Total Non-labor Costs (1,000,000 yuan)		Proportion to Total Revenue (%)	
	1986	1987	1986	1987	1986	1987	1986	1987
Total	5915	7261	16300	21103	10203	13937	62.60	66.04
Primary Industry	1059	1552	1766	2639	815	1384	46.15	52.44
Crop Farming	75	79	217	233	88	101	40.55	43.35
Forestry	30	46	53	58	19	23	35.85	39.66
Animal Husbandry	55	65	118	177	76	122	64.41	68.93
Fishery	899	1362	1378	2171	632	1138	45.86	52.42
Secondary Industry	3347	4111	11434	14707	7552	10200	66.05	69.35
Industry	3095	3842	9985	13037	6747	9190	67.57	70.49
Construction	252	269	1449	1670	805	1010	55.56	60.48
Tertiary Industry	1509	1598	3100	3757	1836	2353	59.23	62.63
Transportation	1041	1035	1506	1673	823	959	54.65	57.32
Commerce, Food Services and Service Trade	324	402	1173	1590	763	1099	65.05	69.12
Others	144	161	421	494	250	295	59.38	59.72

Note:
*** Rural economic associations (Nongchun Jingji Lianheti) refer to the economic organizations that farmers voluntarily joined since 1979, to deal with farm crops production, processing farm crops, selling products and other business. The members of those associations jointly manage the associations and share the costs and benefits.**

FINANCIAL INDICATORS OF RURAL ECONOMIC ASSOCIATIONS* BY SECTOR
(continued)

Item	Pre-tax Income (1,000,000 yuan)		Taxes (1,000 yuan)		Collective Retained Income (1,000,000 yuan)		Earnings of Association Members (1,000,000 yuan)	
	1986	1987	1986	1987	1986	1987	1986	1987
Total	6098	7165	705	860	653	835	4740	5470
Primary Industry	951	1254	37	53	90	124	824	1077
Crop Farming	129	132	6	6	17	21	106	105
Forestry	34	35	2	2	6	6	26	27
Animal Husbandry	42	54	1	2	4	7	37	45
Fishery	746	1033	28	43	63	90	655	900
Secondary Industry	3881	4507	525	640	445	568	2911	3299
Industry	3237	3847	471	582	398	512	2368	2753
Construction	644	660	54	58	47	56	543	546
Tertiary Industry	1266	1404	143	167	118	143	1005	1094
Transportation	684	714	74	81	57	64	553	569
Commerce, Food Services and Service Trade	410	491	51	66	41	59	318	366
Others	172	199	18	20	20	20	134	159

6.5 *RURAL ECONOMIC ASSOCIATION* INCOME PER MEMBER* *1987*

(yuan)

	Income			
Item	Subtotal	Taxes	Collective Retained Income	Earnings of Association Members
Overall	2472	297	288	1887
Primary Industry	2801	118	277	2406
Crop Farming	2215	101	352	1762
Forestry	1273	73	218	982
Animal Husbandry	3396	126	440	2830
Fishery	2997	125	261	2611
Secondary Industry	2287	325	288	1674
Industry	2429	367	323	1738
Construction	1706	150	145	1412
Tertiary Industry	2926	348	298	2280
Transportation	3363	382	301	2680
Commerce, Food Services and Service Trade	2720	366	327	2028
Others	2285	230	230	1825

Note:
*** Rural economic associations (Nongchun Jingji Lianheti) refer to the economic organizations that farmers voluntarily joined since 1979, to deal with farm crops production, processing farm crops, selling products and other business. The members of those associations jointly manage the associations and share the costs and benefits.**

6.6 *FINANCIAL INDICATORS OF RURAL ECONOMIC ASSOCIATIONS* BY REGION* *1987*

(1,000,000 yuan)

Region	Total Revenue	Total Non-labor Costs	Pre-tax Income			
			Subtotal	Taxes	Collective Retained Income	Earnings of Association Member
Total	**21102.156**	**13936.730**	**7165.425**	**859.839**	**834.989**	**5470.597**
Beijing	14.167	8.647	5.520	0.642	1.067	3.810
Tianjin	402.517	253.519	148.998	24.781	15.880	108.337
Hebei	4920.246	3181.266	1738.980	170.413	162.016	1406.551
Shanxi	431.032	275.382	155.650	24.862	20.597	110.191
Inner Mongolia	68.758	40.433	28.325	3.330	5.292	19.703
Liaoning	555.606	355.967	199.639	24.997	18.481	156.161
Jilin	74.500	49.274	25.226	3.285	3.209	18.732
Heilongjiang	50.745	27.985	22.760	1.873	2.325	18.562
Shanghai	17.597	13.175	4.422	1.205	0.327	2.890
Jiangsu	636.370	428.098	208.272	33.355	17.053	157.864
Zhejiang	2113.230	1486.160	627.070	104.980	68.910	453.180
Anhui	647.141	411.532	235.609	28.231	29.233	178.145
Fujian	2027.337	1490.230	537.107	73.723	73.432	389.952
Jiangxi	234.149	148.967	85.182	12.297	7.700	65.185
Shandong	1545.425	840.730	704.695	58.327	73.365	573.003
Henan	2195.645	1504.756	690.889	81.408	108.205	501.276
Hubei	327.411	211.923	115.488	14.418	11.389	89.681
Hunan	549.318	335.962	213.356	25.361	22.771	165.224
Guangdong	2559.694	1706.766	852.927	95.055	121.528	636.345
Guangxi	196.709	118.439	78.270	9.445	12.360	56.465
Sichuan	629.485	454.448	175.037	30.385	20.599	124.053
Guizhou	91.218	47.977	43.241	6.178	5.133	31.930
Yunnan	130.382	78.608	51.774	5.261	4.168	42.345
Tibet	0.000	0.000	0.000	0.000	0.000	0.000
Shaanxi	484.911	353.667	131.244	16.792	20.096	94.356
Gansu	163.096	89.437	73.659	7.425	8.057	58.177
Qinghai	8.627	5.098	3.528	0.458	0.437	2.633
Ningxia	14.071	9.333	4.738	0.791	0.716	3.231
Xinjiang	12.770	8.951	3.819	0.563	0.642	2.615

Note:
*** Rural economic associations (Nongchun Jingji Lianheti) refer to the economic organizations that farmers voluntarily joined since 1979, to deal with farm crops production, processing farm crops, selling products and other business. The members of those associations jointly manage the associations and share the costs and benefits.**

Section VII

INCOME AND LIVING EXPENDITURE OF RURAL HOUSEHOLDS

7.1 RURAL HOUSEHOLDS SIZE AND INCOME PER CAPITA

Item	Unit	1980	1985	1986	1987	1987 as Percentage of 1986
Number of Households Surveyed	household	15914	66642	66836	66912	100.1
Number of Permanent Residents	person	881	3415	3387	3350	98.9
Average Number of Permanent Residents per Household	person	5.54	5.12	5.07	5.01	98.8
Average Number of Full and Part-time Laborers per Household	person	2.45	2.95	2.95	2.95	100.0
Average Number of Persons Supported by Each Laborer	yuan	2.26	1.74	1.72	1.70	98.6
Average Income per Capita	yuan	191.33	397.60	423.76	462.55	109.2
Labor and Non-labor Income from Collectives	yuan	108.37	33.37	36.15	42.09	116.4
Labor and Non-labor Income from Economic Associations	yuan		3.69	2.92	3.49	119.5
From Household Business	yuan	62.55	322.53	345.28	383.57	111.1
Other Non-labor Income*	yuan	20.41	38.01	39.41	33.40	84.7
Average Labor Income Per Capita	yuan	166.39	350.07	374.68	418.35	111.7
Average Cash and Savings Balance Per Capita at Year End	yuan	26.55	112.55	149.16	191.74	128.5

Note:
*** Non-labor income refers to income from the government relief funds, government subsidies, wages of houshold members who work at non-agricultural units, and gifts from relatives or friends.**

7.2 RURAL HOUSEHOLD TOTAL EXPENDITURE PER CAPITA

Item	Per Capita Expenditure (yuan)		Percentage	
	1986	1987	1986	1987
Total Expenditure	535.82	603.99	100.0	100.0
Household Business Expenditure	132.65	150.59	24.8	24.9
Taxes	8.07	8.84	1.5	1.5
Contribution to Collectives According to Contract	11.80	13.85	2.2	2.3
Purchasing Productive Fixed Assets	16.66	20.52	3.1	3.4
Living Expenditure	356.95	398.29	66.6	65.9
Other Non-production Expenditures	9.69	11.90	1.8	2.0
Given to Other Members out of Household	1.11	1.30	0.2	0.2
Given to Relatives and Friends out of Rural Area	2.19	2.31	0.4	0.4
Others	6.39	8.29	1.2	1.4

7.3 *RURAL HOUSEHOLD LIVING EXPENDITURE PER CAPITA*

Item	1980	1985	1986	1987	1987 as Percentage of 1986
Total Living Expenditure (yuan)	162.21	317.42	356.95	398.29	111.6
Consumer Goods	157.95	308.35	345.71	378.14	109.4
Food	100.19	183.33	201.17	219.67	109.2
Clothing	19.99	31.34	33.74	34.23	101.5
Fuel	9.66	18.16	18.57	19.29	103.9
Housing	12.80	39.46	51.23	57.76	112.8
Daily Articles and Others	15.31	36.06	41.00	47.19	115.1
Services and Recreation	4.26	9.07	11.24	20.15	197.3
Percentage	100.0	100.0	100.0	100.0	
Consumer Goods	97.4	97.1	96.9	94.9	
Food	61.8	57.7	56.3	55.2	
Clothing	12.3	9.9	9.5	8.6	
Fuel	6.0	5.7	5.2	4.8	
Housing	7.9	12.4	14.4	14.5	
Daily Articles and Others	9.4	11.4	11.5	11.8	
Services and Recreation	2.6	2.9	3.1	5.1	

7.4 PER CAPITA CONSUMPTION OF MAJOR CONSUMER GOODS BY RURAL HOUSEHOLDS

Item	Unit	1980	1985	1986	1987	1987 as Percentage of 1986
Grain	kg	257.00	257.00	259.00	259.00	100.0
Rice and Wheat	kg	163.00	209.00	212.00	211.00	99.5
Vegetables	kg	127.00	131.00	134.00	130.00	97.0
Edible Oil	kg	2.49	4.04	4.19	4.69	111.9
Edible Vegetable Oil	kg	1.40	2.60	2.63	3.11	118.3
Pork, Beef and Mutton	kg	7.75	10.97	11.79	11.65	98.8
Pork	kg	7.27	10.32	11.14	10.98	98.6
Poultry	kg	0.66	1.03	1.14	1.15	100.9
Fresh Eggs	kg	1.20	2.03	2.08	2.25	108.2
Fish and Shrimps	kg	1.10	1.64	1.87	1.96	104.8
Sugar	kg	1.06	1.46	1.59	1.70	106.9
Liquor	kg	1.89	4.37	4.96	5.48	110.5
Cigarettes	pack		23.72	25.99	26.42	101.7
Tea	kg		0.24	0.27	0.29	107.4
Cotton Cloth	m	4.30	2.54	1.98	1.57	79.3
Chemical Fiber Cloth	m	0.94	2.50	2.53	2.28	90.1
Woolen Fabric	m	0.06	0.14	0.13	0.12	92.3
Silk and Satins	m	0.06	0.07	0.06	0.05	83.3
Cotton	kg	0.38	0.43	0.34	0.52	152.9
Knitting Wool and Woolen Knitware	kg	0.05	0.04	0.05	0.07	140.0
Rubber, Gym and Leather Shoes	pair	0.51	0.55	0.66	0.68	103.0

7.5 *PER CAPITA EXPENDITURE ON CONSUMER GOODS BY RURAL HOUSEHOLDS*

Item	1980	1985	1986	1987	1987 as Percentage of 1986
Expenditure on Consumer Goods	157.95	308.35	345.71	378.41	109.5
Purchased Goods	79.62	185.62	216.97	243.75	112.3
Food	31.13	76.46	88.61	101.90	115.0
Cloth	19.61	30.70	33.11	33.56	101.4
Fuel	2.77	3.92	4.07	4.46	109.6
Housing	11.36	38.66	50.33	56.80	112.9
Daily Articles and Others	14.75	35.88	40.85	47.03	115.1
Self-Produced Goods	78.33	122.73	128.74	134.39	104.4
Food	69.06	106.87	112.56	117.77	104.6
Clothes	0.38	0.64	0.63	0.67	106.3
Fuel	6.89	14.24	14.50	14.83	102.3
Housing	1.44	0.80	0.90	0.96	106.7
Daily Articles and Others	0.56	0.18	0.15	0.16	106.7
Percentage (total expenditure on each item=item)					
Purchased Goods	50.4	60.2	62.8	64.5	102.7
Food	31.1	41.7	44.1	46.4	105.2
Cloth	98.1	98.0	98.1	98.0	99.9
Fuel	28.7	21.6	21.9	23.1	105.5
Housing	88.8	98.0	98.1	98.3	100.2
Daily Articles and Others	96.3	99.5	99.6	99.7	100.1
Self-Produced Goods	49.6	39.8	37.2	35.5	95.4
Food	68.9	58.3	55.9	53.6	95.9
Clothes	1.9	2.0	1.9	2.0	105.3
Fuel	71.3	78.4	78.1	76.9	98.5
Housing	11.2	2.0	1.8	1.7	94.4
Daily Articles and Others	3.7	0.5	0.4	0.3	75.0

7.6 *POSSESSION OF MAJOR CONSUMER DURABLES PER 100 RURAL HOUSEHOLDS*

Item	1980	1985	1986	1987	1987 as Percentage of 1986
Bicycles	36.87	80.64	90.31	98.52	109.1
Sewing Machines	23.31	43.21	46.99	49.79	106.0
Radios	33.54	54.19	54.24	52.98	97.7
Wrist Watches	37.58	126.32	145.06	161.22	111.1
Television Sets	0.39	11.74	17.28	24.38	141.1
Recorders		4.33	6.60	9.68	146.6
Washing Machines		1.90	3.22	4.78	148.3
Electric Fans		9.66	13.63	19.76	145.0
Refrigerators		0.06	0.20	0.31	153.2

7.7 *HOUSING SPACE OF RURAL HOUSEHOLD*

Item	Unit	1980	1985	1986	1987	1987 as Percentage of 1986
Average Number of Rooms per Household (year-end)	room	4.06	5.11	5.27	5.36	101.7
Average Floor Space per Capita (year-end)	sq.m	11.59	17.34	18.09	18.88	104.4
Living Space	sq.m	9.40	14.70	15.29	16.00	104.6
Made of Brick and Wood	sq.m		7.47	8.15	8.55	104.9
Made of Reinforced concrete	sq.m		0.31	0.37	0.55	148.7
Value per Room (year-end)	yuan		465.75	507.61	537.21	105.8
Value of Each Newly-built Room	yuan		747.43	890.32	1138.22	127.8
Value per Square Meter of Newly-built House	yuan		40.17	47.07	58.39	124.1

7.8 *RURAL HOUSEHOLD PER CAPITA INCOME BY REGION*

(yuan)

Region	1980	1986	1987
Total	**191.33**	**423.76**	**462.55**
Beijing	290.46	823.16	916.38
Tianjin	277.92	635.17	749.41
Hebei	175.78	407.61	444.40
Shanxi	155.78	344.98	376.87
Inner Mongolia	181.32	339.53	388.77
Liaoning	273.02	533.20	599.25
Jilin	236.30	456.70	523.09
Heilongjiang	205.58	476.18	474.46
Shanghai	397.35	936.57	1059.21
Jiangsu	217.94	561.28	626.48
Zhejiang	219.18	609.31	725.13
Anhui	184.82	396.53	429.26
Fujian	171.74	418.51	484.88
Jiangxi	180.94	395.63	429.29
Shandong	194.33	449.27	517.69
Henan	160.73	332.92	377.72
Hubei	169.88	445.13	460.66
Hunan	219.71	439.66	471.30
Guangdong	274.37	546.43	644.21
Guangxi	173.68	316.10	353.95
Sichuan	187.90	337.94	369.46
Guizhou	161.46	303.51	341.84
Yunnan	150.12	338.14	304.57
Tibet		343.57	348.39
Shaanxi	142.49	298.98	329.47
Gansu	153.33	269.40	296.14
Qinghai		369.24	392.15
Ningxia	178.06	374.49	382.71
Xinjiang	198.01	419.88	452.72

7.9 RURAL HOUSEHOLD PER CAPITA LIVING EXPENDITURES BY REGION

(1,000 yuan)

Region	Living Expenditure			Consumer Goods			(1) Food Subtotal		
	1980	1986	1987	1980	1986	1987	*1980*	*1986*	*1987*
Total	**162.21**	**356.95**	**398.29**	**157.95**	**345.71**	**378.14**	**100.19**	**201.17**	**219.07**
Beijing	252.67	644.23	705.56	244.60	622.42	675.22	135.39	291.90	339.86
Tianjin	208.37	480.32	538.89	203.39	466.72	517.31	118.63	235.50	267.66
Hebei	142.01	333.04	365.35	138.83	324.28	348.29	79.62	161.57	176.98
Shanxi	134.38	287.44	312.73	131.82	277.41	296.74	80.48	156.98	162.23
Inner Mongolia	156.60	307.46	349.14	152.51	297.26	330.81	102.37	185.85	208.78
Liaoning	228.14	433.53	471.89	220.85	422.42	449.34	128.52	221.00	236.64
Jilin	216.25	388.77	441.60	214.48	375.66	414.86	140.07	214.66	239.54
Heilongjiang	164.13	338.45	361.04	159.89	327.69	345.59	95.52	190.93	199.25
Shanghai	321.83	895.61	977.49	316.20	877.87	953.87	169.93	405.87	450.43
Jiangsu	194.71	499.33	578.90	189.11	485.80	557.14	112.88	247.16	278.27
Zhejiang	191.88	560.59	659.40	187.06	545.49	611.92	109.03	282.06	320.39
Anhui	162.94	339.98	382.99	156.96	327.49	364.30	97.45	197.05	209.98
Fujian	157.67	394.10	442.83	152.34	378.89	416.32	99.43	237.34	266.09
Jiangxi	156.01	340.58	389.64	151.84	328.53	371.10	97.27	199.61	223.87
Shandong	145.91	364.56	406.33	142.71	355.71	388.73	79.96	182.18	199.22
Henan	135.51	292.16	309.90	132.19	282.53	293.66	78.49	159.99	164.03
Hubei	152.74	373.53	408.69	148.37	360.37	385.99	98.32	217.19	232.22
Hunan	192.85	386.35	434.75	189.15	373.80	412.65	127.70	228.96	245.68
Guangdong	222.22	454.06	531.92	215.65	431.70	449.39	134.12	267.03	301.93
Guangxi	151.11	283.87	309.29	147.96	273.48	293.44	96.44	175.68	191.92
Sichuan	159.44	310.92	348.32	154.82	302.53	331.81	111.65	194.56	215.01
Guizhou	139.25	271.86	304.21	134.07	264.02	292.08	96.45	190.55	212.90
Yunnan	124.56	305.00	325.65	122.00	298.12	314.85	86.93	205.19	217.26
Tibet		257.85	245.85		256.16	243.82		179.68	171.93
Shaanxi	139.83	262.61	285.79	136.65	254.13	270.36	83.57	146.51	158.27
Gansu	126.64	232.79	252.84	123.04	225.26	240.14	81.35	137.84	144.22
Qinghai		313.54	344.93		305.49	327.77		193.08	198.56
Ningxia	135.45	301.18	334.72	132.06	291.46	316.71	85.93	172.18	187.94
Xinjiang	150.62	317.48	359.83	147.01	307.12	337.27	90.60	180.43	197.77

RURAL HOUSEHOLD PER CAPITA LIVING EXPENDITURE BY REGION

(yuan) (continued)

	(1) Food						(2) Clothes		
	Staple Food			Non-Staple Food			1980	1986	1987
Region	*1980*	*1986*	*1987*	*1980*	*1986*	*1987*			
Total	**60.59**	**86.53**	**87.53**	**35.27**	**82.63**	**94.21**	**19.99**	**33.74**	**34.23**
Beijing	71.72	92.57	96.23	41.78	112.59	134.05	32.20	60.73	68.33
Tianjin	70.22	102.83	107.46	28.71	82.06	99.28	31.39	50.55	51.18
Hebei	54.85	88.05	88.49	20.84	47.31	57.79	19.70	35.29	37.47
Shanxi	54.75	85.82	83.89	20.12	43.42	48.56	20.81	37.35	38.79
Inner Mongolia	56.81	86.66	93.83	39.65	73.42	84.83	21.51	32.70	34.43
Liaoning	59.15	89.45	93.80	60.59	96.70	101.96	30.44	47.83	50.98
Jilin	72.61	95.48	103.17	51.78	89.45	100.31	27.61	40.35	43.72
Heilongjiang	58.97	90.31	90.80	34.90	71.75	74.95	27.33	37.15	38.98
Shanghai	71.25	101.72	105.16	77.74	176.18	196.41	36.37	74.13	80.62
Jiangsu	62.13	89.35	88.59	38.74	107.38	132.86	24.39	43.33	40.76
Zhejiang	65.35	81.33	82.04	31.49	127.96	150.61	22.59	48.78	46.20
Anhui	58.88	100.51	97.70	33.10	67.07	77.06	18.81	30.38	31.29
Fujian	59.34	95.58	100.78	35.20	104.83	121.96	16.01	27.35	25.68
Jiangxi	63.16	86.25	86.07	31.67	87.66	106.44	15.59	29.17	28.47
Shandong	49.65	82.47	80.62	26.90	66.06	78.80	23.82	39.88	41.76
Henan	53.96	95.79	93.71	19.12	41.64	44.90	18.48	31.23	31.38
Hubei	61.15	84.23	83.62	35.84	98.57	108.51	17.65	35.04	33.75
Hunan	67.17	82.63	81.10	52.19	115.05	125.53	20.25	36.30	35.16
Guangdong	62.58	77.58	79.40	56.89	145.90	165.12	19.58	21.58	24.85
Guangxi	51.83	65.96	68.84	41.17	90.36	100.06	13.98	18.01	18.07
Sichuan	60.99	83.60	85.37	43.48	86.34	100.12	17.44	29.30	26.91
Guizhou	50.02	90.75	97.20	35.02	79.11	92.62	14.44	23.16	23.72
Yunnan	51.33	78.85	84.15	27.80	99.97	102.16	12.35	22.60	26.02
Tibet		91.13	85.96		47.73	48.83		29.79	27.30
Shaanxi	52.66	81.89	83.94	22.96	43.92	49.83	18.01	30.55	29.70
Gansu	60.29	85.65	85.16	20.92	37.73	41.57	16.85	28.28	26.95
Qinghai		100.12	91.07		66.31	76.41		44.64	46.28
Ningxia	64.11	90.45	87.59	21.79	59.26	74.09	19.29	37.73	38.46
Xinjiang	54.57	84.49	88.52	35.49	67.63	77.86	31.24	51.35	57.20

RURAL HOUSEHOLD PER CAPITA LIVING EXPENDITURE BY REGION

(yuan) (continued)

Region	(3) Fuel			(4) Housing			(5) Daily Articles and Others		
	1980	1986	1987	1980	1986	1987	1980	1986	1987
Total	**9.66**	**18.57**	**19.29**	**12.80**	**51.23**	**57.76**	**15.31**	**41.00**	**47.19**
Beijing	9.03	20.21	22.96	28.96	139.17	129.19	39.02	110.41	114.88
Tianjin	14.07	17.90	18.66	16.46	97.23	112.31	22.84	65.54	67.50
Hebei	8.25	19.09	17.78	14.43	60.71	62.49	16.83	47.63	53.57
Shanxi	6.18	8.68	8.79	9.20	35.59	44.08	15.15	38.81	42.85
Inner Mongolia	8.36	17.79	20.52	2.92	23.03	24.35	17.35	37.89	42.73
Liaoning	15.70	27.27	26.27	16.72	65.95	66.69	29.47	60.37	68.76
Jilin	12.12	22.66	22.50	12.59	52.91	56.97	22.09	45.08	52.13
Heilongjiang	9.29	24.14	26.55	8.70	29.91	33.49	19.05	45.56	47.32
Shanghai	10.88	19.17	20.70	60.72	266.59	266.75	38.30	112.11	136.00
Jiangsu	8.78	21.42	29.35	24.15	117.47	144.22	18.91	56.42	64.54
Zhejiang	11.62	21.26	21.07	26.23	117.81	146.46	17.59	75.58	77.80
Anhui	9.24	20.79	21.98	17.15	44.49	60.73	14.31	34.78	40.32
Fujian	13.17	20.90	22.14	11.54	53.20	53.82	12.19	40.10	48.59
Jiangxi	12.97	21.50	22.76	12.51	45.30	56.06	13.50	32.95	39.94
Shandong	6.76	22.67	21.81	14.42	63.13	72.70	17.75	47.85	53.24
Henan	6.90	14.55	14.95	14.50	45.74	50.30	13.82	31.02	33.00
Hubei	8.55	18.81	19.14	11.61	45.68	52.14	12.24	43.65	48.74
Hunan	14.70	16.15	17.46	12.28	50.50	60.35	14.22	41.89	54.00
Guangdong	18.63	23.85	24.47	21.06	67.79	75.76	22.26	51.46	67.38
Guangxi	11.82	16.67	17.14	10.54	36.26	33.42	15.18	26.86	32.89
Sichuan	8.09	14.72	15.32	6.65	32.26	37.35	10.99	31.69	37.22
Guizhou	10.55	15.61	16.33	5.48	17.36	18.85	7.15	17.34	20.28
Yunnan	8.50	17.25	14.29	7.36	30.45	29.29	6.86	22.63	27.99
Tibet		25.21	25.88		7.43	5.36		14.05	13.35
Shaanxi	10.83	13.75	13.47	11.08	30.98	32.18	13.16	32.34	36.74
Gansu	4.53	13.65	14.00	8.99	17.11	21.25	11.32	28.38	33.72
Qinghai		16.56	20.64		19.98	24.43		31.23	37.86
Ningxia	7.80	11.06	10.29	6.59	26.16	30.23	12.45	44.33	49.79
Xinjiang	9.61	17.85	19.23	3.28	25.12	23.18	12.28	32.37	39.89

RURAL HOUSEHOLD PER CAPITA LIVING EXPENDITURE BY REGION

(yuan) (continued)

	Services and Recreation		
Region	1980	1986	1987
Total	**4.26**	**11.24**	**20.15**
Beijing	8.07	21.81	30.34
Tianjin	4.98	13.60	21.58
Hebei	3.18	8.76	17.06
Shanxi	2.56	10.03	15.99
Inner Mongolia	4.09	10.20	18.33
Liaoning	7.29	11.11	22.55
Jilin	1.77	13.11	26.74
Heilongjiang	4.24	10.76	15.45
Shanghai	5.63	17.74	23.62
Jiangsu	5.60	13.53	21.76
Zhejiang	4.82	15.10	47.48
Anhui	5.98	12.49	18.69
Fujian	5.33	15.21	26.51
Jiangxi	4.17	12.05	18.54
Shandong	3.20	8.85	17.60
Henan	3.32	9.63	16.24
Hubei	4.37	13.16	22.70
Hunan	3.70	12.55	22.10
Guangdong	6.57	22.36	37.53
Guangxi	3.15	10.39	15.85
Sichuan	4.62	8.39	16.51
Guizhou	5.18	7.84	12.13
Yunnan	2.56	6.88	10.80
Tibet		1.69	2.03
Shaanxi	3.18	8.48	15.43
Gansu	3.60	7.53	12.70
Qinghai		8.05	17.16
Ningxia	3.39	9.72	18.01
Xinjiang	3.61	10.36	22.56

7.10 *PERCENTAGE RURAL HOUSEHOLD PER CAPITAL LIVING EXPENDITURE BY REGION*

(total living expenditure = 100)

	Consumer Goods								
	Subtotal			Food			Clothes		
Region	*1980*	*1986*	*1987*	*1980*	*1986*	*1987*	*1980*	*1986*	*1987*
Nationwide	**97.4**	**96.9**	**94.9**	**61.8**	**56.4**	**55.2**	**12.3**	**9.5**	**8.6**
Beijing	96.8	96.6	95.7	53.6	45.3	48.2	12.7	9.4	9.7
Tianjin	97.6	97.2	96.0	56.9	49.0	49.7	15.1	10.5	9.5
Hebei	97.8	97.4	95.3	56.1	48.5	48.4	13.9	10.6	10.3
Shanxi	98.1	96.5	94.9	59.9	54.6	51.9	15.5	13.0	12.4
Inner Mongolia	97.4	96.7	94.8	65.4	60.5	59.8	13.7	10.6	9.9
Liaoning	96.8	97.4	95.2	56.3	51.0	50.2	13.4	11.0	10.8
Jilin	99.2	96.6	93.9	64.8	55.2	54.2	12.8	10.4	9.9
Heilongjiang	94.4	96.8	95.7	58.2	56.4	55.2	16.6	11.0	10.8
Shanghai	98.3	98.0	97.6	52.8	45.3	46.1	11.3	8.3	8.3
Jiangsu	97.1	97.3	96.2	58.0	49.5	48.1	12.5	8.7	7.0
Zhejiang	97.5	97.3	92.8	56.8	50.3	48.6	11.8	8.7	7.0
Anhui	96.3	95.1	95.1	59.8	54.8	54.8	11.5	8.9	8.2
Fujian	96.6	96.1	94.0	63.1	60.2	60.1	10.1	6.9	5.8
Jiangxi	97.3	96.5	95.2	62.3	58.6	57.5	10.0	8.6	7.3
Shandong	97.8	97.6	95.7	54.8	50.0	49.0	16.3	10.9	10.3
Henan	97.5	96.7	94.8	57.9	54.8	52.9	13.6	10.7	10.1
Hubei	97.1	96.5	94.5	64.4	58.2	56.8	11.5	9.4	8.3
Hunan	98.1	96.8	94.9	66.2	59.3	56.5	10.5	9.4	8.1
Guangdong	97.0	95.1	92.9	60.3	58.8	56.8	8.8	4.8	4.7
Guangxi	97.9	96.3	94.9	63.8	61.9	62.1	9.3	6.4	5.8
Sichuan	97.1	97.3	95.3	70.0	62.6	61.7	10.9	9.4	7.7
Guizhou	96.3	97.1	96.0	69.3	70.1	70.0	10.4	8.5	7.8
Yunnan	97.9	97.7	96.7	69.8	67.3	66.7	9.9	7.4	8.0
Tibet		99.3	99.2		69.7	69.9		11.6	11.1
Shaanxi	97.7	96.8	94.6	59.8	55.8	55.4	12.9	11.6	10.4
Gansu	97.2	96.8	95.0	64.3	59.2	57.0	13.3	12.2	10.7
Qinghai		97.4	95.0		61.6	57.6		14.2	13.4
Ningxia	97.5	96.8	94.6	63.4	57.2	56.2	14.2	12.5	11.5
Xinjiang	97.6	96.7	93.7	60.2	56.8	55.0	20.7	16.2	15.9

PERCENTAGE RURAL HOUSEHOLD PER CAPITAL LIVING EXPENDITURE BY REGION

(continued)

	Consumer Goods								
	Fuel			Housing			Daily Articles and Others		
Region	1980	1986	1987	1980	1986	1987	1980	1986	1987
Nationwide	**6.0**	**5.2**	**4.8**	**7.9**	**14.4**	**14.5**	**9.4**	**11.5**	**11.8**
Beijing	3.6	3.1	3.3	11.5	21.6	18.3	15.4	17.1	16.3
Tianjin	6.7	3.7	3.5	7.9	20.2	20.8	11.0	13.6	12.5
Hebei	5.8	5.7	4.9	10.2	18.2	17.1	11.8	14.3	14.7
Shanxi	4.6	3.0	2.8	6.8	12.4	14.1	11.3	13.5	13.7
Inner Mongolia	5.3	5.8	5.9	1.9	7.5	7.0	11.1	12.3	12.2
Liaoning	6.9	6.3	5.6	7.3	15.2	14.1	12.9	13.9	14.6
Jilin	5.6	5.8	5.1	5.8	13.6	12.9	10.2	11.6	11.8
Heilongjiang	5.7	7.1	7.4	5.3	8.8	9.3	11.6	13.5	13.1
Shanghai	3.4	2.1	2.1	18.9	29.8	27.3	11.9	12.5	13.9
Jiangsu	4.5	4.3	5.1	12.4	23.5	24.9	9.7	11.3	11.2
Zhejiang	6.0	3.8	3.2	13.7	21.0	22.2	9.2	13.5	11.8
Anhui	5.7	6.1	5.7	10.5	13.1	15.9	8.8	10.2	10.5
Fujian	8.4	5.3	5.0	7.3	13.5	12.2	7.7	10.2	11.0
Jiangxi	8.3	6.3	5.8	8.0	13.3	14.4	8.7	9.7	10.3
Shandong	4.6	6.2	5.4	9.9	17.3	17.9	12.2	13.1	13.1
Henan	5.1	5.0	4.8	10.7	15.7	16.2	10.2	10.6	10.7
Hubei	5.6	5.0	4.7	7.6	12.2	12.8	8.0	11.7	11.9
Hunan	7.6	4.2	4.0	6.4	13.1	13.9	7.4	10.8	12.4
Guangdong	8.4	5.3	4.6	9.5	14.9	14.2	10.0	11.3	12.7
Guangxi	7.8	5.9	5.5	7.0	12.8	10.8	10.0	9.5	10.6
Sichuan	5.1	4.7	4.4	4.2	10.4	10.7	6.9	10.2	10.7
Guizhou	7.6	5.8	5.4	3.9	6.4	6.2	5.1	6.4	6.7
Yunnan	6.8	5.6	4.4	5.9	10.0	9.0	5.5	7.4	8.6
Tibet		9.8	10.5		2.9	2.2		5.5	5.4
Shaanxi	7.7	5.2	4.7	7.9	11.8	11.3	9.4	12.3	12.9
Gansu	3.6	5.9	5.5	7.1	7.4	8.4	8.9	12.2	13.3
Qinghai		5.3	6.0		6.4	7.1		10.0	11.0
Ningxia	5.8	3.7	3.1	4.9	8.7	9.0	9.2	14.7	14.9
Xinjiang	6.4	5.6	5.3	2.2	7.9	6.4	8.1	10.2	11.1

PERCENTAGE RURAL HOUSEHOLD PER CAPITAL LIVING EXPENDITURE BY REGION

(continued)

Region	Services and Recreation		
	1980	1986	1987
Nationwide	**2.6**	**3.2**	**5.1**
Beijing	3.2	3.4	4.3
Tianjin	2.4	2.8	4.0
Hebei	2.2	2.6	4.7
Shanxi	1.9	3.5	5.1
Inner Mongolia	2.6	3.3	5.3
Liaoning	3.2	2.6	4.8
Jilin	0.8	3.4	6.1
Heilongjiang	2.6	3.2	4.3
Shanghai	1.7	2.0	2.4
Jiangsu	2.9	2.7	3.8
Zhejiang	2.5	2.7	7.2
Anhui	3.7	3.7	4.9
Fujian	3.4	3.9	6.0
Jiangxi	2.7	3.5	4.8
Shandong	2.2	2.4	4.3
Henan	2.5	3.3	5.2
Hubei	2.9	3.5	5.6
Hunan	1.9	3.3	5.1
Guangdong	3.0	4.9	7.1
Guangxi	2.1	3.7	5.1
Sichuan	2.9	2.7	4.7
Guizhou	3.7	2.9	4.0
Yunnan	2.1	2.3	3.3
Tibet		0.7	0.8
Shaanxi	2.3	3.2	5.4
Gansu	2.8	3.2	5.0
Qinghai		2.6	5.0
Ningxia	2.5	3.2	5.4
Xinjiang	2.4	3.3	6.3

7.11 *RURAL HOUSEHOLD PER CAPITA CONSUMPTION OF MAJOR CONSUMER GOODS BY REGION*

(kg)

	Grain (unhusked)						Vegetables		
	Subtotal			Rice and Wheat			1980	1986	1987
Region	*1980*	*1986*	*1987*	*1980*	*1986*	*1987*			
Nationwide	**257.16**	**259.30**	**259.38**	**162.92**	**212.23**	**211.38**	**127.21**	**133.65**	**130.42**
Beijing	250.12	209.93	216.34	134.90	176.07	172.07	182.35	183.70	185.51
Tianjin	238.42	220.86	223.02	151.12	186.65	183.38	97.77	106.11	121.85
Hebei	226.22	221.54	225.55	68.21	149.42	149.86	113.23	127.56	137.70
Shanxi	241.93	219.26	218.93	48.36	119.22	122.24	85.01	93.82	97.65
Inner Mongolia	253.07	261.37	267.35	75.34	87.01	91.38	140.37	121.46	135.43
Liaoning	259.71	238.39	245.88	50.60	109.01	113.82	224.92	178.62	173.93
Jilin	299.20	288.11	292.48	64.86	115.58	129.60	102.55	215.90	237.15
Heilongjiang	253.88	283.52	279.97	58.44	194.57	170.66	144.79	185.50	169.07
Shanghai	296.92	270.41	267.41	238.51	259.55	247.67	100.43	112.94	132.36
Jiangsu	295.27	290.20	288.48	242.64	262.90	268.37	112.11	122.78	78.20
Zhejiang	312.44	294.83	289.26	271.84	288.49	281.60	116.91	129.46	118.47
Anhui	278.72	278.84	283.97	229.41	267.53	270.80	109.73	104.07	105.77
Fujian	291.92	256.50	257.06	265.74	236.90	222.73	137.30	122.51	114.29
Jiangxi	306.41	325.95	330.96	296.48	319.22	323.89	154.91	174.19	171.46
Shandong	229.37	221.49	225.37	80.38	182.03	180.65	116.21	129.84	122.18
Henan	221.60	240.62	241.43	123.03	197.91	208.76	75.09	74.67	79.74
Hubei	269.96	296.08	295.88	226.98	267.09	272.48	148.25	219.65	224.86
Hunan	334.36	319.79	317.07	304.29	313.00	310.03	185.01	159.61	159.13
Guangdong	291.99	255.63	259.92	266.91	244.96	238.90	115.52	125.37	112.43
Guangxi	257.17	248.05	246.11	234.71	228.38	225.89	125.41	129.76	116.16
Sichuan	258.52	256.18	258.05	184.03	226.56	228.40	147.26	157.94	156.10
Guizhou	224.67	222.36	219.63	149.19	165.77	163.51	142.78	157.64	166.24
Yunnan	221.66	226.39	240.29	131.72	172.69	179.70	126.38	153.12	142.08
Tibet		186.06	176.17		45.71	49.54		15.98	18.19
Shaanxi	205.89	236.98	242.33	90.50	163.97	168.32	69.74	69.04	70.87
Gansu	238.34	236.57	241.08	120.09	199.38	202.06	43.57	44.84	43.31
Qinghai		226.46	229.98		178.31	172.77		49.21	49.59
Ningxia	225.86	260.98	259.95	180.46	233.00	234.35	75.92	93.93	87.01
Xinjiang	211.48	223.25	229.47	126.16	190.70	198.48	72.49	111.16	124.29

RURAL HOUSEHOLD PER CAPITA CONSUMPTION OF MAJOR CONSUMER GOODS BY REGION

(kg) (continued)

Region	Edible Oil			Pork, Beef and Mutton			Poultry		
	1980	1986	1987	1980	1986	1987	1980	1986	1987
Nationwide	**1.40**	**2.63**	**3.11**	**7.75**	**11.79**	**11.65**	**0.66**	**1.14**	**1.15**
Beijing	1.14	3.01	3.99	7.60	9.71	11.38	0.07	0.48	0.35
Tianjin	0.88	3.17	3.95	6.52	8.72	9.77	0.22	0.36	0.41
Hebei	1.03	2.37	3.01	4.54	6.48	6.78	0.08	0.17	0.20
Shanxi	1.01	2.79	2.97	3.11	4.70	4.34	0.07	0.09	0.07
Inner Mongolia	1.18	1.87	2.15	10.36	14.74	15.34	0.15	0.30	0.30
Liaoning	1.24	2.62	2.62	9.69	11.97	11.79	0.29	0.44	0.41
Jilin	1.29	2.90	3.83	8.90	11.25	11.60	0.45	0.55	0.67
Heilongjiang	2.68	4.52	5.08	7.39	8.49	7.92	0.35	0.56	0.59
Shanghai	3.31	4.93	5.78	12.64	18.29	17.91	0.97	4.05	4.55
Jiangsu	2.32	4.29	5.27	6.88	10.57	10.03	0.80	1.76	1.66
Zhejiang	1.46	2.18	2.86	7.63	14.30	13.21	1.00	1.93	2.00
Anhui	2.07	3.14	3.88	6.16	8.79	8.70	2.00	2.14	1.91
Fujian	0.52	1.00	0.87	6.28	11.03	10.71	1.45	2.32	1.99
Jiangxi	2.02	3.14	4.09	6.53	12.77	13.31	1.09	1.28	1.32
Shandong	1.72	3.59	4.32	5.07	7.29	7.00	0.44	0.66	0.61
Henan	1.01	1.88	2.43	4.10	5.72	5.59	0.24	0.43	0.44
Hubei	1.80	4.10	4.81	8.89	15.88	15.99	0.60	1.05	1.15
Hunan	2.24	2.57	2.84	11.15	18.30	18.54	1.20	2.06	1.99
Guangdong	1.80	2.67	3.27	6.55	13.95	14.99	2.15	3.45	3.72
Guangxi	0.95	1.85	1.65	6.43	11.64	11.75	1.83	2.72	2.26
Sichuan	1.07	1.21	1.46	13.32	19.19	18.30	0.52	0.87	0.93
Guizhou	0.68	0.67	0.96	9.97	16.39	17.03	0.38	0.55	0.63
Yunnan	0.34	0.44	0.66	8.10	16.00	15.27	0.68	1.29	1.42
Tibet		2.20	2.21		10.79	14.19		0.01	0.01
Shaanxi	1.06	2.29	2.74	5.44	6.35	6.08	0.13	0.12	0.11
Gansu	1.47	2.45	2.83	8.84	7.70	7.82	0.12	0.17	0.17
Qinghai		4.67	4.92		15.27	16.21		0.06	0.06
Ningxia	1.95	4.08	4.22	3.68	8.01	8.78	0.22	0.45	0.42
Xinjiang	2.23	5.41	7.91	9.36	8.73	8.76	0.16	0.53	0.92

RURAL HOUSEHOLD PER CAPITA CONSUMPTION OF MAJOR CONSUMER GOODS BY REGION

(kg) (continued)

Region	Fresh Eggs			Fish and Shrimp			Sugar		
	1980	1986	1987	1980	1986	1987	1980	1986	1987
Nationwide	**1.20**	**2.08**	**2.25**	**1.10**	**1.87**	**1.96**	**1.06**	**1.59**	**1.70**
Beijing	1.95	6.31	6.18	0.76	1.41	1.39	0.98	1.81	2.49
Tianjin	1.56	3.61	4.06	2.35	3.67	4.29	1.24	1.29	1.49
Hebei	0.86	1.83	2.18	0.22	0.40	0.50	0.44	0.94	0.99
Shanxi	0.85	2.08	2.11	0.02	0.03	0.06	0.44	1.26	1.32
Inner Mongolia	1.25	2.07	2.21	0.12	0.10	0.16	0.51	0.83	1.01
Liaoning	1.95	4.22	3.60	1.69	2.16	1.97	0.55	0.60	0.61
Jilin	1.32	5.09	4.55	0.74	1.50	1.54	0.44	0.59	0.66
Heilongjiang	1.91	2.78	2.81	0.48	1.14	1.10	0.72	0.85	0.97
Shanghai	3.04	5.74	5.35	4.04	8.22	8.12	2.94	4.10	3.51
Jiangsu	1.39	4.64-	4.48	1.94	3.92	4.11	1.06	2.22	2.43
Zhejiang	0.98	2.93	3.06	4.91	7.27	7.16	2.01	3.69	3.74
Anhui	1.62	1.70	1.82	1.31	1.19	1.44	1.13	1.66	1.88
Fujian	0.81	1.64	1.44	4.77	4.33	4.39	2.25	3.31	3.04
Jiangxi	1.03	1.63	1.85	1.51	2.03	2.12	1.00	1.58	2.33
Shandong	1.24	3.48	3.92	0.98	1.01	1.00	0.59	1.20	1.36
Henan	1.03	1.72	2.00	0.28	0.24	0.22	0.67	1.27	1.51
Hubei	1.10	2.48	2.65	1.73	2.51	2.84	0.95	1.44	1.54
Hunan	1.09	2.09	2.17	1.58	2.61	2.67	1.03	1.78	1.68
Guangdong	0.79	1.32	1.35	4.22	9.09	9.72	4.22	4.13	4.17
Guangxi	0.33	0.75	0.64	0.58	1.68	1.56	1.01	1.37	1.32
Sichuan	0.96	1.97	2.17	0.16	0.26	0.29	1.11	1.59	1.62
Guizhou	0.53	0.69	0.79	0.20	0.18	0.19	0.75	0.97	0.93
Yunnan	0.55	1.18	1.21	0.17	0.60	0.62	1.49	1.57	1.78
Tibet		0.50	0.47		0.04	0.01		1.02	1.14
Shaanxi	0.44	1.33	1.29	0.03	0.03	0.01	0.39	0.87	0.98
Gansu	0.63	0.89	0.98	0.01		0.01	0.46	0.46	0.60
Qinghai		0.66	0.55		0.02	0.01		0.69	0.80
Ningxia	0.39	1.48	1.67	0.01	0.08	0.16	0.70	1.36	1.40
Xinjiang	0.80	1.85	1.65	0.04	0.10	0.16	1.06	0.80	1.00

RURAL HOUSEHOLD PER CAPITA CONSUMPTION OF MAJOR CONSUMER GOODS BY REGION

(continued)

Region	Liquor (kg)			Cotton Cloth (m)			Chemical Fiber Cloth (m)		
	1980	1986	1987	1980	1986	1987	1980	1986	1987
Nationwide	**1.89**	**4.96**	**5.48**	**4.30**	**1.98**	**1.57**	**0.94**	**2.53**	**2.28**
Beijing	2.48	6.50	8.28	5.21	2.04	2.19	1.29	3.33	3.55
Tianjin	1.57	3.00	4.37	4.99	2.54	2.09	1.12	2.60	2.33
Hebei	0.90	2.19	2.48	4.73	2.51	2.28	1.13	2.45	2.18
Shanxi	0.46	1.37	1.49	6.01	2.46	2.36	1.00	2.61	2.35
Inner Mongolia	1.19	3.60	3.84	5.11	2.45	2.15	0.79	2.37	2.14
Liaoning	1.87	4.61	4.75	4.69	2.25	1.71	1.45	2.54	2.27
Jilin	1.75	4.76	5.55	5.61	2.36	2.10	0.56	2.50	2.37
Heilongjiang	1.79	4.96	5.85	4.94	2.12	1.24	1.40	2.84	1.67
Shanghai	5.15	14.83	15.92	3.39	1.36	1.41	2.57	4.30	3.72
Jiangsu	2.16	7.00	7.95	4.31	1.69	1.38	1.30	3.81	3.43
Zhejiang	6.44	21.32	22.00	3.76	1.64	1.29	1.52	3.42	2.78
Anhui	1.56	3.29	3.75	4.77	1.62	1.34	0.91	2.67	2.54
Fujian	4.74	7.74	7.90	3.75	0.93	0.73	0.73	2.46	2.44
Jiangxi	1.37	3.80	4.58	3.71	1.59	1.08	0.82	2.82	2.80
Shandong	2.26	4.69	5.26	4.70	2.86	2.34	1.51	2.56	2.32
Henan	0.67	1.68	1.90	3.94	1.84	1.60	1.10	2.10	2.04
Hubei	1.81	4.97	5.30	3.66	1.26	0.97	1.13	2.99	2.47
Hunan	3.61	5.86	6.61	4.09	1.82	1.32	0.94	3.08	2.76
Guangdong	1.54	3.77	4.37	3.30	0.79	0.70	0.80	2.04	2.31
Guangxi	2.40	5.82	6.00	2.91	1.08	0.85	0.51	1.54	1.67
Sichuan	1.95	4.04	4.12	4.17	1.88	1.52	0.61	2.11	1.85
Guizhou	2.60	5.03	5.22	3.60	1.84	1.62	0.26	1.60	1.85
Yunnan	1.73	4.25	4.07	3.83	1.52	1.38	0.28	1.68	1.81
Tibet		38.64	53.69		2.19	3.19		0.41	0.38
Shaanxi	1.11	1.63	2.02	5.14	2.76	1.98	0.81	2.91	2.38
Gansu	0.58	1.00	1.13	5.10	2.94	1.75	0.57	1.71	1.56
Qinghai		1.55	1.76		3.25	2.30		2.94	2.80
Ningxia	0.32	0.74	0.82	4.36	2.31	1.69	0.54	2.46	2.51
Xinjiang	0.46	0.85	0.97	6.45	2.57	2.50	1.18	1.77	1.98

7.12 POSSESSION OF MAJOR CONSUMER DURABLES PER 100 RURAL HOUSEHOLDS BY REGION

	Bicycles			Sewing Machines			Radios		
Region	1980	1986	1987	1980	1986	1987	1980	1986	1987
Nationwide	**36.87**	**90.31**	**98.52**	**23.31**	**46.99**	**49.79**	**33.54**	**54.24**	**52.98**
Beijing	124.51	196.00	204.13	41.91	57.07	60.13	96.34	70.00	64.13
Tianjin	108.28	186.07	210.00	40.81	75.18	80.18	86.65	87.50	91.79
Hebei	75.76	150.43	156.74	32.87	74.21	77.45	58.85	88.38	86.33
Shanxi	62.49	96.62	105.38	36.35	74.43	76.29	25.30	56.48	55.14
Inner Mongolia	63.21	90.82	97.86	46.51	73.08	75.05	43.43	70.60	71.04
Liaoning	69.06	124.87	134.18	55.76	69.74	69.95	62.91	61.06	59.10
Jilin	37.23	92.69	101.38	41.40	65.06	66.13	68.96	68.19	61.50
Heilongjiang	47.10	81.00	83.71	45.44	55.75	59.38	68.20	68.38	68.79
Shanghai	81.32	174.33	190.33	41.28	81.17	82.67	43.79	47.67	46.67
Jiangsu	33.62	117.88	132.24	14.00	37.21	41.41	36.73	63.91	61.06
Zhejiang	13.91	103.85	117.41	14.32	55.78	59.11	12.93	30.04	28.22
Anhui	15.87	70.00	78.61	10.78	35.42	39.71	39.21	68.19	65.32
Fujian	15.94	69.29	77.97	20.44	54.07	57.42	19.25	26.76	24.12
Jiangxi	12.12	70.08	80.49	7.86	22.98	26.86	24.41	66.33	62.61
Shandong	69.99	141.36	145.95	28.37	58.05	61.02	53.13	84.62	81.40
Henan	36.01	103.69	109.76	29.53	58.79	60.83	40.11	74.36	74.90
Hubei	12.36	76.00	83.73	13.42	33.94	36.97	31.17	48.36	44.18
Hunan	3.68	55.95	67.43	10.40	27.27	29.86	11.30	30.86	30.00
Guangdong	103.94	138.95	147.69	53.27	60.87	63.57	76.69	51.71	51.22
Guangxi	54.70	107.37	114.91	19.41	52.72	56.12	12.77	27.24	25.52
Sichuan	8.94	30.27	35.53	3.99	14.85	16.24	12.12	32.04	34.75
Guizhou	3.79	9.29	9.42	6.10	17.86	19.00	3.90	14.11	14.55
Yunnan	7.16	36.58	43.33	7.16	23.00	26.08	13.67	27.17	27.04
Tibet		18.70	25.11		13.45	13.71		26.68	27.22
Shaanxi	32.60	74.91	85.99	18.87	53.51	57.16	18.59	60.68	59.95
Gansu	40.56	71.44	79.94	19.49	44.33	48.72	15.55	49.94	51.39
Qinghai		52.67	60.44		39.56	43.33		43.11	46.89
Ningxia	90.45	135.74	148.33	24.97	64.26	67.04	16.67	60.56	54.63
Xinjiang	45.50	77.66	86.27	36.06	48.71	50.57	35.55	42.42	40.79

POSSESSION OF MAJOR CONSUMER DURABLES PER 100 RURAL HOUSEHOLDS BY REGION

(continued)

	Wrist Watches			Television Sets			Recorders		
Region	1980	1986	1987	1980	1986	1987	1980	1986	1987
Nationwide	**37.58**	**145.06**	**161.22**	**3.99**	**17.28**	**24.38**	**1.51**	**6.60**	**9.68**
Beijing	102.60	200.27	226.13	41.46	72.00	78.07	6.67	27.20	34.13
Tianjin	80.83	203.57	241.25	33.80	43.22	70.18	3.80	13.93	14.11
Hebei	30.61	152.88	187.19	2.40	26.52	37.52	0.42	6.45	9.19
Shanxi	38.98	164.95	179.38	4.18	22.10	24.66	1.18	6.90	10.90
Inner Mongolia	44.75	141.32	155.44	3.26	15.17	23.30	1.52	5.38	8.13
Liaoning	93.15	165.71	175.98	16.00	48.15	58.80	2.18	11.01	14.34
Jilin	75.33	155.69	171.19	7.08	42.44	52.87	2.92	10.69	13.50
Heilongjiang	57.99	136.67	146.93	8.40	27.55	37.21	2.26	7.17	9.92
Shanghai	126.35	229.33	247.33	15.28	59.66	69.70	2.50	12.00	15.60
Jiangsu	56.55	171.88	183.79	2.00	18.88	20.48	0.47	7.18	9.47
Zhejiang	60.64	224.67	239.67	0.98	18.89	28.66	1.37	6.59	9.89
Anhui	20.79	119.45	134.97	1.08	8.62	15.20	0.42	4.23	7.06
Fujian	71.19	198.63	205.99	1.67	14.50	22.65	1.43	7.03	11.21
Jiangxi	34.04	153.59	156.37	0.08	9.63	17.22	0.33	4.65	7.80
Shandong	32.77	133.74	148.45	1.25	21.55	29.68	0.14	5.88	8.43
Henan	15.90	108.81	120.29	0.71	5.85	10.24	0.38	3.86	5.69
Hubei	23.26	147.73	163.39	1.97	20.88	31.12	0.88	6.30	10.39
Hunan	26.01	137.49	150.57	0.26	8.32	15.10	0.39	2.49	5.19
Guangdong	112.11	187.48	196.56	5.23	15.00	20.99	7.97	17.24	22.14
Guangxi	25.09	134.01	146.77	1.27	5.21	9.95	1.18	4.70	7.80
Sichuan	17.17	108.98	148.67	1.63	11.47	17.52	0.58	3.89	6.20
Guizhou	1.24	104.06	115.94	0.99	3.93	5.44	0.93	1.88	3.57
Yunnan	17.16	135.29	154.21	1.97	6.13	8.78	4.43	8.46	7.58
Tibet		37.61	34.18		0.63	1.05		4.41	8.02
Shaanxi	11.58	121.40	148.87	1.42	6.08	10.40	0.61	3.60	5.27
Gansu	23.60	144.72	176.72	1.30	9.39	15.44	0.40	4.83	7.94
Qinghai		145.78	159.44	0.37	10.67	10.84	1.67	10.67	20.89
Ningxia	51.45	172.59	182.22	10.00	23.78	39.07	2.71	11.30	15.06
Xinjiang	37.73	106.69	113.09	1.67	17.74	19.95	2.29	10.73	16.32

POSSESSION OF MAJOR CONSUMER DURABLES PER 100 RURAL HOUSEHOLDS BY REGION

(continued)

Region	Washing Machines			Electric Fans		
	1980	1986	1987	1980	1986	1987
Nationwide	**0.36**	**3.22**	**4.78**	**4.42**	**13.63**	**19.76**
Beijing	5.63	37.47	47.73	17.29	41.33	52.40
Tianjin	0.40	13.39	20.54	15.40	31.43	44.64
Hebei	0.21	6.98	11.45	0.63	10.26	15.52
Shanxi	0.18	4.24	6.71	0.09	2.19	3.24
Inner Mongolia	0.43	4.51	7.14	0.22	0.11	0.16
Liaoning	1.55	15.24	19.42	0.27	3.23	3.92
Jilin	2.08	14.69	18.13	0.28	0.69	0.94
Heilongjiang	3.40	11.08	13.00	0.19	0.71	0.50
Shanghai		5.33	13.00	25.28	75.17	104.67
Jiangsu		2.85	5.41	5.87	26.76	37.38
Zhejiang		0.44	2.30	12.06	53.70	69.96
Anhui		0.39	0.19	0.52	11.74	19.81
Fujian		0.16	1.26	8.33	20.93	37.91
Jiangxi		0.08	0.20	2.08	10.08	16.86
Shandong		2.40	2.81	0.49	11.79	17.76
Henan	0.04	0.50	1.29	0.58	5.81	9.10
Hubei		1.39	2.67	1.56	13.76	18.58
Hunan		0.14	0.41	0.92	11.16	20.68
Guangdong		0.45	1.22	40.47	66.05	85.88
Guangxi		0.13	0.26	5.49	16.29	26.08
Sichuan	0.04	0.64	1.22	0.47	5.80	8.67
Guizhou		0.18	0.27	0.31	0.18	0.67
Yunnan		1.08	1.75	0.33	0.29	1.38
Tibet					1.89	2.53
Shaanxi	0.10	0.45	1.35		0.90	1.67
Gansu		1.61	2.00		0.28	0.50
Qinghai		1.33	2.00	0.37	0.22	2.00
Ningxia	0.42	6.11	8.89			0.37
Xinjiang		4.27	7.03		1.05	1.45

7.13 RURAL HOUSEHOLD PER CAPITA HOUSING SPACE BY REGION

(sq.m)

Region	Floor Space 1980	Floor Space 1986	Floor Space 1987	Living Space per Capita (1987)
Nationwide	**11.59**	**18.09**	**18.88**	**16.00**
Beijing	10.43	17.42	18.58	18.33
Tianjin	10.47	15.73	17.39	16.20
Hebei	11.76	16.35	17.13	15.59
Shanxi	11.11	16.39	17.19	15.01
Inner Mongolia	8.12	14.03	14.53	10.62
Liaoning	11.04	15.78	16.46	14.78
Jilin	9.17	14.31	15.08	12.45
Heilongjiang	8.89	14.00	14.41	12.16
Shanghai	16.56	33.36	35.49	30.36
Jiangsu	11.72	19.93	21.19	18.64
Zhejiang	16.07	26.44	29.42	24.73
Anhui	10.58	15.51	16.27	14.50
Fujian	10.43	17.63	18.55	15.86
Jiangxi	11.20	20.26	21.42	18.47
Shandong	10.98	17.14	18.02	16.48
Henan	10.39	15.70	16.28	14.40
Hubei	13.98	22.63	23.50	20.71
Hunan	15.10	22.96	23.83	20.00
Guangdong	12.14	17.72	18.14	16.05
Guangxi	10.33	16.63	17.10	14.76
Sichuan	13.36	21.95	22.81	17.61
Guizhou	10.86	16.14	16.75	13.15
Yunnan	11.45	20.06	20.56	15.86
Tibet		18.27	18.79	8.69
Shaanxi	9.54	14.84	15.54	13.25
Gansu	13.87	13.44	13.93	10.81
Qinghai		14.57	15.21	11.75
Ningxia	8.80	15.06	15.66	12.38
Xinjiang	11.46	15.92	16.40	12.76

7.14 *RURAL HOUSEHOLD PER CAPITA INCOME, EXPENDITURE AND CONSUMPTION BY ECONOMIC ZONE**

Item	Unit	Nationwide	East Economic Zone	Middle Economic Zone	West Economic Zone
Income per Capita	yuan	462.55	566.53	433.22	357.21
Labor Income	yuan	418.35	504.93	400.24	322.61
Total Expenditure per Capita	yuan	603.99	708.92	584.43	486.01
Production Expenditure	yuan	150.59	171.04	145.76	128.00
Living Expenditure	yuan	398.29	480.13	374.78	316.63
Expenditure on Food	yuan	219.67	248.09	208.47	195.54
Major Food Consumption per Capita					
Grain	kg	259.38	250.76	281.77	240.31
Vegetables	kg	130.42	121.75	147.51	118.79
Pork, Beef and Mutton	kg	11.79	10.57	11.27	13.64
Eggs	kg	2.08	2.76	2.33	1.41
Floor Space per Capita (year-end)	sq.m	18.88	19.45	18.55	18.54

Note:
***The east economic zone includes Beijing, Tianjin, Hebei, Liaoning, Shanghai, Jiangsu, Zhejiang, Fujian, Shandong, Guangdong and Guangxi. The middle economic zone includes Shanxi, Inner Mongolia, Jilin, Heilongjiang, Anhui, Jiangxi, Henan, Hubei and Hunan. The west economic zone includes Sichuan, Guizhou, Yunnan, Tibet, Shaanxi, Gansu, Qinghai, Ningxia and Xinjiang.**

Section VIII

RURAL PRODUCTION CONDITIONS

8.1 *AGRICULTURAL RESOURCES*

Item	Unit	1980
Surface Area of the Country	1,000 sq.k	9600
Mountains	%	33
Plateaus	%	26
Basins	%	19
Plains	%	12
Hills	%	10
Annual Average of Precipitation	mm	630
Annual Volume of Precipitation	1,000,000,000 cu.m	6000.0
Cultivated Area	1,000,000 ha	95.89
Forest Area	1,000,000 ha	115.24
Percentage Forest-covered Land	%	12.0
Forest Growing Stock	1,000,000,000 cu.m	10.26
Prairie Area	1,000,000 ha	319.08
Utilizable Area	1,000,000 ha	224.34
Hydrology and Water Conservancy		
Annual Flow of Rivers	1,000,000,000 cu.m	2614.4
Fresh Water Area	1,000,000 ha	16.64
Cultivable Area	1,000,000 ha	5.03
Cultivated Area	1,000,000 ha	3.26
Hydropower Resources	1,000,000 kw	676
Developable Resources	1,000,000 kw	379
Developed Resources	1,000,000 kw	24
Area of Marine Fishing	1,000 sq.naut.miles	818
Cultivable Area in Marine Water	1,000 ha	492
Cultivated Area	1,000 ha	246
Coastline of the Mainland	km	18000

8.2 *CULTIVATED AREA BY REGION*

Region	Total (1,000 mu*)		1987 over 1986	
	1987	1986	Volume Change (1,000 mu*)	Percentage Change
National Total	**1438330**	**1443448**	**-5118**	**-0.4**
Beijing	6266	6283	-17	-0.3
Tianjin	6577	6621	-44	-0.7
Hebei	98648	98880	-232	-0.2
Shanxi	55790	55977	-187	-0.3
Inner Mongolia	72764	73424	-660	-0.9
Liaoning	52384	52942	-558	-1.1
Jilin	59408	59600	-192	-0.3
Heilongjiang	132881	133035	-154	-0.1
Shanghai	4963	4995	-32	-0.6
Jiangsu	68697	68862	-165	-0.2
Zhejiang	26174	26303	-129	-0.5
Anhui	65954	66208	-254	-0.4
Fujian	18659	18754	-95	-0.5
Jiangxi	35428	35458	-30	-0.1
Shandong	103865	104466	-601	-0.6
Henan	104589	104983	-394	-0.4
Hubei	52770	53175	-405	-0.8
Hunan	49770	49958	-188	-0.4
Guangdong	44459	44906	-447	-1.0
Guangxi	38474	38457	17	
Sichuan	94884	95121	-237	-0.2
Guizhou	27859	27938	-79	-0.3
Yunnan	41863	41638	225	0.5
Tibet	3330	3337	-07	-0.2
Shaanxi	53440	53851	-411	-0.8
Gansu	52186	52206	-20	0.0
Qinghai	8469	8449	20	0.2
Ningxia	11864	11867	-03	0.0
Xinjiang	45915	45754	161	0.4

Note:
*** 1 mu = 1/15 hectare.**

CULTIVATED AREA BY REGION

(continued)

	Cultivated Area (1,000 mu*)			
	Paddy Field		Dry Land	
Region	*1987*	*1986*	*1987*	*1986*
National Total	**376562**	**375827**	**1061768**	**318444**
Beijing	536	563	5730	4131
Tianjin	542	488	6035	4570
Hebei	1970	1932	96678	52115
Shanxi	145	147	55645	16018
Inner Mongolia	413	407	72351	15154
Liaoning	7991	7464	44393	3387
Jilin	5486	5145	53922	5807
Heilongjiang	8674	7653	124207	2819
Shanghai	4451	4462	512	452
Jiangsu	41553	41702	27144	9335
Zhejiang	21290	21345	4884	2103
Anhui	25955	25797	39999	7948
Fujian	15093	15166	3566	
Jiangxi	30024	30047	5404	
Shandong	1874	2006	101991	65339
Henan	5660	5823	98929	42899
Hubei	27678	27714	25092	7849
Hunan	39327	39428	10443	1595
Guangdong	32710	33178	11749	
Guangxi	23968	24078	14506	813
Sichuan	48403	48544	46481	
Guizhou	11703	11759	16156	23
Yunnan	14759	14824	27104	1495
Tibet	20	09	3310	2260
Shaanxi	2487	2510	50953	14923
Gansu	109	171	52077	11997
Qinghai			8469	2470
Ningxia	2640	2431	9224	1177
Xinjiang	1101	1034	44814	41765

Note:
*** 1 mu = 1/15 hectare.**

8.3 *RURAL LABOR FORCE OF SOCIETY**

(1,000)

Item	1986	1987	1987 over 1986	
			Volume Change	Percentage Change
Rural Labor Force of Society*	387824	398013	10189	2.6
Rural Labor Force (non-state owned Units)*	379898	390004	10106	2.7
Forestry, Animal Husbandry, Sideline Production and Fishery	304680	308700	4020	1.3
Industry	31393	32972	1579	5.0
Construction	13086	14313	1227	9.4
Transportation	5061	5625	564	11.1
Commerce, Food Services and Service Trade	5318	6069	751	14.1
Culture, Education, Health Care and Social Welfare	5796	5952	156	2.7
Scientific Researchers	154	156	2	1.3
Community Administration	1034	1196	162	15.7
Others	13376	15021	1645	12.3
Staff and Workers of State-owned Units in Primary Industry	7926	8009	83	1.0

Note:
*** Rural labor force of society includes laborers working at state-owned and non-state-owned units; rural labor force includes laborers working at non-state-owned units only.**

8.4 *RURAL LABOR FORCE BY REGION*
(1,000 persons)

	1980	1986	1987
Total	**318359**	**379898**	**390004**
Beijing	1644	1895	1898
Tianjin	1512	1761	1762
Hebei	17666	21071	21642
Shanxi	7026	8068	8228
Inner Mongolia	4430	5096	5158
Liaoning	6780	8234	8298
Jilin	3381	4865	5147
Heilongjiang	4385	4921	4882
Shanghai	2822	2637	2599
Jiangsu	22645	26323	26910
Zhejiang	14964	19145	19551
Anhui	16705	20362	20812
Fujian	7291	8894	9259
Jiangxi	9293	12293	12769
Shandong	26529	30790	31496
Henan	25054	29982	30963
Hubei	15006	16685	16992
Hunan	19975	23197	23893
Guangdong	19625	23157	23806
Guangxi	13001	15857	16373
Sichuan	37276	44180	45513
Guizhou	9293	11578	12044
Yunnan	11990	14669	15207
Tibet	818	896	902
Shaanxi	8908	10694	10969
Gansu	5740	7423	7602
Qinghai	1036	1216	1246
Ningxia	994	1238	1288
Xinjiang	2570	2763	2795

RURAL LABOR FORCE BY REGION *1987*

(1,000 persons) (continued)

Region	Total	Agriculture, Forestry, Animal Husbandry and Sideline Production	Industry	Construction	Transportation, Postal Services and Telecommunications	Commerce, Food Services and Service Trades
Total	**390004**	**308700**	**32972**	**14313**	**5625**	**6069**
Beijing	1898	851	538	116	58	49
Tianjin	1762	899	541	94	54	43
Hebei	21642	16245	2175	986	402	471
Shanxi	8228	5724	916	349	288	163
Inner Mongolia	5158	4585	152	79	50	46
Liaoning	8298	5848	1041	384	200	203
Jilin	5147	4447	251	90	70	63
Heilongjiang	4882	4202	254	83	65	53
Shanghai	2599	875	1241	80	39	34
Jiangsu	26910	16193	5505	1973	655	431
Zhejiang	19551	12604	3997	730	379	348
Anhui	20812	17640	1049	574	258	299
Fujian	9259	7247	584	450	171	183
Jiangxi	12769	10624	917	357	156	174
Shandong	31496	23659	2985	1690	524	607
Henan	30963	25828	1599	1181	407	489
Hubei	16992	13560	1274	557	227	275
Hunan	23893	20433	1356	614	215	308
Guangdong	23806	17110	2288	1353	435	606
Guangxi	16373	15045	371	248	107	167
Sichuan	45513	39396	2053	1345	307	545
Guizhou	12044	11082	423	99	77	79
Yunnan	15207	13807	363	296	133	105
Tibet	902	848	10	4	6	9
Shaanxi	10969	8961	762	368	184	180
Gansu	7602	6187	202	220	76	79
Qinghai	1246	1091	34	31	25	14
Ningxia	1288	1128	28	31	26	14
Xinjiang	2795	2581	64	31	31	32

RURAL LABOR FORCE BY REGION

(1,000 persons) (continued)

Region	Administration of Real Estate, Public Utilities, Resident and Consultancy Services	Health Care, Sports and Social Welfare	Education, Culture, Art, Broadcasting and Television	Scientific Research and Comprehensive Technical Services	Banking and Insurance	Township Administration Economic Organization
Total	**1381**	**1270**	**3139**	**156**	**162**	**1196**
Beijing	24	8	8	2	1	11
Tianjin	6	6	6	1	1	10
Hebei	49	81	152	7	20	74
Shanxi	22	44	109	5	7	109
Inner Mongolia	2	15	59	2	1	13
Liaoning	12	31	90	3	5	75
Jilin	3	17	58	1	3	15
Heilongjiang	2	24	92	2	3	17
Shanghai	59	17	12	11		13
Jiangsu	121	99	198	14	15	65
Zhejiang	498	39	79	8	5	86
Anhui	43	65	187	8	6	28
Fujian	18	33	53	3	3	25
Jiangxi	140	41	131	6	6	69
Shandong	29	137	321	8	10	68
Henan	20	139	405	11	14	63
Hubei	57	63	195	5	10	53
Hunan	38	50	153	7	14	41
Guangdong	27	78	147	8	11	84
Guangxi	14	37	79	3	4	39
Sichuan	127	112	238	29	11	75
Guizhou	9	22	76	1	2	10
Yunnan	33	27	69	7	3	57
Tibet	1	4	3			2
Shaanxi	11	41	121	1	5	63
Gansu	12	25	63	1		15
Qinghai		4	10	1	1	2
Ningxia	1	4	9			3
Xinjiang	3	7	16	1	1	11

8.5 NUMBER OF STAFF AND WORKERS OF STATE-OWNED UNITS IN PRIMARY INDUSTRY BY REGION

(1,000 persons)

Region	1986	1987
Total	**7925.9**	**8008.7**
Beijing	70.7	70.6
Tianjin	44.1	41.3
Hebei	203.1	214.6
Shanxi	78.7	77.1
Inner Mongolia	327.0	348.1
Liaoning	439.6	436.8
Jilin	223.9	230.6
Heilongjiang	932.9	956.6
Shanghai	175.4	167.1
Jiangsu	377.0	374.5
Zhejiang	136.0	136.6
Anhui	191.7	190.0
Fujian	159.7	161.5
Jiangxi	367.0	380.9
Shandong	154.1	154.3
Henan	163.0	165.8
Hubei	579.5	590.6
Hunan	377.6	403.6
Guangdong	954.3	946.4
Guangxi	231.6	237.6
Sichuan	174.1	171.1
Guizhou	72.6	70.7
Yunnan	229.8	231.4
Tibet	9.0	9.9
Shaanxi	83.8	83.0
Gansu	105.7	108.8
Qinghai	50.7	47.5
Ningxia	66.9	63.7
Xinjiang	945.8	940.7

8.6 MAJOR AGRICULTURAL MACHINERY AT YEAR-END

Item	Unit	1980	1985	1986	1987	1987 as Percentage of 1986
Total Power of Agricultural Machinery	1,000,000,000 w	147.46	209.13	229.50	248.36	108.2
Large and Medium Tractors	1,000	744.9	852.4	866.5	881	101.7
	1,000,000,000 w	23.69	27.44	28.07	28.76	102.5
Small and Walk Tractors	1,000	1874	3824	4526	5300	117.1
	1,000,000,000 w	16.16	33.67	40.03	47.13	117.7
Large and Medium Tractor-towed Farm Machines	1,000	1369	1128	1006	1035	102.9
Small Tractor-towed Farm Machines	1,000	2191	3202	3830	4134	107.9
Boat Tractors	1,000	102.0	515	47.2	45	96.1
	1,000,000,000 w	569.938	317.922	297.185	278.356	93.7
Motor-Driven Rice Transplanters	1,000	82.4	12.8	13.0	12.0	89.8
	1,000,000,000 w	203.878	31.709	30.656	31.680	103.3
Motors for Agricultural Drainage and Irrigation	1,000	5630	6163	6507	6839	105.1
	1,000,000,000 w	54.91	57.59	60.44	62.58	103.5
Diesel Engines	1,000	2899	2865	3043	3202	105.2
	1,000,000,000 w	2720	2568	2690	2818	104.8
Electric Motors	1,000	2583	3216	3369	3547	105.3
	1,000,000,000 w	2713	3151	3291	3397	103.2
Pumps for Agricultural Use	1,000	4566	5195	5504	5792	105.2
Sprinkler Machines	1,000 sets	270.7	268.3	267.9	285.1	107.8
Combine Harvesters	1,000	27.0	34.6	30.9	33.8	109.2
	1,000,000,000 w	1.06	1.63	1.40	1.73	123.6
Motor Driven Harvesters	1,000	73.5	86.1	116.4	160.0	137.5
Motor Driven Threshers	1,000	2498	3441	3676	3971	108.0
Seed Selecting Machines	1,000	16.6	16.3	16.4	15.5	94.2
Grain Drying Machines	1,000	10.7	5.4	3.7	3.6	96.2
Rice and Wheat Mills	1,000	3025	3259	3349	3451	103.0
Cotton Ginning Mills	1,000	265	222	206	200	97.6
Oil Pressers	1,000	226	273	274	280	102.2
Trucks for Agricultural Use	1,000	137.7	429.6	499.2	550.2	110.2
	1,000,000,000 w	8.97	30.76	35.81	39.66	110.8
Large and Medium Sized Trailers	1,000	546	804	902	777	86.1
Motor Cargo-transpot Boats	1,000	107.9	236.0	263.6	300.6	114.1
	1,000 tns	1117	3217	3792	4914	129.6
	1,000,000 w	1.14	2.34	2.75	3.16	114.9
Motor Driven Sprayers	1,000	279	306	310	310	100.0
	1,000,000 w	0.53	0.56	0.53	0.53	100.0
Fodder Grinders	1,000	1392	1087	1137	1169	102.8
Forage Grass Harvesters	1,000	14.1	12.5	14.2	15.6	110.1
Excavators	unit	530	409	353	650	184.1
Tree Planters	unit	1650	1305	1472	1368	92.9
Weeders	unit	1366	1219	1152	2984	259.0
Moter-fishing Boats	1,000	61.0	172.6	205.9	238.6	115.9
	1,000 tns	1536	2170	2560	2831	110.6
	1,000,000 w	2.58	3.67	4.24	4.86	114.6
Animal Drawn Carts wtih Rubber Tire	1,000	2398	2875	3051	3482	114.1
Hand Carts with Rubber Tire	1,000	3517	6114	62413	65107	104.3

8.7 MAJOR AGRICULTURAL MACHINERY AT YEAR-END BY REGION

Region	Total Power (1,000,000,000 w)			Large and Medium Tractors (unit)			Small and Walking Tractors (1,000)		
	1980	1986	1987	1980	1986	1987	1980	1986	1987
Total	**147.46**	**229.50**	**248.36**	**744865**	**866463**	**880952**	**1874**	**4526**	**5303**
Beijing	2.35	3.45	3.88	7705	11664	12170	25	37	42
Tianjin	2.13	3.61	3.83	12819	12860	12523	9	14	19
Hebei	12.55	22.22	24.07	42133	36074	34881	111	362	429
Shanxi	5.42	8.53	8.95	32667	33526	32908	31	126	142
Inner Mongolia	4.21	5.39	6.14	33202	40929	42860	15	112	149
Liaoning	5.69	9.38	9.88	42033	57271	57612	46	104	118
Jilin	3.68	5.29	5.35	25961	39257	41069	26	115	143
Heilongjiang	7.09	9.35	10.95	68487	85732	92159	31	199	270
Shanghai	2.15	2.47	2.57	7319	11097	11397	32	31	30
Jiangsu	11.15	18.11	19.74	16238	18669	19368	256	538	605
Zhejiang	5.35	8.89	9.75	9837	8713	8394	96	210	241
Anhui	6.65	9.17	10.36	17562	15554	15221	117	300	377
Fujian	2.40	4.56	5.08	7527	8038	7793	65	120	131
Jiangxi	3.29	5.60	6.10	19806	24546	24677	55	72	80
Shandong	13.72	25.38	27.36	114504	135945	133874	112	321	382
Henan	11.78	17.38	18.66	59666	89655	59485	128	449	528
Hubei	7.73	10.02	10.65	36412	63650	75238	109	159	175
Hunan	5.87	10.59	10.54	19529	16704	14621	64	136	158
Guangdong	6.66	10.45	11.54	19988	16513	15972	127	268	303
Guangxi	3.91	5.57	6.25	22335	22275	19926	104	160	182
Sichuan	6.56	10.13	10.88	22538	21604	20933	99	152	168
Guizhou	1.32	2.15	2.31	8519	12049	12451	9	19	22
Yunnan	3.22	4.75	5.13	17234	18128	17770	33	86	100
Tibet	0.30	0.35	0.39	1983	2620	2386	5	6	6
Shaanxi	4.72	5.81	6.23	20325	20006	19979	69	171	194
Gansu	3.56	4.59	4.95	17126	20760	21724	55	124	147
Qinghai	0.70	0.94	1.03	6364	5073	4902	14	35	42
Ningxia	0.84	1.38	1.50	5811	8011	5831	16	51	58
Xinjiang	2.49	3.96	4.29	29208	41540	42928	15	49	59

MAJOR AGRICULTURAL MACHINERY AT YEAR-END BY REGION

(continued)

Region	Motors for Agricultural Drainage and Irrigations (1,000,000,000 w)			Combine Harvesters (unit)			Motor-driven Harvesters (unit)		
	1980	1986	1987	1980	1986	1987	1980	1986	1987
Total	**54.90**	**60.44**	**62.58**	**27045**	**30945**	**33802**	**73521**	**116352**	**159990**
Beijing	0.71	0.69	0.75	535	1767	2059	4896	225	447
Tianjin	1.01	1.07	1.13	108	78	87	885	367	490
Hebei	7.96	11.65	12.60	397	587	702	875	20254	27885
Shanxi	1.82	1.43	1.43	80	202	280	4939	4588	5306
Inner Mongolia	0.92	0.95	1.04	2814	1503	1768	1367	780	1142
Liaoning	1.64	1.70	1.72	69	38	38	175	38	144
Jilin	0.80	0.74	0.69	145	136	124	116	124	124
Heilongjiang	0.75	0.88	0.91	14081	16970	18853	781	7542	6814
Shanghai	0.26	0.31	0.31	182	783	1100	6019	61	149
Jiangsu	4.43	4.69	4.69	485	897	984	4386	3671	6363
Zhejiang	1.19	1.42	1.45	200	229	203	2807	574	407
Anhui	3.65	2.53	2.60	424	536	529	984	6651	12088
Fujian	0.50	0.59	0.58	67	107	90	216	73	111
Jiangxi	1.54	1.34	1.38	159	66	50	1481	206	183
Shandong	6.79	10.23	10.83	344	372	433	18736	25853	34322
Henan	5.75	5.33	5.41	799	985	901	5547	36316	52848
Hubei	2.11	2.96	2.87	602	484	552	7983	759	837
Hunan	2.57	3.04	3.14	270	91	60	92	33	26
Guangdong	1.73	1.61	1.84	343	153	147	669	386	513
Guangxi	0.70	0.55	0.55	906	82	121	278	87	67
Sichuan	2.69	2.60	2.68	51	36	31	420	34	30
Guizhou	0.63	0.36	0.34			1	321	61	27
Yunnan	0.68	0.58	0.61	184	53	42	690	520	144
Tibet	0.08	0.03	0.03	92	64	16	993	339	419
Shaanxi	1.89	1.56	1.38	167	175	163	3444	2648	3786
Gansu	1.46	1.00	1.00	221	376	375	1863	2781	3602
Qinghai	0.08	0.08	0.07	363	437	438	648	84	59
Ningxia	0.14	0.11	0.13	252	307	188	1265	441	522
Xinjiang	0.42	0.41	0.42	3335	3431	3467	695	856	1135

MAJOR AGRICULTURAL MACHINERY AT YEAR-END BY REGION

(continued)

Region	Motor-driven Threshers (1,000)			Trucks for Agricultural Use (unit)		
	1980	1986	1987	1980	1986	1987
Total	**2498**	**3676**	**3971**	**137668**	**499164**	**500192**
Beijing	28	27	26	4581	12754	14726
Tianjin	20	21	23	2253	13414	14436
Hebei	229	356	393	5498	36075	36665
Shanxi	45	56	58	6655	32273	34863
Inner Mongolia	27	22	24	4536	9728	11513
Liaoning	61	83	90	6902	29953	31245
Jilin	61	34	73	2766	8755	8441
Heilongjiang	4	53	63	9837	11595	12351
Shanghai	86	125	130	1665	7661	8986
Jiangsu	410	746	795	3343	13102	15803
Zhejiang	332	685	753	2004	9940	11156
Anhui	88	111	125	4287	17404	21476
Fujian	25	18	19	3029	9186	10881
Jiangxi	31	28	32	6011	17861	19525
Shandong	208	395	415	7084	40153	43772
Henan	119	211	236	6631	38408	42022
Hubei	174	147	145	5546	12814	14129
Hunan	31	155	149	8023	42918	43586
Guangdong	134	143	161	13395	32327	39040
Guangxi	77	40	38	3129	11244	13205
Sichuan	125	48	44	5743	31072	35582
Guizhou	4	1	1	2016	6323	6982
Yunnan	54	34	32	3464	12610	14668
Tibet	9	5	4	649	2284	2410
Shaanxi	74	96	106	3484	11526	12995
Gansu	16	10	10	3710	9302	10268
Qinghai	8	4	4	1930	3454	3432
Ningxia	12	15	14	1041	2857	3112
Xinjiang	6	7	8	5533	12168	12922

MAJOR AGRICULTURAL MACHINERY AT YEAR-END BY REGION

(continued)

Region	Motor-driven Freight Boats (unit)					
	1980		1986		1987	
	Unit	*Capacity (1,000 tns)*	*Unit*	*Capacity (1,000 tns)*	*Unit*	*Capacity (1,000 tns)*
Total	**107903**	**1117**	**263598**	**3792**	**300642**	**4914**
Beijing					4	3
Tianjin	11		22		20	
Hebei	17		27		30	
Shanxi			29		44	1
Inner Mongolia			26		27	
Liaoning	433	8	856	18	742	16
Jilin	2		66	2	57	4
Heilongjiang	75	13	152		318	
Shanghai	4676	67	2159	52	2188	55
Jiangsu	60584	490	94978	1208	110923	1190
Zhejiang	16880	132	64753	697	74270	753
Anhui	3494	48	21592	527	23104	644
Fujian	1551	29	10064	155	10945	180
Jiangxi	1532	41	7604	165	8109	176
Shandong	651	14	3319	111	3284	102
Henan	28		486	7	750	43
Hubei	3381	36	6043	139	9391	144
Hunan	5324	78	13304	173	14805	195
Guangdong	7717	126	27573	355	29544	409
Guangxi	1198	26	7044	106	8312	127
Sichuan	192	6	2419	66	2734	53
Guizhou	62	1	276	4	334	13
Yunnan	73	2	588	6	398	4
Tibet						
Shaanxi	22		157	1	223	2
Gansu			61		86	
Qinghai						
Ningxia						
Xinjiang						

MAJOR AGRICULTURAL MACHINERY AT YEAR-END BY REGION

(continued)

Region	Fodder Grinders (1,000)			Forage Grass Harvesters (unit)		
	1980	1986	1987	1980	1986	1987
Total	**1392**	**1137**	**1169**	**14058**	**14196**	**15632**
Beijing	15	9	8		380	
Tianjin	9	4	4	36	93	12
Hebei	97	62	62	37	60	385
Shanxi	30	19	18	43	151	44
Inner Mongolia	33	19	21	3659	9118	10641
Liaoning	54	29	28	193	138	17
Jilin	40	37	46	638	564	359
Heilongjiang	46	35	35	1185	1136	929
Shanghai	7	5	5			
Jiangsu	119	70	67		10	8
Zhejiang	33	31	32			
Anhui	21	15	16	1	10	5
Fujian	19	24	27		4	
Jiangxi	8	10	12		5	7
Shandong	207	144	139			
Henan	114	100	106	36	17	25
Hubei	82	58	58			
Hunan	31	25	23			
Guangdong	60	57	55			
Guangxi	63	87	96		7	
						2
Sichuan	128	147	155	199	46	39
Guizhou	7	8	10	3	5	13
Yunnan	36	37	37			31
Tibet				66		
Shaanxi	66	47	49	23	6	11
Gansu	46	41	43	26	79	83
Qinghai	7	5	5	80	26	83
Ningxia	7	4	4	39	28	24
Xinjiang	7	7	8	2794	2313	2914

MAJOR AGRICULTURAL MACHINERY AT YEAR-END BY REGION
(continued)

	Motor-fishing Boats					
	1980		1986		1987	
Region	*Unit*	*Capacity (1,000 tns)*	*Unit*	*Capacity (1,000 tns)*	*Unit*	*Capacity (1,000 tns)*
Total	**61022**	**1536**	**205923**	**2560**	**238628**	**2831**
Beijing	31		38		38	
Tianjin	478	33	529	32	1208	39
Hebei	1684	49	4250	56	4977	74
Shanxi	14		27		23	
Inner Mongolia	25		37		42	
Liaoning	5495	125	15448	208	17518	221
Jilin	80	1	146	2	172	2
Heilongjiang	265	1	2043	3	2559	5
Shanghai	1436	70	1480	74	1920	77
Jiangsu	5796	156	20334	368	25220	340
Zhejiang	12857	395	32274	616	35476	675
Anhui	854	14	5034	52	5808	65
Fujian	7255	165	27339	269	34426	364
Jiangxi	181	3	6457	18	7612	23
Shandong	10690	182	20977	278	23599	281
Henan	160	1	503	1	471	1
Hubei	608	3	2674	17	4005	17
Hunan	548	4	3155	6	4409	11
Guangdong	10760	283	54122	463	59430	533
Guangxi	1158	49	6635	90	7602	93
Sichuan	98	1	339	2	401	1
Guizhou	9		2		16	
Yunnan	391	1	1777	4	1306	8
Tibet					16	
Shaanxi	56		15		20	
Gansu	17		4		5	
Qinghai	5		16		15	
Ningxia	6					
Xinjiang	65		270	1	334	

MAJOR AGRICULTURAL MACHINERY AT YEAR-END BY REGION

(continued)

Region	Animal Drawn Carts With Rubber Tire (1,000)			Hand Carts With Rubber Tire (unit)		
	1980	1986	1987	1980	1986	1987
Total	**2398**	**3051**	**3482**	**35170**	**62413**	**65107**
Beijing	49	54	56	509	677	685
Tianjin	43	58	63	232	562	548
Hebei	481	558	605	4409	6939	7047
Shanxi	89	102	110	1042	1982	2017
Inner Mongolia	179	185	197	411	1236	1623
Liaoning	281	585	587	481	1247	1338
Jilin	209	290	530	55	455	567
Heilongjiang	285	428	438	420	943	879
Shanghai				91	231	251
Jiangsu	20	14	13	1942	3881	4011
Zhejiang				1329	1835	2094
Anhui	16	1	3	2311	3983	4436
Fujian	7	2	6	518	896	936
Jiangxi	5	1	2	409	1010	1102
Shandong	234	190	204	5783	13722	13925
Henan	199	108	128	17892	10347	10643
Hubei	17	8	7	697	2260	2429
Hunan	2	2	3	269	172	196
Guangdong	12	36	59	519	1161	1199
Guangxi	3	13	16	92	467	460
Sichuan	5	6	6	126	123	117
Guizhou	15	44	45	70	83	86
Yunnan	39	31	32	632	925	977
Tibet	11	14	17	41	33	33
Shaanxi	46	36	36	2168	3068	3180
Gansu	43	49	49	1611	2224	2313
Qinghai	15	42	43	205	274	300
Ningxia	14	5	5	216	456	464
Xinjiang	79	189	222	690	1226	1251

8.8 *EDUCATIONAL LEVEL OF RURAL LABOR FORCE OF SOCIETY*

Level of Education Completed	Percentage of Rural Labor Force
Total	**100.00**
Higher Education	0.06
Secondary Specialized School	0.37
Senior Middle School	6.79
Junior Middle School	29.39
Primary School	38.40
Illiterate and Semi-illiterate	24.99

8.9 *POSSESSION OF MAJOR AGRICULTURAL MACHINERY BY RURAL HOUSEHOLDS*

Item	Unit	Volume	Proportion to National Total (%)
Large and Medium Tractors	unit	607878	69.0
	1,000 ,000 kw	16.40	57.0
Small Walking Tractors	1,000	4963	9.36
	1,000,000 kw	44.15	93.7
Motor-driven Threshers	1,000	2794	70.4
Trucks for Agricultural Use	unit	360093	65.4
	1,000,000 kw	26.23	66.1
Carts with Rubber Tire	1,000	3351	96.2
Hand Carts with Rubber Tire	1,000	63903	98.2
Motors for Agricultural Drainage and Irrigation	1,000	4139	60.5
	1,000,000 kw	29.24	46.7
Diesel Engines	1,000	2406	75.1
	1,000,000 kw	18.95	67.2
Electric Motors	1,000	1692	47.7
	1,000,000 kw	10.24	30.2
Pumps for Agricultural Use	1,000	3362	58.0

8.10 POSSESSION OF MAJOR AGRICULTURAL MACHINERY BY RURAL HOUSEHOLD BY REGION 1987

(1,000 mu*)

Region	Large and Medium Tractors for Agricultural Use (unit)	Small Sized Tractors and Walking Tractors (1,000)	Motor-driven Threshers (1,000)	Trucks for Agricultural Use (unit)	Motors for Drainage Irrigation (1,000,000 kw)
Total	**607878**	**4963**	**2794**	**360093**	**29.24**
Beijing	2055	36	1	2545	0.01
Tianjin	6962	17	6	5527	0.11
Hebei	19216	423	321	28228	9.28
Shanxi	25357	137	34	25923	0.15
Inner Mongolia	32990	143	22	7754	0.71
Liaoning	47533	114	83	22268	0.66
Jilin	34115	140	69	6571	0.49
Heilongjiang	56911	253	59	5777	0.56
Shanghai	356	9	5	579	
Jiangsu	6536	485	399	6476	0.45
Zhejiang	5562	207	682	6976	0.23
Anhui	10452	372	107	15638	1.03
Fujian	6458	127	12	8794	0.21
Jiangxi	17774	73	25	11396	0.23
Shandong	85805	363	267	20368	6.70
Henan	42541	525	172	35331	3.61
Hubei	60700	156	83	8039	0.61
Hunan	9965	153	144	30825	1.35
Guangdong	10959	280	119	25303	0.66
Guangxi	16224	177	25	10765	0.14
Sichuan	15931	161	29	26455	1.01
Guizhou	10876	42	1	5621	0.21
Yunnan	11868	96	19	10467	0.16
Tibet	2031	6	4	2098	0.02
Shaanxi	15185	192	83	9974	0.43
Gansu	16460	144	6	7362	0.07
Qinghai	3791	22	4	2683	0.03
Ningxia	4413	56	7	2283	0.04
Xinjiang	28782	54	6	8067	0.08

Note:
*** 1 mu = 1/15 hectare.**

8.11 *AGRICULTURAL MECHANIZATION, ELECTRICITY, FERTILIZER APPLICATION AND IRRIGATION*

	Unit	1980	1985	1986	1987
Level of Mechanization in Agriculture					
Tractor-plowed Areas	1,000,000 mu*	614.86	516.637	546.417	575.901
Machine-sown Areas	1,000,000 mu*	224.66	181.632	194.358	209.112
Rice-transplanted Areas	1,000,000 mu*	2.354	1.903	2.438	2.961
Machine-harvested Areas	1,000,000 mu*	65.43	71.317	82.602	91.814
Electricity Consumed in Rural Areas					
Electricity Consumed in Rural Areas	1,000,000,000 kwh	32.08	50.89	58.67	65.88
Number of Hydropower Stations Run by Township	1,000	12.2	12.1	12.0	12.0
Generation Capacity	1,000 kw	1749	2599	2650	2774
Number of Hydropower Stations Run by Village	1,000	68.1	43.7	42.2	40.0
Generating Capacity	1,000 kw	1292	1203	1229	1167
Application of Chemical Fertilizer					
Consumption of Chemical Fertilizer					
Gross Weight	1,000,000 tns	58.649	73.105	79.960	83.772
Effective Element Weight	1,000,000 tns	12.694	17.758	19.306	19.993
Irrigation of Farmland					
Effectively Irrigated Areas	1,000,000 mu*	673.32	660.539	663.387	666.045
Power-irrigated Areas	1,000,000 mu*	379.72	369.438	375.478	372.368
Proportion to Effectively Irrigated Areas	%	56.4	55.9	56.6	55.9
Power-pumped Wells	1,000	2599	2628	2674	2623
Rural Methane-generating Pits	1,000		3752	3578	3475

Note:
*** 1 mu = 1/15 hectare.**

8.12 AGRICULTURAL MECHANIZATION, ELECTRICITY, FERTILIZER APPLICATION AND IRRIGATION BY REGION

(1,000 mu*)

Region	Tractor-plowed Area			Machine-sown Area			Machine-harvested Area		
	1980	1986	1987	1980	1986	1987	1980	1986	1987
Total	**614857**	**546417**	**575901**	**224657**	**194358**	**209912**	**65429**	**82602**	**91814**
Beijing	4660	4538	4518	3520	3411	3494	546	914	1110
Tianjin	5858	5327	5679	2122	1309	1241	233	114	385
Hebei	57293	44353	49173	25884	18481	21194	3650	5940	7699
Shanxi	26666	28158	29094	5414	3895	4752	683	2032	2513
Inner Mongolia	24460	14874	17726	11270	5990	6890	4694	3586	3520
Liaoning	31256	29175	31664	11110	3823	4526	18	21	64
Jilin	21208	22929	21862	18170	14871	16189	180	164	158
Heilongjiang	90005	82022	79484	59520	59622	58159	32233	32554	31563
Shanghai	4671	4533	4031	110	153	215	210	429	549
Jiangsu	43503	50785	51626	5982	6490	7821	1255	2137	3433
Zhejiang	14491	11304	11272	9			189	87	247
Anhui	15572	16741	23011	1136	910	820	632	2036	3107
Fujian	6463	5538	5710	13	2	1	36	105	22
Jiangxi	10281	7231	7056	39			89	48	21
Shandong	68447	68930	71419	27615	21828	25613	5345	7859	10147
Henan	49850	41481	47602	7800	6538	7431	1751	8328	10023
Hubei	17898	8155	7229	3159	753	608	1297	839	819
Hunan	10069	6251	7237	161	11	17	81	28	30
Guangdong	17290	11863	11854	36	12	141	193	70	61
Guangxi	11739	8585	9217	59	2	4	105	10	17
Sichuan	11682	7919	7806	295	58	69	115	260	135
Guizhou	441	90	85	5	5		10	2	
Yunnan	3524	2758	4155	108	4	12	84	3	53
Tibet	928	272	240	547	276	270	126	4	130
Shaanxi	18909	20416	21501	10215	12155	13970	450	1424	1806
Gansu	9755	9866	11354	2947	4685	5433	618	1083	1216
Qinghai	2505	2054	2180	2358	1825	1943	636	1024	1048
Ningxia	4734	2792	3486	1757	2079	2421	301	324	352
Xinjiang	30699	27477	29130	23296	25160	26670	9759	11137	11586

Note:
*** 1 mu = 1/15 hectare.**

AGRICULTURAL MECHANIZATION, ELECTRICITY, FERTILIZER APPLICATION AND IRRIGATION BY REGION

(continued)

Region	Electricity Consumed in Rural Areas (1,000,000,000 kwh)			Consumption of Chemical Fertilizer					
	1980	1986	1987	Gross Weight			Effective Weight		
				1980	1986	1987	1980	1986	1987
Total	**32.08**	**58.67**	**65.88**	**58649**	**79960**	**83772**	**12694**	**19306**	**19993**
Beijing	0.77	1.81	1.59	588	462	488	110	90	100
Tianjin	0.67	1.13	1.16	276	275	273	54	43	43
Hebei	3.22	4.76	5.02	3428	5110	5357	747	1153	1165
Shanxi	1.36	1.77	2.04	1429	1697	1779	303	407	407
Inner Mongolia	0.46	0.72	0.82	284	599	675	36	217	239
Liaoning	2.38	3.38	3.87	2984	2640	2652	618	727	673
Jilin	0.97	1.39	1.49	1202	1791	1958	303	607	677
Heilongjiang	1.45	1.52	1.59	1069	1208	1316	346	477	522
Shanghai	1.22	2.44	2.88	1036	854	917	207	153	172
Jiangsu	3.32	7.12	8.52	5768	7700	8126	1182	1698	1780
Zhejiang	1.75	4.38	5.70	2990	3809	4101	618	787	861
Anhui	1.07	1.53	1.68	2457	5612	5942	549	1150	1202
Fujian	0.64	1.47	1.41	1806	2365	2560	370	572	624
Jiangxi	0.52	0.96	1.17	1853	2086	2230	371	624	664
Shandong	2.01	5.13	5.79	6967	7797	8264	1354	1889	1961
Henan	1.72	3.33	3.73	3862	6775	6374	724	1487	1356
Hubei	0.96	1.84	1.98	2431	4488	5062	558	1041	1180
Hunan	0.97	1.81	1.80	3610	4321	4578	797	1012	1066
Guangdong	1.31	3.11	3.77	3491	4293	4752	828	1222	1381
Guangxi	0.48	0.96	0.95	1830	2473	2684	397	570	636
Sichuan	1.28	3.05	3.28	4853	7137	7000	1095	1573	1480
Guizhou	0.29	0.32	0.40	772	1060	1096	208	328	334
Yunnan	0.61	0.80	0.87	1143	1744	1766	273	461	443
Tibet	0.01	0.01	0.01	16	17	18	3	5	5
Shaanxi	1.21	1.89	2.18	1233	1889	1982	296	437	436
Gansu	0.82	1.17	1.06	604	838	852	141	249	234
Qinghai	0.08	0.09	0.11	150	119	125	38	34	37
Ningxia	0.15	0.22	0.26	177	269	283	46	74	79
Xinjiang	0.38	0.66	0.75	340	532	562	122	219	236

AGRICULTURAL MECHANIZATION, ELECTRICITY, FERTILIZER APPLICATION AND IRRIGATION BY REGION

(1,000 mu*) (continued)

	Effective Irrigated Area			Power-irrigated Area		
Region	1980	1986	1987	1980	1986	1987
Total	**673321**	**663387**	**666045**	**379718**	**375478**	**372368**
Beijing	5105	5059	5070	4107	4269	4261
Tianjin	5689	5109	5113	5679	5100	5111
Hebei	54334	53310	54085	49484	47893	49507
Shanxi	16727	15811	16163	11629	11343	11689
Inner Mongolia	16561	15085	15567	5606	8352	9256
Liaoning	11396	10962	11534	8946	9018	9416
Jilin	10960	10762	11293	6619	6356	6845
Heilongjiang	10057	10795	11494	6643	6285	6473
Shanghai	5238	4902	4903	5238	4902	4903
Jiangsu	51192	53067	52277	46818	48504	47904
Zhejiang	22870	22449	22444	17371	16854	14881
Anhui	36570	31384	32349	25380	21318	21844
Fujian	13216	13704	13825	2600	2056	2263
Jiangxi	25044	27212	27321	7447	5887	5733
Shandong	66113	68202	67213	54486	57699	57378
Henan	53044	48191	48751	41611	35982	35403
Hubei	35175	33792	33171	19957	20706	19864
Hunan	36238	41576	39976	15634	19400	15540
Guangdong	31619	28698	27823	8455	8229	7701
Guangxi	21490	20250	20611	4331	3579	3351
Sichuan	45343	40944	41175	8789	8234	8820
Guizhou	6853	7975	8070	1200	926	934
Yunnan	13697	14500	14597	1727	1707	1969
Tibet	2227	1825	1941	66	127	105
Shaanxi	18272	18677	18887	11357	11683	11842
Gansu	12803	12387	12514	4713	4311	4428
Qinghai	2394	2455	2470	292	243	251
Ningxia	3487	3690	3795	404	617	766
Xinjiang	39158	40614	41113	3124	3897	3930

Note:
*** 1 mu = 1/15 hectare.**

8.13 *IRRIGATION, RESERVOIRS, WATERLOGGING PREVENTION, WATER AND SOIL CONSERVATION AND IMPROVEMENT OF SALINE-ALKALINE SOIL*

	Unit	1980	1985
Number of Irrigation System (year-end)		5299	5343
Above 33,000 Hectares		70	70
7,000-33,000 Hectares		552	550
1,000-7,000 Hectares		4677	4723
Effectively Irrigated Area		20869	21144
Above 33,000 Hectares	1,000 ha	5988	6014
7,000-33,000 Hectares	1,000 ha	6745	6811
1,000-7,000 Hectares	1,000 ha	8137	8319
Number of Reservoirs		82716	82870
Large Reservoirs (above 100,000,000 cu.m)		350	353
Medium Reservoirs (10,000,000-100,000,000 cu.m)		2415	2428
Small Reservoirs (10,000-10,000,000 cu.m)		79951	80089
Capacity of Reservoirs	1,000,000,000 cu.m	443.16	447.54
Large Reservoirs	1,000,000,000 cu.m	319.87	323.34
Medium Reservoirs	1,000,000,000 cu.m	66.63	67.23
Small Reservoirs	1,000,000,000 cu.m	56.66	56.97
Irrigated Area of Reservoirs	1,000 ha	15749	15902
Large Reservoirs	1,000 ha	6408	6449
Medium Reservoirs	1,000 ha	4189	4257
Small Reservoirs	1,000 ha	5152	5196
Total Area Liable to Waterlogging	1,000 ha	24229	24337
Area with Waterlogging Prevention Measures	1,000 ha	18761	18958
Proportion to Total Area Liable to Waterlogging	%	77.4	77.9
Total Area of Water Loss and Soil Erosion	1,000 sq.m	1310	1320
Areas with Water Loss and Soil Erosion	1,000 sq.m	479	495
Proportion to Total Area of Water Loss and Soil Erosion	%	36.0	37.0
Total Area of Saline-alkaline Cultivated Land	1,000 ha	7607	7636
Improved Area	1,000 ha	4623	4755
Porportion to Total Area of Saline-alkaline Land	%	60.8	62.3
Total Length of Dunes and Embankments	1,000 ha	185	200
Land Protected by Dunes and Embankments	1,000 ha	31666	32204

8.14 WATER CONSERVANCY FACILITIES AND AREAS WITH WATERLOGGING PREVENTION MEASURES AND IMPROVED AREAS OF SALINE AND ALKALINE LAND BY REGION

	Number of Reservoirs		Capacity of Reservoirs (1,000,000 cu.m)		Areas with Waterlogging Prevention (1,000 ha)		Proportion to Total Area Liable to Waterlogging (%)	
	1986	1987	1986	1987	1986	1987	1986	1987
National Total	**82716**	**82870**	**443161**	**447544**	**18761**	**18958**	**77.4**	**77.9**
Beijing	83	83	7380	7380	155	156	93.6	93.6
Tianjin	75	89	2457	2492	405	402	95.3	95.7
Hebei	1182	1167	14550	14272	1542	1541	82.7	82.6
Shanxi	794	784	3962	3960	87	87	76.9	76.9
Inner Mongolia	503	508	5905	5928	169	193	65.2	52.5
				3				
Liaoning	978	979	29122	0057	967	967	96.6	96.6
Jilin	1312	1302	29621	29831	963	957	93.6	92.6
Heilongjiang	480	480	6113	6128	2263	2357	56.0	58.3
Shanghai					60	62	90.0	91.2
Jiangsu	1133	1140	18987	19015	2758	2768	93.9	94.3
Zhejiang	3496	3511	31767	33215	417	422	80.5	81.4
Anhui	4361	4365	17998	17991	1907	1917	80.5	80.9
Fujian	2537	2585	6368	6658	101	102	46.7	47.5
Jiangxi	9410	9412	22805	22933	300	301	64.5	64.9
Shandong	5490	5495	19108	19138	2343	2368	76.4	77.2
				49365				
Henan	2464	2467	49344		1620	1647	77.0	78.3
Hubei	6348	6353	48418	48372	1163	1158	83.7	83.7
Hunan	12725	12727	21091	21091	431	433	83.0	82.7
Guangdong	7268	7281	43095	44319	497	498	84.3	84.5
Guangxi	4582	4585	21464	21522	177	179	51.6	51.5
				11676				
Sichuan	8983	9015	11481		77	79	46.4	47.6
Guizhou	1849	1846	5033	5054	33	34	37.7	39.2
Yunnan	4146	4184	6559	6600	155	158	63.5	69.6
Tibet								
				4486				
Shaanxi	1414	1415	4484		135	135	80.2	81.2
Gansu	298	291	8528	8530	11	11	34.8	34.8
Qinghai	132	133	200	201				
Ningxia	194	194	1750	1751				
Xinjiang	479	479	5574	5579	25	26	35.2	38.1

WATER CONSERVANCY FACILITIES AND AREAS WITH WATERLOGGING PREVENTION MEASURES AND IMPROVED AREAS OF SALINE AND ALKALINE LAND BY REGION

(continued)

	Improved Area of Saline and Alkaline Land (1,000 ha)		Proportion to Total Saline and Alkaline Land (%)	
	1986	1987	1986	1987
National Total	**4623**	**4755**	**60.8**	**62.3**
Beijing	39	40	79.5	82.2
Tianjin	205	205	85.3	86.0
Hebei	707	721	69.4	70.8
Shanxi	164	172	50.6	53.1
Inner Mongolia	227	229	46.1	43.6
Liaoning	285	287	74.0	74.5
Jilin	135	135	49.4	49.4
Heilongjiang	183	182	32.5	32.3
Shanghai	18	25	36.5	60.7
Jiangsu	588	593	84.6	85.2
Zhejiang				
Anhui	95	95	84.1	84.1
Fujian	19	19	51.8	51.8
Jiangxi				
Shandong	716	740	74.7	77.2
Henan	605	615	75.8	77.0
Hubei				
Hunan				
Guangdong				
Guangxi	34	39	12.2	13.6
Sichuan	1	1	33.3	33.3
Guizhou				
Yunnan	2	2	50.0	50.0
Tibet				
Shaanxi	55	55	65.6	66.4
Gansu	61	63	50.3	51.9
Qinghai	9	9	46.4	50.0
Ningxia	53	53	60.8	61.2
Xinjiang	423	475	41.7	46.8

8.15 RURAL NON-STATE-OWNED PRODUCTIVE FIXED ASSETS

	Value (1,000,000,000 yuan)			Percentage		
	1983	1986	1987	1983	1986	1987
Total Original Value of Productive fixed Assets at Year-end	**163.21**	**239.31**	**269.38**	**100.0**	**100.0**	**100.0**
By Use of Production						
House and Buildings for Production	47.14	71.67	77.80	28.9	29.9	28.9
Draught Animals and Product Animals	49.03	59.34	60.76	30.0	24.8	22.6
Machinery for Agriculture, Forestry, Animal Husbandry and Fishery	23.82	28.34	30.66	14.6	11.8	11.4
Machinery for Industry and Construction	26.68	49.47	66.01	16.3	20.7	24.5
Machinery for Transportation	16.54	30.49	34.15	10.2	12.7	12.6
By Ownership						
Collective-owned	83.10	119.67	141.31	50.9	50.0	52.5
Household-owned	80.11	119.64	128.07	49.1	50.0	47.5

8.16 FIXED ASSETS OF TOWNSHIP AND VILLAGE ENTERPRISES

	1980	1985	1986	1987
Value (1,000,000,000 yuan)				
Total Original Value of Fixed Assets at Year-end	32.63	75.04	94.67	122.66
Township Enterprises	20.03	46.70	59.08	75.00
Village Enterprises	12.60	28.34	35.59	47.66
Total Net Value of Fixed Assets at Year-end	26.59	58.98	74.32	95.98
Township Enterprises	16.06	38.59	45.60	57.60
Village Enterprises	10.53	23.09	28.72	38.38
Percentage				
Total Original Value of Fixed Assets at Year-end				
Township Enterprises	61.39	62.23	62.41	61.14
Village Enterprises	38.61	37.77	37.59	38.86
Total Net Value of Fixed Assets at Year-end				
Township Enterprises	60.40	60.85	61.37	60.01
Village Enterprises	39.60	39.15	38.63	39.99

8.17 ORIGINAL VALUE OF FIXED ASSETS OF TOWNSHIP AND VILLAGE ENTERPRISES BY REGION

(1,000,000,000,000 yuan)

Region	1980	1986	1987
Total	**32632.06**	**94674.64**	**122664.57**
Beijing	572.66	2730.62	3450.01
Tianjin	441.27	1602.36	2193.58
Hebei	1755.04	4554.60	5726.83
Shanxi	943.29	3040.44	3750.97
Inner Mongolia	327.20	604.34	723.84
Liaoning	1427.84	4578.42	6024.01
Jilin	570.47	1298.01	1660.29
Heilongjiang	787.25	1751.00	2034.20
Shanghai	1305.58	4750.70	5514.28
Jiangsu	3579.11	13636.21	18277.50
Zhejiang	1817.15	7999.02	10680.75
Anhui	773.17	2347.40	3057.53
Fujian	792.54	2269.57	2894.56
Jiangxi	765.71	1739.35	2009.40
Shandong	3509.79	11124.18	14656.99
Henan	2031.28	4383.86	5590.20
Hubei	2065.80	4545.04	5477.85
Hunan	2251.10	3542.85	4426.70
Guangdong	2037.86	7114.34	10234.20
Guangxi	647.42	836.08	1033.35
Sichuan	2064.83	5367.81	6525.09
Guizhou	188.70	525.73	672.40
Yunnan	485.30	1174.99	2050.07
Tibet			
Shaanxi	716.38	1694.11	2157.54
Gansu	308.28	728.68	926.94
Qinghai	98.65	111.62	156.95
Ningxia	122.04	159.71	192.95
Xinjiang	246.35	463.50	565.59

8.18 *ORIGINAL VALUE OF FIXED ASSETS OF RURAL ECONOMIC ASSOCIATIONS * 1987*

	Original Value of Fixed Assets (1,000,000 yuan)	Average Original Value of Fixed Assets Per Association (yuan)	Average Original Value of Fixed Assets Per Employee (yuan)
Total	**7260**	**14999**	**1702**
Crop Farming	79	8144	1091
Forestry	46	10698	1386
Livestock and Animal Husbandry	65	14444	3218
Fishery	1362	20858	3721
Industry	3842	16259	1480
Construction	269	7752	456
Transportation	1035	16274	4413
Commerce, Food Services and Service Trade	402	8272	1778
Others	160	9415	1410

Note:
*** Rural economic associations (Nongchun Jingji Lianheti) refer to the economic organizations that farmers voluntarily joined since 1979, to deal with farm crops production, processing farm crops, selling products and other business. The members of those associations jointly manage the associations and share the costs and benefits.**

8.19 *ORIGINAL VALUE OF FIXED ASSETS OF ECONOMIC ASSOCIATIONS* BY REGION* 1987

(1,000 yuan)

Region	Total Original Value of Fixed Assets						
	Total	Crop Farming	Forestry	Animal Husbanry	Fishery	Industry	Construction
Total	**7260103**	**79256**	**45774**	**65232**	**1361854**	**3841762**	**268822**
Beijing	2197	10		3		669	10
Tianjin	102603	331	323	2360	3907	40617	2943
Hebei	1522155	7197	4307	4433	103594	944420	60926
Shanxi	169017	573	373	299	418	113143	5427
Inner Mongolia	43684	7332	879	631	550	25967	1003
Liaoning	190657	7902	746	1987	102777	69496	7269
Jilin	44476	2538	183	5976	310	25616	695
Heilongjiang	54564	5686	68	1506	2469	10885	843
Shanghai	3020	63	25	901	85	1415	125
Jiangsu	149472	488	35	837	21502	84522	4619
Zhejiang	446650	1650	930	1470	124520	237350	5480
Anhui	230402	703	1430	528	5008	146180	8735
Fujian	910443	11577	9025	4761	368651	370592	11291
Jiangxi	72626	568	193	429	1377	38631	3349
Shandong	673428	3173	5220	9288	26075	222310	27740
Henan	819685	1939	1922	2699	3431	565390	47586
Hubei	71511	270	145	94	2917	39395	5426
Hunan	134597	2138	1234	559	871	81984	11071
Guangdong	982611	19645	11345	20952	329014	397720	24631
Guangxi	90474	1277	2810	336	26213	46569	1532
Sichuan	226237	989	268	2205	835	141724	6829
Guizhou	43223	85	1383	161	209	29073	1970
Yunnan	25882	572	335	295	482	37916	2780
Tibet							
Shaanxi	138796	524	749	1001	1003	94296	16801
Gansu	88720	1037	1665	1378	607	59570	7512
Qinghai	7396	741		50	5	47150	610
Ningxia	7029	101	181	68	338	3516	1210
Xinjiang	8843	147		25	11	7431	409

Note:
*** Rural economic associations (Nongchun Jingji Lianheti) refer to the economic organizations that farmers voluntarily joined since 1979, to deal with farm crops production, processing farm crops, selling products and other business. The members of those associations jointly manage the associations and share the costs and benefits.**

ORIGINAL VALUE OF FIXED ASSETS OF ECONOMIC ASSOCIATIONS* BY REGION 1987

(1,000 yuan) (continued)

Region	Total Original Value of Fixed Assets		
	Transportation	Commerce, Food Services and Service Trade	Others
Total	**1034541**	**401745**	**161117**
Beijing	141	282	1082
Tianjin	37354	3719	11049
Hebei	278518	81973	36787
Shanxi	41800	5836	1148
Inner Mongolia	4492	2598	232
Liaoning	24254	9068	2738
Jilin	5000	2383	522
Heilongjiang	2387	1348	390
Shanghai	220	156	30
Jiangsu	28404	5406	3659
Zhejiang	59710	10820	4720
Anhui	43670	18346	5802
Fujian	86701	30316	17529
Jiangxi	24093	2919	1067
Shandong	91722	40291	12934
Henan	120536	45694	30488
Hubei	17279	3308	2677
Hunan	21828	11502	3410
Guangdong	78164	86475	14670
Guangxi	5464	4723	1530
Sichuan	23672	11449	2686
Guizhou	8541	2273	781
Yunnan	6999	4491	694
Tibet			
Shaanxi	12685	8703	2404
Gansu	9492	5851	1608
Qinghai	232	746	297
Ningxia	741	818	56
Xinjiang	442	251	127

Note:
*** Rural economic associations (Nongchun Jingji Lianheti) refer to the economic organizations that farmers voluntarily joined since 1979, to deal with farm crops production, processing farm crops, selling products and other business. The members of those associations jointly manage the associations and share the costs and benefits.**

8.20 NUMBER OF AGRICULTURAL METEOROLOGICAL SERVICE STATIONS

	1980	1986	1987
Agricultural Meteorological Observation Stations	750	1247	1252
Crop Growth Period Observation Stations	476	878	980
Soil Humidity Observation Stations	388	909	953
Phenolgical Observation Stations	262	682	660
Agricltural and Meteorological Experiment Stations		64	64
Crop Farming		53	54
Forestry		4	4
Animal Husbandry		7	6
Stations Sending Agricultural Weather Report Every Ten Days	9097	1062	904
Weather Stations		1512	1391

8.21 AREAS COVERED AND AFFECTED BY NATURAL DISASTERS

(1,000,000 mu*)

	1980	1986	1987
Total Areas Covered by Natural Disasters	667.89	707.03	631.29
Drought	391.67	465.63	373.80
Flood	137.19	137.33	130.29
Typhoon and Hail	103.49	73.95	89.71
Frost	35.54	30.12	37.49
Total Areas Affected by Natural Disasters	334.76	354.84	305.89
Drought	187.28	221.47	195.49
Flood	75.38	84.02	61.56
Typhoon and Hail	54.45	40.79	34.30
Frost	17.65	8.56	14.54
Areas with Total Loss of Crops	58.41	100.11	55.03
Drought		54.76	35.92
Flood		31.37	10.29
Typhoon and Hail		9.45	6.08
Frost		4.53	2.74

Note:
*** 1 mu = 1/15 hectare.**

8.22 AREAS COVERED AND AFFECTED BY DISASTERS BY REGION

(1,000,000 mu*)

Region	Total Disasters Covered 1980	Covered 1986	Covered 1987	Affected 1980	Affected 1986	Affected 1987
Total	**667.89**	**707.03**	**631.29**	**334.76**	**354.84**	**305.89**
Beijing	4.38	0.99	0.52	1.59	0.46	0.18
Tianjin	5.76	0.39	2.84	3.48	0.12	1.32
Hebei	62.01	61.31	51.31	39.33	32.27	29.74
Shanxi	46.44	37.48	42.49	20.33	20.60	18.63
Inner Mongolia	45.02	39.75	33.66	25.82	21.77	23.22
Liaoning	22.92	13.81	19.77	13.97	9.72	12.69
Jilin	31.97	33.10	15.99	16.80	23.79	9.07
Heilongjiang	46.82	34.72	54.33	24.18	15.37	22.20
Shanghai	3.00	0.02	0.07	2.40	0.01	
Jiangsu	27.00	25.79	26.96	13.00	12.28	8.67
Zhejiang	8.65	12.27	16.16	4.15	4.62	5.57
Anhui	32.76	32.26	20.36	17.03	10.78	10.88
Fujian	10.12	11.22	7.63	2.91	4.66	3.43
Jiangxi	9.90	18.24	11.81	3.81	10.26	6.00
Shandong	58.04	60.77	49.48	21.58	26.69	25.93
Henan	39.23	78.66	43.98	20.72	43.15	16.70
Hubei	38.48	31.84	21.08	25.71	18.83	8.72
Hunan	30.56	36.20	31.31	16.66	18.13	14.28
Guangdong	21.96	30.65	19.58	4.93	16.16	6.44
Guangxi	17.78	16.61	13.78	5.92	6.55	4.83
Sichuan	31.15	32.85	44.59	12.41	13.16	15.06
Guizhou	9.87	8.16	16.12	5.48	4.50	8.87
Yunnan	11.66	23.34	17.79	4.15	7.83	8.64
Tibet	0.64	0.73	1.27	0.22	0.06	0.52
Shaanxi	29.82	24.68	32.07	14.10	12.44	23.86
Gansu	11.12	25.33	22.23	8.93	12.19	15.10
Qinghai	2.37	2.02	1.70	1.23	1.51	0.80
Ningxia	2.46	5.08	6.37	1.25	1.53	1.76
Xinjiang	6.00	8.76	6.04	2.67	3.60	2.78

Note:
*** 1 mu = 1/15 hectare.**

AREAS COVERED AND AFFECTED BY DISASTERS BY REGION

(1,000,000 mu*) (continued)

	Drought					
	Covered			Affected		
Region	1980	1986	1987	1980	1986	1987
Total	**391.67**	**465.63**	**373.80**	**187.28**	**221.47**	**195.49**
Beijing	3.78	0.52	0.43	1.45	0.25	0.13
Tianjin	4.22	0.13	0.41	2.31	0.04	0.30
Hebei	54.12	40.80	41.00	35.03	20.13	24.30
Shanxi	38.84	32.00	35.71	16.70	17.00	17.00
Inner Mongolia	33.82	29.07	27.26	19.56	15.64	19.46
Liaoning	16.86	4.20	10.64	10.66	2.50	6.93
Jilin	16.46		7.58	7.93		5.14
Heilongjiang	37.60	10.72	19.72	20.00	4.36	7.35
Shanghai						
Jiangsu	3.42	13.40	4.70	0.20	3.58	3.00
Zhejiang		6.15		2.55		
Anhui	3.00	23.00	4.97	0.61	7.30	2.61
Fujian	5.14	6.87	2.95	1.47	3.30	0.80
Jiangxi	2.75	15.32	5.04		11.09	2.64
Shandong	34.00	54.00	37.41	10.05	22.20	19.84
Henan	21.03	75.00	29.97	11.50	41.00	11.85
Hubei	9.09	22.72	1.45	6.22	13.16	0.75
Hunan	15.04	27.53	18.31	8.73	13.09	9.21
Guangdong	11.37	16.87	11.37	1.24	6.56	4.49
Guangxi	15.54	10.18	11.21	5.17	3.40	3.89
Sichuan	22.91	17.29	29.40	8.56	8.50	8.01
Guizhou	0.91	3.90	13.43	0.54	2.30	7.62
Yunnan	7.40	6.03	13.20	2.00	1.76	6.96
Tibet	0.20	0.73	0.99	0.09	0.06	0.52
Shaanxi	21.67	19.00	19.40	9.63	10.00	16.53
Gansu	6.10	20.00	18.36	5.48	9.05	13.40
Qinghai	1.45	0.10	0.84	0.60		0.32
Ningxia	2.05	4.10	6.00	1.05	0.95	1.62
Xinjiang	3.00	6.00	2.05	0.50	2.00	0.82

Note:
*** 1 mu = 1/15 hectare.**

AREAS COVERED AND AFFECTED BY DISASTERS BY REGION

(1,000,000 mu*) (covered)

	Flood					
	Covered			Affected		
Region	1980	1986	1987	1980	1986	1987
Total	**137.19**	**137.33**	**130.29**	**75.38**	**84.02**	**61.56**
Beijing		0.14			0.07	
Tianjin			0.10			0.05
Hebei		2.60	2.36	0.26	2.30	1.51
Shanxi	0.79	1.02	1.09	0.26	0.31	0.74
Inner Mongolia	2.82	6.29	2.50	1.46	4.26	1.85
Liaoning	0.40	7.20	7.38	0.16	6.12	4.96
Jilin	2.47	26.79	3.66	1.38	20.74	2.62
Heilongjiang	2.32	18.73	22.06	0.82	8.85	7.91
Shanghai	2.40	0.01	0.01	2.00		
Jiangsu	18.00	9.48	4.55	12.60	7.23	2.97
Zhejiang	3.75	1.23	8.25	1.60	0.69	2.64
Anhui	23.30	6.06	10.55	13.47	1.96	6.05
Fujian	2.26	1.56	2.20	0.37	0.80	1.40
Jiangxi	6.27	1.30	2.53	3.36	0.78	1.25
Shandong	2.75	1.56	2.10	0.96	0.90	1.16
Henan	11.80	3.21	4.60	5.35	2.05	3.40
Hubei	24.75	8.31	13.49	16.39	5.42	5.56
Hunan	14.37	5.35	8.43	7.31	3.05	2.98
Guangdong	4.85	13.35	6.41	1.43	9.50	1.10
Guangxi	1.26	5.44	1.41	0.43	2.88	0.31
Sichuan	3.70	6.64	9.51	1.00	2.06	5.32
Guizhou	1.36	2.41	1.78	0.25	0.76	0.73
Yunnan	1.11	4.65	1.72	0.50	1.72	0.47
Tibet	0.08		0.10	0.02		
Shaanxi	4.09	2.29	7.97	2.84	0.72	3.95
Gansu	1.81	1.38	2.65	1.11	0.55	1.06
Qinghai	0.01	0.21	0.07	0.01	0.20	0.07
Ningxia	0.01	0.12			0.10	
Xinjiang	0.46		2.81	0.30		1.50

Note:
*** 1 mu = 1/15 hectare.**

AREAS COVERED AND AFFECTED BY DISASTERS BY REGION

(1,000,000 mu*) (continued)

	Typhoon and Hail					
	Covered			Affected		
Region	1980	1986	1987	1980	1986	1987
Total	**103.49**	**73.95**	**89.71**	**54.45**	**40.79**	**34.30**
Beijing	0.60	0.29	0.09	0.14	0.10	0.05
Tianjin	1.54	0.24	2.33	1.17	0.08	0.97
Hebei	7.89	17.35	7.48	4.30	9.71	3.63
Shanxi	3.66	4.06	5.29	2.97	3.16	0.69
Inner Mongolia	7.75	4.39	1.95	4.36	1.87	0.32
Liaoning	4.91	2.17	1.75	2.72	1.10	0.80
Jilin	13.04	4.23	4.75	7.49	2.79	1.31
Heilongjiang	7.00	1.17	8.45	3.36	0.59	4.30
Shanghai	0.01	0.01	0.06		0.01	
Jiangsu	3.92	2.49	5.21	0.15	1.67	1.74
Zhejiang	4.00	2.89	3.36	2.00	1.03	0.96
Anhui	1.60	2.60	3.82	0.69	1.30	1.69
Fujian	0.95	0.88	1.49	0.21	0.56	0.64
Jiangxi	0.58	1.56	2.50	0.28	0.17	1.18
Shandong	15.82	5.12	9.20	7.88	3.53	4.72
Henan	6.28	0.35	8.47	3.82	0.04	0.83
Hubei	1.47	0.80	2.18	0.82	0.25	0.72
Hunan	0.35	2.93	3.21	0.12	1.84	1.32
Guangdong	4.68	0.16	1.80	1.66	0.10	0.85
Guangxi	0.84	0.54	1.16	0.30	0.27	0.63
Sichuan	4.28	6.57	4.96	2.79	1.70	1.34
Guizhou	2.96	1.70	0.74	1.77	1.44	0.44
Yunnan	0.52	0.51	2.28	0.25	0.08	0.79
Tibet	0.16		0.17	0.02		
Shaanxi	3.18	2.56	4.36	1.24	1.72	3.15
Gansu	3.04	3.91	0.97	2.20	2.59	0.57
Qinghai	0.49	1.41	0.44	0.32	1.04	0.28
Ningxia	0.29		0.30	0.15		0.08
Xinjiang	1.67	2.31	0.94	1.27	1.60	0.30

Note:
* 1 mu = 1/15 hectare.

AREAS COVERED AND AFFECTED BY DISASTERS BY REGION

(1,000,000 mu*) (continued)

Region	Frost					
	Covered			Affected		
	1980	1986	1987	1980	1986	1987
Total	**35.54**	**30.12**	**37.49**	**17.65**	**8.56**	**14.54**
Beijing		0.04			0.04	
Tianjin		0.02				
Hebei		0.56	0.47			0.30
Shanxi	3.15	0.40	0.40	0.40	0.13	0.20
Inner Mongolia	0.63		1.95	0.44	0.13	1.59
Liaoning	0.75	0.24		0.43		
Jilin		2.08			0.26	
Heilongjiang		4.10	4.10		1.57	2.64
Shanghai	0.59			0.40		
Jiangsu	1.66	0.42	12.50	0.05	0.10	0.96
Zhejiang	0.90	2.00	4.55	0.55	0.35	1.97
Anhui	4.86	0.60	1.02	2.26	0.22	0.53
Fujian	1.77	1.91	0.99	0.86		0.59
Jiangxi	0.30	0.06	1.74	0.17	0.02	0.93
Shandong	5.47	0.09	0.77	2.69	0.06	0.21
Henan	0.12	0.10	0.94	0.05	0.06	0.62
Hubei	3.17	0.01	3.96	2.28		1.69
Hunan	0.80	0.39	1.36	0.50	0.15	0.77
Guangdong	1.05	0.27		0.60		
Guangxi	0.14	0.45		0.02		
Sichuan	0.26	2.35	0.72	0.06	0.90	0.39
Guizhou	4.64	0.15	0.17	2.92		0.08
Yunnan	2.63	12.15	0.59	1.40	4.27	0.42
Tibet	0.20		0.01	0.09		
Shaanxi	0.88	0.83	0.34	0.39	0.27	0.23
Gansu	0.17	0.04	0.25	0.14	0.03	0.07
Qinghai	0.42	0.30	0.35	0.30		0.13
Ningxia	0.11	0.11	0.07	0.05		0.06
Xinjiang	0.87	0.45	0.24	0.60		0.16

Note:
*** 1 mu = 1/15 hectare.**

Section IX

RURAL CULTURE, EDUCATION, HEALTH CARE AND SOCIAL WELFARE

9.1 NUMBER OF CULTURAL AND RECREATIONAL ORGANIZATIONS

Item	Unit	1986	1987
Rural Township Cultural Stations		49815	49805
Rural Town Cultural Centers		10586	10808
Rural Mass Amateur Organizations			
Number of Amateur Art Performance Groups		54128	52877
Number of Persons Engaged in Amateur Art Creations	1,000	345	374
Number of Households Specializing in Cultural Activities	1,000	172	208

9.2 PERFORMANCES BY ART PERFORMANCE TROUPES IN RURAL AREAS

Item	Number of Performance in Rural Areas (1,000)		Rural Audience (1,000,000 person-times)	
	1986	1987	1986	1987
Total	395.3	387.9	419.62	425.66
State-run Troupes in Cultural Departments	167.2	173.9	199.39	196.39
Collective-run Troupes in Cultural Departments	228.1	214.0	220.23	229.27
By Type of Performances				
Drama, Children and Comedy Troupes	1.8	3.2	2.14	2.74
Opera, Ballet and Dance Troupes	5.9	8.2	6.08	6.49
Cultural and Performance Troupes and Ulanmuchi Art Troupes	25.9	21.5	18.28	18.82
Philharmonic and Chorus Troupes	0.3	0.2	0.77	0.46
Local Opera Troupes	285.7	288.6	369.77	379.05
Recitation and Ballad-singing, Acrobatics, Puppet Show and Shadow Show	75.6	66.2	22.58	18.10

9.3 NUMBER OF RURAL TOWN CULTURAL CENTERS AND HOUSEHOLDS SPECIALIZING IN CULTURAL ACTIVITIES BY REGION

Region	Town Cultural Centers		Households Specializing in Cultural Activities	
	1986	1987	1986	1987
Total	**10586**	**10808**	**172439**	**207893**
Beijing	28	23	16	167
Tianjin	26	31	161	186
Hebei	337	361	37671	40603
Shanxi	350	369	10760	17153
Inner Mongolia	178	146	2319	2896
Liaoning	403	419	13576	14587
Jilin	306	474	4875	5694
Heilongjiang	339	356	2780	4646
Shanghai	131	130	7	17
Jiangsu	1346	1464	6879	9316
Zhejiang	745	739	2633	3594
Anhui	816	805	6966	7051
Fujian	692	542	3209	3888
Jiangxi	356	424	12140	15776
Shandong	774	774	12322	14958
Henan	547	494	11541	12843
Hubei	349	407	8401	6681
Hunan	970	994	10270	15802
Guangdong	806	792	7029	7693
Guangxi	258	275	2581	3761
Sichuan			9599	11761
Guizhou	81	112	1586	2933
Yunnan	95	108	326	424
Tibet				
Shaanxi	315	325	3172	3290
Gansu	139	146	985	1360
Qinghai	31	32	27	121
Ningxia	20	15	149	80
Xinjiang	148	51	459	612

9.4 *PERFORMANCES BY ART PERFORMANCE TROUPES IN RURAL AREAS BY REGION*

Region	Number of Performances (1,000)		Rural Audience (1,000,000 person-times)	
	1986	1987	1986	1987
Total	**395.3**	**387.9**	**419.62**	**425.66**
Organizations under the Ministry of Culture	0.3	0.2	0.41	0.19
Beijing	0.7	0.7	0.70	0.59
Tianjin	1.6	1.0	2.98	1.90
Hebei	37.0	36.1	31.36	53.03
Shanxi	40.0	43.9	77.69	72.12
Inner Mongolia	12.0	11.6	9.47	16.34
Liaoning	6.0	5.4	6.25	8.90
Jilin	8.9	10.5	7.15	8.01
Heilongjiang	7.0	6.2	4.11	3.68
Shanghai	20.0	16.2	6.76	3.68
Jiangsu	48.0	46.1	16.04	17.92
Zhejiang	20.0	16.0	8.64	8.72
Anhui	10.0	9.8	8.40	8.47
Fujian	15.7	14.8	23.40	19.93
Jiangxi	6.6	8.4	7.76	9.45
Shandong	18.5	15.1	25.20	20.40
Henan	49.5	49.3	78.34	72.18
Hubei	8.2	7.5	4.84	5.71
Hunan	11.4	13.1	6.48	7.51
Guangdong	16.0	20.0	19.67	17.64
Guangxi	4.7	5.8	4.87	5.78
Sichuan	8.9	8.3	5.12	4.16
Guizhou	0.9	1.3	0.61	0.71
Yunnan	4.5	4.4	3.57	4.12
Tibet	0.9	1.1	0.57	0.77
Shaanxi	19.5	17.4	28.31	26.26
Gansu	10.8	11.4	23.71	21.99
Qinghai	10.8	0.9	1.41	1.17
Ningxia	1.7	2.0	2.25	2.55
Xinjiang	5.2	3.4	3.55	2.41

9.5 *NUMBER OF STUDENTS AND TEACHERS IN REGULAR SECONDARY AND PRIMARY SCHOOLS*

Item	Unit	1986	1987
Senior Middle Schools			
Number of Schools		54900	56330
Number of Classes	1,000	36	38
Graduates	1,000	537	620
New Students Enrolled	1,000	676	704
Total Students Enrollled	1,000	1946	2043
Full-time Teachers	1,000	120	133
Junior Middle Schools			
Number of Schools		635120	626900
Number of Classes	1,000	582	553
Graduates	1,000	6639	7284
New Students Enrolled	1,000	9691	9709
Total Students Enrollled	1,000	28080	28550
Full-time Teachers	1,000	1449	1503
Primary Schools			
Number of Schools	1,000	763	744
Number of Classes	1,000	3465	3410
Graduates	1,000	16269	16361
New Students Enrolled	1,000	18655	17064
Total Students Enrollled	1,000	109139	104635
Teachers, Workers and Staff	1,000	4764	4715
Teachers	1,000	4326	4281
Workers and Staff	1,000	438	434

9.6 *BASIC STATISTICS OF RURAL ADULT EDUCATION*

Item	Unit	1986	1987
Higher Education			
Number of Institutions		5	5
Graduates	person	507	566
New Students Enrolled	person	705	369
Total Students Enrolled	person	1334	1104
Full-time Teachers	person	185	174
Secondary Specialized Schools			
Number of Institutions		269	288
Graduates	person	17856	15582
New Students Enrolled	person	45263	29813
Total Students Enrolled	person	84458	54800
Full-time Teachers	person	4114	4444
Number of Technical Training Schools		273480	272890
Graduates	1,000	3057	5245
Correspondence and Part-time	1,000	2516	4487
New Students Enrolled	1,000	3202	5260
Correspondence amd Part-time	1,000	2751	4654
Total Students Enrolled	1,000	3364	5289
Correspondence and Part-time	1,000	2994	4923
Teachers, Staff and Workers	1,000	44	55
Full-time Teachers	1,000	26	33
Part-time Teachers	1,000	74	102
Secondary Schools			
Number of Schools		9584	5968
Graduates	1,000	254	290
New Students Enrolled	1,000	386	292
Total Students Enrolled	1,000	642	475
Full-time Teachers	1,000	9	9
Primary Schools			
Number of Schools		297727	173020
Graduates	1,000	8031	11015
New Students Enrolled	1,000	9738	11851
Total Students Enrolled	1,000	12459	13356
Full-time Teachers	1,000	78	82

9.7 *BASIC STATISTICS OF RURAL VOCATIONAL MIDDLE SCHOOLS*

Item	Unit	1986	1987
Number of Independent Set-up Schools		4502	4411
Senior Middle Schools		2940	2877
Combined Senior and Junior Middle Schools		276	311
Junior Middle Schools		1286	1223
Number of Classes Attached to Regular Middle Schools		5390	13019
Senior Middle Schools		4667	12344
Junior Middle Schools		723	675
Graduates		287690	338771
Senior Middle Schools	person	204512	243602
Junior Middle Schools	person	83178	95169
New Students Enrolled	person	518696	525931
Senior Middle Schools	person	383614	381404
Junior Middle Schools	person	135055	144527
Total of Students Enrolled	person	1174322	1189910
Senior Middle Schools	person	802225	816261
Junior Middle Schools	person	372097	373649

9.8 NUMBER OF TOWNSHIP HOSPITALS, BEDS AND MEDICAL PERSONNEL

Item	Unit	1986	1987
Total of Hospitals		46967	47177
Central Hospitals		10762	10144
Township Hospitals		36205	37033
Total of Beds		711234	722979
Central Hospitals		311247	295670
Township Hospitals		399987	427309
Total of Personnel in Health Care Institutions	person	882923	876559
Central Hospitals	person	357061	331278
Township Hospitals	person	525862	545281
Total of Medical Personnel	person	764200	761269

9.9 NUMBER OF RURAL COLLECTIVE OWNED HOSPITALS, BEDS AND MEDICAL PERSONNEL

Item	Unit	1986	1987
Total of Hospitals		30101	30326
Central Hospitals		1551	1524
Township Hospitals		28550	28802
Total of Beds		349042	353357
Central Hospitals		51983	52353
Township Hospitals		297059	301004
Total of Personnel in Health Care Institutions	person	465212	461837
Central Hospitals	person	66612	66581
Township Hospitals	person	398600	395256
Total of Medical Personnel	person	409340	407650

9.10 *CLASSIFICATION OF MEDICAL PERSONNEL IN TOWNSHIP HOSPITALS*

(person)

Item	1986	1987
Total of Personnel in Health Care Institutions	**882923**	**867559**
Medical Personnel	764200	761269
Senior Doctors of Chinese Medicine	27363	26849
Senior Doctors of Western Medicine	56155	55187
Senior Doctors of Combined Chinese and Western Therapautics	40	45
Senior Nurses	1361	2037
Senior Pharmacists of Chinese Medicine	2284	2380
Senior Pharmacists of Western Medicine	1218	1263
Senior Laboratory Technicians	516	604
Other Senior Technicians	859	982
Junior Doctors of Chinese Medicine	64212	61814
Junior Doctors of Western Medicine	128676	128624
Junior Nurses	73768	73533
Midwives	28418	28487
Junior Pharmacists of Chinese Medicine	18251	18416
Junior Pharmacists of Western Medicine	14034	13854
Junior Laboratory Technicians	9687	9712
Other Junior Technicians	9818	9814
Other Doctors of Chinese Medicine	23110	21707
Nursing Staff	55358	56661
Staff Pharmacists of Chinese Medicine	41654	42442
Staff Pharmacists of Western Medicine	39007	38431
Laboratory Staff	14972	15114
Other Primary Medical Personnel	153439	153292
Other Technical Personnel	584	579
Administrative Personnel	67184	65664
Logistics Workers	50955	49047

9.11 *NUMBER OF MEDICAL PERSONNEL IN RURAL INDIVIDUALLY RUN CLINICS*

(person)

Item	1986	1987
Total of Personnel in Health Care Institutions	**103535**	**104665**
Medical Personnel	103535	104665
Senior Doctors of Chinese Medicine	2056	2049
Senior Doctors of Western Medicine	1553	1731
Senior Doctors of Combined Chinese and Western Therapautics	5	13
Senior Nurses	7	12
Senior Pharmacists of Chinese Medicine	45	67
Senior Pharmacists of Western Medicine	24	25
Senior Laboratory Technicians	1	3
Other Senior Technicians	85	103
Junior Doctors of Chinese Medicine	14161	14152
Junior Doctors of Western Medicine	11468	10693
Junior Nurses	105	188
Midwives	434	447
Junior Pharmacists of Chinese Medicine	475	380
Junior Pharmacists of Western Medicine	167	112
Junior Laboratory Technicians	36	14
Other Junior Technicians	4860	4807
Other Doctors of Chinese Medicine	22903	23424
Nursing Staff	119	177
Staff Pharmacists of Chinese Medicine	1938	1844
Staff Pharmacists of Western Medicine	420	523
Laboratory Staff	10	16
Other Primary Medical Personnel	42663	43585

9.12 NUMBER OF TOWNSHIP HOPITALS, BEDS AND MEDICAL PERSONNEL BY REGION

	Hospitals		Beds		Medical Personnel (person)	
Region	1986	1987	1980	1986	1980	1986
Total	**46967**	**47177**	**711234**	**722979**	**882923**	**876559**
Beijing	173	176	2770	3229	5234	5320
Tianjin	119	115	2085	2075	3337	3273
Hebei	2623	2661	32379	33532	29049	29454
Shanxi	1891	1891	26772	27106	29450	29540
Inner Mongolia	1332	1332	15503	15273	19955	19587
Liaoning	1055	1166	24663	25153	29720	29497
Jilin	890	889	17995	17838	23303	22825
Heilongjiang	845	845	13776	13862	18424	18719
Shanghai	176	174	6759	6740	10298	10088
Jiangsu	1999	1996	59197	60629	72638	73281
Zhejiang	2883	2958	26832	27322	36803	36760
Anhui	2855	2772	37192	37655	44872	43907
Fujian	854	861	16236	16021	23384	23481
Jiangxi	1664	1661	22600	22358	31157	31146
Shandong	1989	1983	50640	50715	69454	67164
Henan	2032	2023	51479	56710	56444	53977
Hubei	1317	1321	43754	43783	52376	52718
Hunan	3535	3540	47816	48295	55274	54476
Guangdong	1651	1648	37833	37646	67174	66632
Guangxi	1079	1063	17246	17315	23329	23213
Sichuan	7089	7152	76192	77491	91860	91642
Guizhou	3072	3045	15968	16435	22983	23307
Yunnan	1341	1339	21045	21244	18687	18757
Tibet	291	313	537	620	458	421
Shaanxi	1963	2066	19277	19040	22607	22863
Gansu	1162	1195	9023	9341	10589	11048
Qinghai	314	287	1677	1660	2249	2168
Ningxia	203	129	1777	1643	2563	2075
Xinjiang	570	576	12031	12248	9252	9220

9.13 *NUMBER OF VILLAGE MEDICAL ORGANIZATIONS BY REGION* *1987*

	Village Medical Clinics					
	Subtotal	Run by Village or Village Residents	Run Jointly by Doctors and Medical Workers	Set up by Township	Run by Individuals	Others
Total	**807844**	**300315**	**82966**	**29141**	**363285**	**32137**
Beijing	4738	2211	493	47	1867	120
Tianjin	4266	1856	481	39	1695	204
Hebei	64068	12476	7112	795	39286	4399
Shanxi	30875	20637	3831	797	4498	1112
Inner Mongolia	14816	2840	1317	457	9984	218
Liaoning	17977	7065	3188	281	6680	763
Jilin	10103	5435	1693	137	2653	185
Heilongjiang	15954	12624	1047	204	1871	208
Shanghai	3010	2284	5	9	261	451
Jiangsu	34945	23314	5918	826	4094	793
Zhejiang	31920	7519	2007	1545	19659	1190
Anhui	42088	2151	3320	801	34660	1156
Fujian	20650	5878	2933	1114	4391	6334
Jiangxi	26915	2578	3537	736	19253	881
Shandong	97834	65970	7864	1072	21986	942
Henan	87030	45432	2040	1116	37304	1138
Hubei	30236	14116	2408	871	12216	625
Hunan	45146	7022	6841	5293	23583	2407
Guangdong	31909	4880	4377	3002	18267	1383
Guangxi	23425	4887	2225	280	15184	849
Sichuan	71072	11336	7678	4554	46039	1465
Guizhou	11369	1179	620	1369	7845	356
Yunnan	16941	7233	3509	324	5147	728
Tibet	1397	40	128	896	300	33
Shaanxi	34472	12293	4871	794	13904	2610
Gansu	20798	12764	1318	352	6190	174
Qinghai	4126	1887	129	119	1626	365
Ningxia	2778	1151	201	13	1176	237
Xinjiang	6986	1257	1875	1307	1666	881

9.14 *NUMBER OF DOCTORS, MEDICAL WORKERS AND MIDWIVES IN TOWNSHIPS AND VILLAGES BY REGION* *1987*

(person)

Region	Doctors and Medical Workers in Townships and Villages			Midwives
	Total	Doctors in Townships and Villages	Medical Workers	
Total	**1278449**	**723799**	**554700**	**481630**
Beijing	6686	2896	3790	1115
Tianjin	7403	6315	1088	1789
Hebei	100629	83355	17274	23051
Shanxi	51939	32244	19695	24484
Inner Mongolia	21785	11262	10523	4016
Liaoning	29393	23342	6051	10577
Jilin	24075	14657	9418	11179
Heilongjiang	32463	17528	14935	16233
Shanghai	7313	4202	3111	340
Jiangsu	68992	38414	30578	6091
Zhejiang	38985	14932	24053	14242
Anhui	51524	21401	30123	22209
Fujian	31579	14000	17579	14939
Jiangxi	40885	20579	20306	25740
Shandong	143506	95378	48128	39703
Henan	144913	104849	40064	27133
Hubei	63037	31924	31113	27003
Hunan	63066	28465	34601	45612
Guangdong	41725	22424	19311	21242
Guangxi	41685	25289	16396	34114
Sichuan	110927	34614	76313	25783
Guizhou	18039	7150	10889	17915
Yunnan	30591	14681	15910	19026
Tibet	3326	1441	1885	275
Shaanxi	52237	24537	27700	21306
Gansu	31875	17178	14697	15649
Qinghai	5520	4183	1337	4262
Ningxia	4518	2209	2309	2275
Xinjiang	9873	4350	5523	4327

9.15 *RURAL PERSONS ENJOYING FIVE GUARANTEES**

Item	Unit	1980	1985
Number of Persons Enjoying Five Guarantees	person	2931957	2869966
Old People	person	2413117	2388543
Orphans	person	108297	101534
Disabled People	person	410543	379889
Number of Five Guarantees Persons Supported by Collectives	person	2204205	2189686
Proportion to Total Five Guarantees Persons	%	75.6	76.3
Number of Persons in Elderly People's Homes	person	285186	313448
Proportion to Total Five Guarantees Persons	%	9.7	10.9
Number of Persons Individually Supported	person	1919019	1876238
Proportion to Total Five Guarantees Persons	%	65.5	65.4
Number of Persons Receiving Periodical and Fixed-amount of Relief Funds from Government	person	220329	214311
Proportion to Total Five Guarantees Persons Individually Supported	%	8.3	11.4

Note:
*** The five guarantees refer to food, clothing, housing, medical care and funeral expenses (or education for children). They are provided for disabled people, childless old people and orphaned children.**

9.16 *NUMBER OF RURAL PERSONS ENJOYING FIVE GUARANTEES* BY REGION* *1987*

(person)

Region	Total	Elderly	Disabled	Orphans
Total	2869966	2388543	379889	101534
Beijing	11132	9938	1049	145
Tianjin	10290	9447	690	153
Hebei	123122	107234	13725	2163
Shanxi	45200	34084	10219	897
Inner Mongolia	62681	54033	7098	1559
Liaoning	59746	50072	6758	2916
Jilin	52387	45935	4783	1669
Heilongjiang	64372	56397	5647	2328
Shanghai	4855	4289	485	81
Jiangsu	203642	183065	17103	3474
Zhejiang	68383	57351	9392	1640
Anhui	207685	171028	32412	4245
Fujian	57816	47232	7067	3517
Jiangxi	184236	149523	23986	10927
Shandong	166437	134941	29511	1985
Henan	292649	243380	45107	4162
Hubei	197577	161738	29443	5936
Hunan	301807	238704	46624	16479
Guangdong	35513	30031	4498	984
Guangxi	125102	104100	12363	8039
Sichuan	297515	256780	29700	11035
Guizhou	73309	61843	6389	5077
Yunnan	82721	65488	14246	2987
Tibet	7644	6184	1050	410
Shaanxi	55649	44811	8921	1917
Gansu	37964	30804	5624	1536
Qinghai	4441	3638	365	438
Ningxia	5636	4861	572	203
Xinjiang	30455	21312	5071	4072

Note:
*** The five guarantees refer to food, clothing, housing, medical care and funeral expenses (or education for children). They are provided for disabled people, childless old people and orphaned children.**

9.17 COLLECTIVE SUPPLY FOR RURAL PERSONS ENJOYING FIVE GUARANTEES* BY REGION 1987

(person)

Region	Persons in Elderly People's Homes	Persons Supported Individually	Persons Supported by Collectives	Persons Receiving Government Periodical and Fixed Amount of Relief Funds
Total	313448	1876238	2189686	214311
Beijing	3473	3399	6872	2006
Tianjin	2537	4104	6641	130
Hebei	19375	51885	71260	3506
Shanxi	4493	19849	24342	5744
Inner Mongolia	9981	40120	50101	8853
Liaoning	18411	33854	52265	3199
Jilin	16884	30568	47452	200
Heilongjiang	17849	36584	54433	1089
Shanghai	3378	1313	4691	93
Jiangsu	24346	154903	179249	1420
Zhejiang	6550	37278	43828	3734
Anhui	15742	151905	167647	18717
Fujian	3345	42959	46304	11747
Jiangxi	26146	105958	132604	43804
Shandong	23012	99838	122850	2252
Henan	25520	174408	199928	3604
Hubei	33586	130928	164514	2163
Hunan	10690	228954	239644	7583
Guangdong	2155	24239	26394	2689
Guangxi	326	62900	63266	23752
Sichuan	25417	239708	265125	23158
Guizhou	558	52336	52894	10065
Yunnan	5610	61406	67016	21993
Tibet	337		337	3582
Shaanxi	6652	38069	44721	1587
Gansu	1935	23203	25138	4844
Qinghai	324	2955	3279	277
Ningxia	1559	2572	4131	1540
Xinjiang	2757	20043	22800	980

Note:
*** The five guarantees refer to food, clothing, housing, medical care and funeral expenses (or education for children). They are provided for disabled people, childless old people and orphaned children.**

9.18 *ELDERLY PEOPLE'S HOMES RUN BY RURAL COLLECTIVES*

Item	Unit	1986	1987
Number of Elderly People's Homes		26678	28014
Number of Workers and Staff	person	63502	66234
Persons Admitted at Year End	person	285186	313448
Old People	person	255453	281058
Orphans	person	6612	6716
Disabled	person	23121	25674
Value of Collective Supplies	1,000,000 yuan	111.61	1383.59

9.19 *ELDERLY PEOPLE'S HOMES RUN BY RURAL COLLECTIVES BY REGION*

Region	Number of Elderly People's Homes		Number of Persons Admitted at Year End	
	1986	1987	1986	1987
Total	**26678**	**28014**	**285186**	**313488**
Beijing	264	265	3495	3473
Tianjin	229	230	2552	2537
Hebei	1938	2192	17050	19375
Shanxi	648	729	4090	4493
Inner Mongolia	796	792	10174	9981
Liaoning	808	846	16433	18411
Jilin	636	632	17539	16884
Heilongjiang	744	712	17839	17849
Shanghai	179	183	2894	3378
Jiangsu	2321	2496	22528	24346
Zhejiang	566	656	5830	6550
Anhui	1658	1744	14681	15742
Fujian	266	315	2720	3345
Jiangxi	1544	1727	22395	26646
Shandong	3051	2487	23251	23012
Henan	2125	2443	17138	25520
Hubei	2957	3088	29277	33586
Hunan	1034	1079	10674	10690
Guangdong	304	232	3047	2155
Guangxi	39	50	200	326
Sichuan	2230	2532	22192	25417
Guizhou	73	83	446	558
Yunnan	512	561	5161	5610
Tibet	37	45	276	337
Shaanxi	998	1016	7116	6652
Gansu	243	341	1600	1935
Qinghai	21	45	218	324
Ningxia	239	231	1676	1559
Xinjiang	212	262	2606	2757

9.20 *SUPPORT FOR RURAL POOR HOUSEHOLDS*

Item	Unit	1986	1987
Receiving Government Relief Funds and Collective Subsidies			
Number of Poor Households Supported	1,000	8726	8430
Proportion to Total of Poor Households	%	39.0	40.0
Number of Persons in Poor Households	1,000	39902	37033
Proportion to Total of Persons in Poor Households	%	39.0	38.0
Collective Subsidy	1,000 yuan	172797	167902
Poor Household Support Programs			
Support Programs Undertaken by Township (commune)		50252	48887
Number of Households Entering the Programs This Year	1,000	3930	3584
Number of Households Leaving the Programs This Year	1,000	2255	2698
Total Number of Households in the Programs at the Year-end	1,000	5389	6688

9.21 *SUPPORT FOR RURAL POOR HOUSEHOLDS BY REGION*

	Number of Poor Households Receiving Government Relief Funds and Collective Subsidies				Value of Collective Subsidies (1,000 yuan)	
	Households (1,000)		Persons (1,000)		1986	1987
Region	*1986*	*1987*	*1986*	*1987*		
Total	**8726**	**8430**	**39902**	**37033**	**172797**	**167902**
Beijing	4	5	11	15	675	606
Tianjin	12	11	53	45	278	284
Hebei	299	337	1075	1280	5177	6745
Shanxi	199	286	838	1136	3568	1946
Inner Mongolia	214	210	880	976	969	1289
Liaoning	119	130	513	558	5825	5411
Jilin	166	120	740	548	4068	3039
Heilongjiang	221	184	1004	853	16267	7277
Shanghai	3	2	8	4	530	1033
Jiangsu	459	417	1789	1568	13641	13646
Zhejiang	196	169	794	670	4994	4889
Anhui	362	298	1573	1257	4294	3290
Fujian	250	231	1096	1053	1342	1162
Jiangxi	292	258	1404	1196	5258	3684
Shandong	228	295	878	1188	9657	19552
Henan	885	793	3814	3388	16586	6738
Hubei	373	299	1705	1391	9991	9897
Hunan	603	523	2631	2269	13926	9681
Guangdong	200	190	804	883	1319	9567
Guangxi	622	545	2956	2167	590	225
Sichuan	817	690	4831	3199	8863	53021
Guizhou	883	802	4079	3595	319	723
Yunnan	536	681	2569	3274	35001	321
Tibet	10	24	46	119	760	
Shaanxi	341	322	1581	1415	1208	1303
Gansu	221	326	1152	1620	5137	405
Qinghai	49	61	256	343	68	76
Ningxia	41	81	223	463	206	142
Xinjiang	143	144	595	559	2174	1950

9.22 *RURAL SOCIAL RELIEF FUNDS AND NATURAL DISASTER RELIEF FUNDS*

Item	Unit	1980	1985
Rural Social Relief Funds	1,000,000,000 yuan	213.44	202.60
Funds for Five Guarantees*	1,000,000,000 yuan	42.44	44.31
Relief Funds for Poor Households	1,000,000,000 yuan	163.22	150.06
Relief Funds for Leprosy	1,000,000,000 yuan	7.78	8.23
Natural Disaster Relief Funds	1,000,000,000 yuan	1070.26	987.15
Funds for Living	1,000,000,000 yuan	609.96	614.51
Funds for Rescuing, Transfering and Settling Natural Disaser Victims	1,000,000,000 yuan	40.84	23.87
Funds for Reopening Production	1,000,000,000 yuan	116.88	106.39
Others	1,000,000,000 yuan	302.58	242.38
Supporting the Poor Households	1,000,000,000 yuan	286.80	222.86
Proportion to Total Expenditure of Civil Administration			
Rural Social Relief Funds	%	6.2	5.6
Natural Disaster Relief Funds	%	31.1	27.5

Note:
*** The five guarantees refer to food, clothing, housing, medical care and funeral expenses (or education for children). They are provided for disabled people, childless old people and orphaned childred.**

9.23 *RURAL SOCIAL RELIEF FUNDS BY REGION*

(1,000 yuan)

Region	Relief Funds					
	Subtotal		Funds for Five Guarantees*		Funds for Poor Households	
	1986	*1987*	*1986*	*1987*	*1986*	*1987*
Total	**213443**	**202595**	**42438**	**44309**	**163216**	**150557**
Beijing	2188	3221	120	76	2068	3145
Tianjin	3021	1814	176	230	2841	1580
Hebei	6835	5928	1082	1136	5722	4760
Shanxi	6232	5096	1392	1194	4838	3901
Inner Mongolia	4172	4088	1797	1959	2372	2125
Liaoning	10593	9101	1142	1099	9374	7879
Jilin	4187	3638	702	555	3481	3058
Heilongjiang	10033	8946	977	771	9036	8156
Shanghai	423	260			36	019
Jiangsu	14613	15544	2359	2386	11272	12166
Zhejiang	11870	11394	1693	1600	9875	9477
Anhui	7847	7610	2147	2263	5328	4884
Fujian	7749	6991	1574	1639	5875	5067
Jiangxi	10789	11201	3581	3917	6138	6403
Shandong	9868	8615	1870	1679	7998	6936
Henan	6720	6752	1324	1342	5572	5358
Hubei	6927	6207	942	876	5324	4869
Hunan	5394	4502	1384	1390	3571	2661
Guangdong	8571	8973	2691	2635	4206	4527
Guangxi	15149	12882	2959	4302	11793	8124
Sichuan	20168	17909	3004	3160	16034	13734
Guizhou	5823	5162	1190	1259	4100	3440
Yunnan	11048	11717	2850	3258	8187	8434
Tibet	3795	5301	2094	2417	1650	2704
Shaanxi	3642	2886	675	620	2942	2238
Gansu	4845	4293	934	964	3878	3300
Qinghai	3323	2360	284	354	3038	2006
Ningxia	2313	2196	562	471	1751	1725
Xinjiang	5305	8014	663	756	4592	7201

Note:
*** The five guarantees refer to food, clothing, housing, medical care and funeral expenses (or education for children). They are provided for disabled people, childless old people and orphaned childred.**

9.24 *NATURAL DISASTER RELIEF FUNDS BY REGION*

(1,000 yuan)

Region	1986	1987
Total	**1070255**	**987154**
Beijing	3980	3725
Tianjin	2736	3220
Hebei	28886	51893
Shanxi	17627	26730
Inner Mongolia	46422	34145
Liaoning	80456	35691
Jilin	70867	65622
Heilongjiang	54144	36890
Shanghai	4513	121
Jiangsu	35125	29391
Zhejiang	13395	26783
Anhui	47286	37491
Fujian	15512	21198
Jiangxi	22259	32606
Shandong	41651	47109
Henan	101637	110672
Hubei	36369	30615
Hunan	47239	36289
Guangdong	54161	51511
Guangxi	39008	33305
Sichuan	61802	58324
Guizhou	47010	49443
Yunnan	75510	54081
Tibet	7406	6797
Shaanxi	33905	33203
Gansu	46222	40923
Qinghai	9216	6948
Ningxia	9115	8414
Xinjiang	16737	14014

9.25 *RURAL POSTAL AND TELECOMMUNICATION FACILITIES*

Item	Unit	1986	1987
Number of Rural Post Offices		44517	44315
Lenghth of Rural Postal Routes	1,000 km	4203	4182
Number of Rural Post Boxes	1,000	137	138
Total Capacity of Rural Switchboards	1,000 lines	2919	3094
Number of Rural Telephone Subscribers	1,000	999	977
Number of Telephones	1,000	1618	1774
Number of Rural Mail and Newspaper Stations	1,000	222	249

9.26 RURAL POSTAL AND TELECOMMUNICATION FACILITIES BY REGION

Region	Number of Post Offices		Number of Post Boxes		Total Capacity of Rural Switchboard (1,000 lines)	
	1986	1987	1986	1987	1986	1987
Total	**44517**	**44315**	**136794**	**138199**	**2919**	**3094**
Beijing	217	216	988	959	23	24
Tianjin	137	136	784	791	21	25
Hebei	2470	2289	3896	3861	199	200
Shanxi	1550	1518	2489	2479	107	109
Inner Mongolia	1380	1386	2523	2625	73	74
Liaoning	1276	1261	6249	6346	133	141
Jilin	913	911	7407	7201	83	86
Heilongjiang	1228	1230	7804	7883	74	80
Shanghai	238	250	2346	2389	54	62
Jiangsu	2550	2539	6151	6267	247	275
Zhejiang	3156	3182	10877	11477	268	295
Anhui	2143	2157	5212	5296	94	98
Fujian	1556	1553	10295	10359	72	76
Jiangxi	1603	1631	5205	5182	87	93
Shandong	2174	2176	5661	5465	227	246
Henan	2178	2172	4183	4217	148	149
Hubei	1888	1896	8635	8637	172	166
Hunan	2358	2349	7276	7312	160	164
Guangdong	2561	2508	10980	11527	246	294
Guangxi	1195	1201	5215	5329	64	66
Sichuan	5497	5571	8999	8913	123	129
Guizhou	1112	1093	1682	1646	37	37
Yunnan	1501	1494	3559	3567	66	67
Tibet	32	27	55	58	2	1
Shaanxi	1417	1430	3637	3662	69	70
Gansu	943	936	2166	2218	33	33
Qinghai	171	142	470	454	4	4
Ningxia	164	167	408	412	6	6
Xinjiang	909	894	1624	1658	26	25

RURAL POSTAL AND TELECOMMUNICATION FACILITIES BY REGION

(continued)

Region	Number of Rural Telephone Subscribers		Number of Telephones (1,000)		Number of Households With Telephone	
	1986	1987	1986	1987	1986	1987
Total	**998707**	**976760**	**1618**	**1774**	**36113**	**69139**
Beijing	1569	1546	15	16	34	13
Tianjin	1776	1837	13	15	54	59
Hebei	25135	27426	90	92	576	692
Shanxi	15289	15891	43	44	81	116
Inner Mongolia	15943	16540	33	34	156	366
Liaoning	61447	65319	85	92	755	1706
Jilin	27790	30671	61	67	1071	2154
Heilongjiang	25738	27012	38	46	80	262
Shanghai	37001	40651	47	52	383	763
Jiangsu	53256	59055	166	187	780	1521
Zhejiang	62935	72806	146	168	4157	8109
Anhui	23324	24781	34	40	262	346
Fujian	47326	29931	38	40	1323	2264
Jiangxi	23323	23871	46	48	266	394
Shandong	55345	58670	115	125	981	1355
Henan	26659	50583	57	59	1082	1460
Hubei	52977	57332	87	90	573	963
Hunan	29130	30454	86	90	149	315
Guangdong	13572	160446	156	200	22241	44429
Guangxi	47968	31746	40	40	535	1062
Sichuan	50807	52223	77	82	184	290
Guizhou	18132	15555	23	22	36	32
Yunnan	55170	34166	43	45	152	168
Tibet	198	371	1	1		
Shaanxi	16267	16722	33	33	89	145
Gansu	9589	9844	16	16	28	46
Qinghai	8372	9749	3	3	6	27
Ningxia	1571	1639	4	4	9	18
Xinjiang	9783	9923	23	23	52	64

9.27 *NUMBER OF NEWSPAPER AND MAGAZINE SUBSCRIPTIONS IN RURAL AREAS BY REGION*

(1,000)

	Subscriptions			
	Subtotal		Personal Subscriptions	
Region	*1986*	*1987*	*1986*	*1987*
National Total	**97512**	**105618**	**37761**	**42524**
Beijing	1295	2306	569	745
Tianjin	700	772	202	209
Hebei	3535	4289	987	1250
Shanxi	2253	1944	937	697
Inner Mongolia	1589	2232	626	1432
Liaoning	3400	4314	1286	1647
Jilin	2382	2542	946	1044
Heilongjiang	3525	4475	2035	3141
Shanghai	2374	2797	659	659
Jiangsu	8664	9226	2780	3887
Zhejiang	5381	5646	1890	2059
Anhui	3737	4877	893	1009
Fujian	2421	2991	980	1199
Jiangxi	3219	3039	821	907
Shandong	8929	8290	3186	2921
Henan	5411	5701	1756	1817
Hubei	5114	5570	1963	1925
Hunan	6101	5677	2935	2688
Guangdong	5521	5934	3277	3110
Guangxi	3371	4084	1784	1751
Sichuan	8959	9414	3619	4285
Guizhou	1063	1269	491	613
Yunnan	1897	2051	676	748
Tibet	48	7	5	1
Shaanxi	2189	2336	718	816
Gansu	1099	1134	403	481
Qinghai	323	148	8	37
Ningxia	1530	1012	572	609
Xinjiang	1482	1541	757	837

9.28 *RURAL WIRE BROADCASTING*

Item	Unit	1986	1987
Number of Rural Broadcasting Institutions			
Broadcasting Stations at County Level	1,000	2.214	2.154
Service Stations at County Level	1,000	1.702	1.732
District Broadcasting Stations under County's Jurisdiction	1,000	2.315	1.588
Broadcasting and Amplifying Stations at Township Level	1,000	50.604	48.586
Broadcasting Stations at Village Level	1,000	225.420	233.870
Status of Rural Wire Broadcasting			
Number of Villages with Wire Broadcasting		549712	546478
Proportion to Total Villages	%	71.9	71.0
Number of Households with Loudspeakers	1,000	79753	80250
Proportion to Total Rural Households	%	41.6	41.0
Number of Rural Loudspeakers	1,000	81887	83160
Installed in Households	1,000	80241	8025
Regularly Working	1,000	67936	6947
Proportion to All	%	84.7	87.0
Number of Small Broadcasting Networks		21114	14242
Number of Amplifiers	unit/kwh	273312/60763	229985/51988

9.29 RURAL WIRE BROADCASTING BY REGION

Region	Number of Broadcasting and Amplifying Stations at Township Level		Number of Broadcasting Stations at Village Level		Number of Villages with Access to Wire Broadcasting		Proportion of Villages with Access to Wire Broadcasting to Total Villages (%)	
	1986	1987	1986	1987	1986	1987	1986	1987
Total	**50604**	**48586**	**225420**	**233870**	**549712**	**546478**	**72**	**71**
Beijing	275	267	3467	3340	4083	3758	94	86
Tianjin	223	223	3564	2805	3616	3701	94	96
Hebei	3617	3608	29797	31472	39289	40310	78	80
Shanxi	1894	1900	10925	6204	29975	28669	85	84
Inner Mongolia	1145	1077	2460	2750	6896	6411	29	24
Liaoning	1253	1240	13481	13410	13107	12388	82	76
Jilin	909	904	7677	7804	8890	9035	89	90
Heilongjiang	1099	1105	10113	10884	11878	12432	82	86
Shanghai	227	229	2058	2106	2975	2941	99	97
Jiangsu	2017	2074	17695	18436	35133	35506	97	98
Zhejiang	3187	3204	23075	23049	42954	43062	99	99
Anhui	3360	3375	5317	6214	28160	29357	85	84
Fujian	918	924	6824	7050	10042	10252	69	70
Jiangxi	1762	1775	2836	2735	11321	9843	55	48
Shandong	2389	2427	26325	32656	71348	73041	80	82
Henan	2072	2056	17561	18495	37383	35367	77	75
Hubei	3253	1913	11807	12516	23293	23455	70	70
Hunan	3408	3433	9261	9051	36142	36264	75	79
Guangdong	1997	1091	5217	5783	11326	12351	51	39
Guangxi	1052	1065	1394	1282	5008	4802	34	33
Sichuan	7798	7733	2232	3512	60379	60565	80	79
Guizhou	896	846	117	68	4579	3900	13	15
Yunnan	947	1179	3209	2980	4919	3868	37	30
Tibet	20	20	100	100	1100	100	11	10
Shaanxi	2424	2428	6091	6104	27452	26774	82	82
Gansu	1320	1345	1094	1000	9613	9148	55	52
Qinghai	218	205	557	546	2175	1899	55	47
Ningxia	254	239	234	224	1869	1891	77	78
Xinjiang	670	701	932	1294	4807	5388	64	65

RURAL WIRE BROADCASTING BY REGION
(continued)

Region	Number of Households with Loudspeakers		Proportion of Households with Loudspeakers to Total Households (%)	
	1986	1987	1986	1987
Total	**7975**	**8025**	**42**	**41**
Beijing	10	11	9	10
Tianjin	1	1	1	1
Hebei	289	296	25	25
Shanxi	386	372	75	72
Inner Mongolia	66	62	20	19
Liaoning	295	283	50	53
Jilin	203	218	68	74
Heilongjiang	234	224	66	63
Shanghai	100	101	81	77
Jiangsu	952	974	73	74
Zhejiang	601	610	67	67
Anhui	136	113	14	11
Fujian	163	161	34	33
Jiangxi	120	94	21	16
Shandong	939	973	57	58
Henan	804	832	55	57
Hubei	329	342	39	40
Hunan	424	458	35	38
Guangdong	178	173	15	17
Guangxi	102	90	16	13
Sichuan	1028	1056	49	49
Guizhou	9	8	2	1
Yunnan	38	33	7	5
Tibet	4	3	11	10
Shaanxi	313	301	57	54
Gansu	145	137	43	40
Qinghai	21	19	41	37
Ningxia	27	28	46	48
Xinjiang	58	52	26	23

Section X

THE RANKING OF REGIONS BY SELECTED INDICATORS

10.1 *TOTAL OUTPUT VALUE OF RURAL SOCIETY*

Region	1987		1986	
	Value (1,000,000,000 yuan)	Rank	Value (1,000,000,000 yuan)	Rank
Beijing	12.413	21	9.818	22
Tianjin	11.854	23	8.633	24
Hebei	47.700	7	37.830	7
Shanxi	16.617	19	15.291	17
Inner Mongolia	11.124	24	9.542	23
Liaoning	40.835	9	31.804	11
Jilin	19.721	16	15.058	19
Heilongjiang	22.280	14	2.024	12
Shanghai	21.644	15	16.401	15
Jiangsu	124.503	1	96.386	1
Zhejiang	70.572	4	54.732	4
Anhui	40.437	11	33.304	10
Fujian	24.242	12	19.110	14
Jiangxi	22.311	13	19.126	13
Shandong	87.084	2	68.776	2
Henan	60.432	6	46.016	6
Hubei	42.843	8	35.961	8
Hunan	40.774	10	33.666	9
Guangdong	75.356	3	56.674	3
Guangxi	18.342	18	15.859	16
Sichuan	61.786	5	51.700	5
Guizhou	12.156	22	10.796	21
Yunnan	15.092	20	12.876	20
Tibet	1.131	29	1.073	29
Shaanxi	18.507	17	15.095	18
Gansu	9.550	26	7.974	25
Qinghai	2.004	28	1.853	28
Ningxia	2.124	27	1.919	27
Xinjiang	9.727	25	0.791	26

10.2 *GROSS OUTPUT VALUE OF AGRICULTURE*

	1987		1986	
Region	Value (1,000,000,000 yuan)	Rank	Value (1,000,000,000 yuan)	Rank
Beijing	3.442	25	2.814	25
Tianjin	3.293	26	2.692	26
Hebei	20.066	10	17.438	10
Shanxi	6.142	23	5.882	22
Inner Mongolia	8.774	20	7.725	20
Liaoning	16.922	11	14.203	11
Jilin	12.081	16	9.843	16
Heilongjiang	13.700	14	13.717	12
Shanghai	3.884	24	3.376	24
Jiangsu	38.025	4	33.267	3
Zhejiang	22.812	9	19.204	9
Anhui	25.534	6	22.192	7
Fujian	13.297	15	10.707	15
Jiangxi	14.435	12	12.479	13
Shandong	41.318	1	36.118	1
Henan	32.362	5	25.949	5
Hubei	24.968	8	21.910	8
Hunan	25.339	7	22.268	6
Guangdong	38.987	2	31.486	4
Guangxi	13.792	13	11.869	14
Sichuan	38.894	3	33.898	2
Guizhou	9.225	19	7.931	19
Yunnan	11.125	17	9.601	17
Tibet	1.029	29	0.992	29
Shaanxi	10.339	18	8.720	18
Gansu	6.551	22	5.640	23
Qinghai	1.594	17	1.411	28
Ningxia	1.476	28	1.416	27
Xinjiang	8.164	21	6.553	21

10.3 *RURAL HOUSEHOLD INCOME*

Region	1987		1986	
	Yuan/Person	Rank	Yuan/Person	Rank
Beijing	916.38	2	823.16	2
Tianjin	749.41	3	635.17	3
Hebei	444.40	15	407.61	15
Shanxi	376.87	22	344.98	20
Inner Mongolia	388.77	19	339.53	22
Liaoning	599.25	7	533.20	7
Jilin	523.09	8	456.70	9
Heilongjiang	474.46	11	476.18	8
Shanghai	1059.21	1	936.57	1
Jiangsu	626.48	6	561.28	5
Zhejiang	725.13	4	609.31	4
Anhui	429.26	17	396.53	16
Fujian	484.88	10	418.51	14
Jiangxi	429.29	16	395.63	17
Shandong	517.69	9	449.27	10
Henan	377.72	21	332.92	25
Hubei	460.66	13	445.13	11
Hunan	471.30	12	439.66	12
Guangdong	644.21	5	546.43	6
Guangxi	353.95	25	316.10	26
Sichuan	369.46	23	337.94	24
Guizhou	341.84	27	303.51	27
Yunnan	364.57	24	338.14	23
Tibet	348.39	26	343.57	21
Shaanxi	329.47	28	298.98	28
Gansu	296.14	29	269.40	29
Qinghai	392.15	18	369.24	19
Ningxia	382.71	20	374.49	18
Xinjiang	452.72	14	374.88	13

10.4 *OUTPUT OF GRAIN BY REGION*

	1987		1986	
Region	Amount (1,000 tns)	Rank	Amount (1,000 tns)	Rank
Beijing	227.0	25	216.5	25
Tianjin	167.7	26	157.6	26
Hebei	1920.0	8	1965.5	8
Shanxi	712.5	19	732.4	19
Inner Mongolia	607.0	21	528.5	23
Liaoning	1276.3	14	1222.2	14
Jilin	1675.8	11	1397.7	13
Heilongjiang	1737.6	10	1776.3	9
Shanghai	232.6	24	236.9	24
Jiangsu	3257.7	3	3339.6	2
Zhejiang	1589.0	12	1605.1	11
Anhui	2428.7	6	2371.9	6
Fujian	839.3	18	751.5	18
Jiangxi	1562.8	13	1453.8	12
Shandong	3393.7	2	3250.0	3
Henan	2948.4	4	2545.7	5
Hubei	2320.7	7	2304.5	7
Hunan	2593.7	5	2631.5	4
Guangdong	1848.2	9	1717.8	10
Guangxi	1210.2	15	1118.1	15
Sichuan	3921.3	1	3923.8	1
Guizhou	673.2	20	672.3	20
Yunnan	934.8	17	870.0	17
Tibet	46.7	29	45.4	29
Shaanxi	987.9	16	965.5	16
Gansu	529.4	23	551.0	21
Qinghai	104.1	28	98.4	28
Ningxia	139.0	27	154.0	27
Xinjiang	588.0	22	547.7	22

10.5 *OUTPUT OF GRAIN PER CAPITA BY REGION*

	1987		1986	
Region	Kg/Person	Rank	Kg/Person	Rank
Beijing	231	25	224	27
Tianjin	203	28	194	28
Hebei	339	14	352	13
Shanxi	267	22	277	18
Inner Mongolia	297	19	262	22
Liaoning	340	13	330	14
Jilin	721	1	606	1
Heilongjiang	519	2	535	3
Shanghai	188	29	193	29
Jiangsu	516	3	535	2
Zhejiang	388	10	396	10
Anhui	463	4	457	6
Fujian	303	18	275	19
Jiangxi	442	7	417	8
Shandong	433	8	420	7
Henan	375	12	328	15
Hubei	462	5	465	5
Hunan	452	6	465	4
Guangdong	289	20	273	20
Guangxi	304	17	286	17
Sichuan	377	11	383	11
Guizhou	222	27	225	26
Yunnan	268	21	254	23
Tibet	227	26	226	25
Shaanxi	322	16	319	16
Gansu	254	23	268	21
Qinghai	251	24	240	24
Ningxia	324	15	367	12
Xinjiang	422	9	399	9

10.6 *OUTPUT OF OIL-BEARING CROPS BY REGION*

	1987		1986	
Region	Amount (tn)	Rank	Amount (tn)	Rank
Beijing	32930	28	30937	28
Tianjin	52156	26	58612	27
Hebei	688740	8	617502	9
Shanxi	308124	17	351743	15
Inner Mongolia	539622	9	660488	7
Liaoning	192045	19	316211	16
Jilin	352592	15	388461	14
Heilongjiang	126027	24	190317	21
Shanghai	162096	22	149485	23
Jiangsu	1210978	5	1167739	4
Zhejiang	396612	13	429420	11
Anhui	1510522	3	1316053	3
Fujian	174844	21	171828	22
Jiangxi	356974	14	315869	17
Shandong	2342899	1	2076205	1
Henan	1365650	4	989873	5
Hubei	755418	6	818584	6
Hunan	530649	10	471749	10
Guangdong	586850	7	656561	8
Guangxi	185732	20	237405	20
Sichuan	1615091	2	1589865	2
Guizhou	463410	11	418985	13
Yunnan	135175	23	109780	24
Tibet	11820	29	11617	29
Shaanxi	315119	16	301317	18
Gansu	294459	18	298740	19
Qinghai	103774	25	103646	25
Ningxia	44479	27	62219	26
Xinjiang	422988	12	426449	12

10.7 *OUTPUT OF SUGAR BY REGION*

Region	1987 Amount (tn)	1987 Rank	1986 Amount (tn)	1986 Rank
Beijing			481	26
Tianjin				27
Hebei	57836	22	78893	22
Shanxi	192867	20	272167	17
Inner Mongolia	1678324	8	1590267	9
Liaoning	283685	17	218267	18
Jilin	690021	12	597567	12
Heilongjiang	3304055	5	3897929	5
Shanghai	2189	26		28
Jiangsu	297029	16	323545	16
Zhejiang	1087733	10	1321618	10
Anhui	115394	21	130491	21
Fujian	4134624	4	4729044	4
Jiangxi	1907887	7	1720300	7
Shandong	38419	23	58812	23
Henan	198271	18	195415	19
Hubei	416647	14	523769	13
Hunan	1230388	9	1662412	8
Guangdong	18120432	1	20443000	1
Guangxi	11674203	2	11213970	2
Sichuan	2415014	6	2488734	6
Guizhou	195618	19	192481	20
Yunnan	5587985	3	5298452	3
Tibet				
Shaanxi	24450	24	48715	24
Gansu	563182	13	521338	14
Qinghai	6193	25	7558	25
Ningxia	316601	15	326285	15
Xinjiang	965028	11	663603	11

10.8 *NUMBER OF LARGE DOMESTIC ANIMALS AT YEAR-END BY REGION*

	1987		1986	
Region	Number (1,000 heads)	Rank	Number (1,000 heads)	Rank
Beijing	282	27	264	27
Tianjin	274	28	263	28
Hebei	4923	14	4752	14
Shanxi	2717	22	2701	20
Inner Mongolia	7308	4	7513	4
Liaoning	3153	17	3139	18
Jilin	2745	21	2849	19
Heilongjiang	3146	18	3140	17
Shanghai	71	29	68	29
Jiangsu	857	24	875	24
Zhejiang	747	26	758	26
Anhui	5054	13	4862	12
Fujian	1236	23	1212	23
Jiangxi	2845	19	2679	22
Shandong	5387	12	4801	13
Henan	10008	2	9574	2
Hubei	3471	16	3391	16
Hunan	3802	15	3662	15
Guangdong	5525	11	5379	10
Guangxi	6510	5	6181	6
Sichuan	10265	1	10108	1
Guizhou	5976	7	5720	7
Yunnan	9233	3	9045	3
Tibet	5633	8	5558	8
Shaanxi	2836	20	2700	21
Gansu	5561	9	5389	9
Qinghai	6025	6	6213	5
Ningxia	778	25	787	25
Xinjiang	5543	10	5378	11

10.9 *OUTPUT OF PORK, BEEF AND MUTTON BY REGION*

	1987		1986	
Region	Amount (1,000 tns)	Rank	Amount (1,000 tns)	Rank
Beijing	129	26	131	25
Tianjin	65	28	68	28
Hebei	953	7	918	7
Shanxi	206	23	208	22
Inner Mongolia	407	17	374	17
Liaoning	573	15	588	13
Jilin	343	18	345	18
Heilongjiang	321	19	331	19
Shanghai	188	24	179	24
Jiangsu	1349	3	1399	3
Zhejiang	762	11	811	8
Anhui	769	16	768	9
Fujian	520	10	481	16
Jiangxi	781	9	729	11
Shandong	1264	5	1309	4
Henan	803	8	742	10
Hubei	1146	6	1100	6
Hunan	1638	2	1559	2
Guangdong	1271	4	1188	5
Guangxi	711	12	636	12
Sichuan	3360	1	3155	1
Guizhou	597	13	550	15
Yunnan	596	14	567	14
Tibet	88	27	75	27
Shaanxi	319	20	319	20
Gansu	308	21	293	21
Qinghai	133	25	113	26
Ningxia	47	29	40	29
Xinjiang	213	22	195	23

10.10 OUTPUT OF PORK, BEEF AND MUTTON PER CAPITA BY REGION

	1987		1986	
Region	Yuan/Person	Rank	Kg/Person	Rank
Beijing	12.5	23	13.5	23
Tianjin	7.9	28	8.4	28
Hebei	16.8	15	16.4	15
Shanxi	7.6	29	7.9	29
Inner Mongolia	19.8	9	18.5	10
Liaoning	15.3	17	15.9	17
Jilin	14.7	21	15.0	18
Heilongjiang	5.4	27	10.0	25
Shanghai	14.9	19	14.6	20
Jiangsu	21.4	7	22.4	5
Zhejiang	18.7	12	20.0	8
Anhui	14.6	22	14.8	19
Fujian	18.7	11	17.6	12
Jiangxi	22.0	6	20.9	7
Shandong	16.0	16	16.9	13
Henan	10.2	26	9.6	26
Hubei	22.0	5	22.2	6
Hunan	28.5	4	27.5	4
Guangdong	19.9	8	18.9	9
Guangxi	17.9	13	16.3	16
Sichuan	32.3	2	30.8	2
Guizhou	19.5	10	18.4	11
Yunnan	17.0	14	16.5	14
Tibet	42.9	1	37.3	1
Shaanxi	10.4	25	10.6	24
Gansu	14.8	20	14.3	21
Qinghai	31.4	3	27.6	3
Ningxia	11.0	24	9.5	27
Xinjiang	15.0	18	14.2	22

10.11 OUTPUT OF AQUATIC PRODUCTS BY REGION

	1987		1986	
Region	Amount (tn)	Rank	Amount (tn)	Rank
Beijing	30237	20	22177	20
Tianjin	81323	16	67286	16
Hebei	179328	13	155063	14
Shanxi	5428	26	4003	26
Inner Mongolia	23123	21	20688	21
Liaoning	806023	6	669542	6
Jilin	45061	18	38339	18
Heilongjiang	101533	15	84274	15
Shanghai	263849	9	237062	9
Jiangsu	921927	5	804787	5
Zhejiang	1249810	2	1172086	2
Anhui	240688	10	207417	11
Fujian	982034	4	809927	4
Jiangxi	225879	12	192849	12
Shandong	1106641	3	914411	3
Henan	76178	17	66074	17
Hubei	582686	7	466603	7
Hunan	443790	8	381747	8
Guangdong	1666000	1	1465012	1
Guangxi	240305	11	211759	10
Sichuan	171692	14	158391	13
Guizhou	18185	22	13965	22
Yunnan	38111	19	31160	19
Tibet			203	29
Shaanxi	11909	25	8931	24
Gansu	1875	29	1160	28
Qinghai	2260	28	4580	25
Ningxia	5031	27	3217	27
Xinjiang	14500	24	11312	23
China Aquatic Products Corporation	18069	23		

10.12 MAIN RURAL ECONOMIC INDICATORS BY REGIONAL ANNUAL PER CAPITA INCOME

Region	Percentage Income Per Capita (income per capita =100)				Percentage Gross Output Value (rural total product of society=100)		
	From Collectives	From New Economic Associations*	From Household Business	Others	Agriculture	Industry and Construction	Transportation, Commerce and Food Services
Nationwide	**9.10**	**0.75**	**82.93**	**7.22**	**49.57**	**42.50**	**7.93**
Regions with Per Capita Income over 500 Yuan	15.49	0.87	76.18	7.47	38.96	53.94	7.10
Shanghai	51.74	0.10	35.66	12.50	17.94	77.12	4.94
Beijing	41.48	0.40	45.11	13.03	27.73	60.81	11.46
Tianjin	31.69	1.48	59.17	7.66	27.78	62.60	9.62
Zhejiang	17.07	2.73	73.06	7.14	32.32	62.40	5.27
Guangdong	6.17	0.70	84.18	9.03	51.74	38.23	10.03
Jiangsu	22.11	0.35	71.10	6.44	30.54	63.98	5.48
Liaoning	13.17	0.55	78.22	8.06	41.44	49.68	8.88
Jilin	4.44	0.14	90.71	4.72	61.26	29.46	9.28
Shandong	11.98	0.55	81.18	6.28	47.45	45.95	6.60
Regions with Per Capita Income 350-500 Yuan	5.23	0.80	87.21	6.76	59.31	32.01	8.69
Fujian	5.40	1.35	84.80	8.44	54.85	35.76	9.39
Heilongjiang	4.52	0.08	91.27	4.12	61.49	26.90	11.61
Hunan	4.22	1.60	89.44	4.74	62.14	29.92	7.93
Hubei	6.18	0.26	89.15	4.42	58.28	32.75	8.97
Xinjiang	1.78	0.07	93.08	5.07	83.93	10.32	5.75
Hebei	9.83	2.62	80.23	7.33	42.07	50.88	7.05
Jiangxi	5.12	0.33	89.21	5.34	64.70	27.29	8.01
Anhui	4.34	0.50	89.34	5.82	63.15	28.84	8.01
Qinghai	1.43	0.09	89.23	9.25	29.54	13.52	6.94
Inner Mongolia	2.82	0.12	92.66	4.40	78.87	13.78	7.34
Ningxia	2.36	0.36	88.45	8.84	69.49	18.88	11.63
Henan	4.91	0.89	86.33	7.87	53.55	35.83	10.62
Shanxi	12.65	0.64	73.66	13.05	36.96	49.70	13.34
Sichuan	5.14	0.32	86.98	7.57	62.95	28.99	8.06
Yunnan	2.44	0.16	89.23	8.17	73.71	19.14	7.15
Guangxi	0.59	0.21	91.33	7.50	75.19	17.98	6.83
Regions with Per Capita Income Less than 350 Yuan	2.52	0.24	88.38	8.87	65.65	25.16	9.18
Tibet	0.95	0.01	90.08	9.31	90.98	4.60	4.42
Guizhou	1.63	0.38	91.09	6.90	75.89	16.97	7.14
Shaanxi	2.77	0.10	87.47	9.65	55.87	33.33	10.80
Gansu	3.90	0.23	84.86	11.02	68.60	22.19	9.21

Note:
* Rural economic associations (Nongchun Jingji Lianheti) refer to the economic organizations that farmers voluntarily joined since 1979, to deal with farm crops production, processing farm crops, selling products and other business. The members of those associations jointly manage the associations and share the costs and benefits.

MAIN RURAL ECONOMIC INDICATORS BY REGIONAL ANNUAL PER CAPITA INCOME

(continued)

	Percentage Employment (total =100)			Percentage Laborers by Education Level (total =100)			
	Primary Industry	Secondary Industry	Tertiary Industry	Illiterates or Semi-illiterates	Primary School Gradutes	Junior Middle School Graduates	Senior Middle School Graduates and over
Nationwide	**79.57**	**11.88**	**8.55**	**24.99**	**38.40**	**29.39**	**7.22**
Regions with Per Capita Income over 500 Yuan	68.57	19.99	11.44	20.04	39.29	32.57	8.10
Shanghai	37.67	47.76	14.57	14.72	34.80	41.12	9.36
Beijing	46.81	33.22	19.96	9.87	26.96	51.80	11.37
Tianjin	52.14	35.21	12.64	10.10	36.51	43.61	9.78
Zhejiang	64.17	24.01	11.28	20.37	44.26	29.56	5.81
Guangdong	72.95	14.71	12.34	17.80	43.68	29.11	9.41
Jiangsu	60.72	27.04	12.24	27.88	31.15	33.04	7.93
Liaoning	71.95	16.31	11.73	8.71	47.29	36.69	7.31
Jilin	86.98	6.34	6.68	12.50	44.90	33.88	8.72
Shandong	75.24	14.77	9.99	22.39	36.90	32.57	8.14
Regions with Per Capita Income 350-500 Yuan	84.36	8.42	7.22	24.96	39.31	28.80	6.93
Fujian	78.64	10.98	10.38	31.08	40.65	21.28	6.99
Heilongjiang	88.35	5.77	5.87	17.17	38.00	35.99	8.84
Hunan	85.76	8.11	6.13	15.38	47.89	29.22	7.51
Hubei	80.48	10.41	9.11	21.03	40.33	31.16	7.48
Xinjiang	94.27	2.54	3.19	28.19	43.92	21.67	6.22
Hebei	75.31	14.46	10.23	16.04	36.14	35.56	11.26
Jiangxi	83.69	9.69	6.62	26.45	42.88	23.88	6.79
Anhui	84.90	7.73	7.38	36.19	29.64	27.99	6.18
Qinghai	88.02	5.03	6.96	53.94	26.77	17.03	2.26
Inner Mongolia	89.58	4.20	6.22	20.85	41.19	30.80	7.16
Ningxia	88.19	4.35	7.45	39.30	33.23	22.97	4.50
Henan	83.50	8.93	7.57	26.74	30.85	33.55	8.86
Shanxi	69.85	15.23	14.92	11.91	38.93	39.88	9.28
Sichuan	86.61	7.44	5.95	28.62	43.29	24.76	3.33
Yunnan	90.93	4.26	4.81	42.01	39.00	16.49	2.50
Guangxi	92.01	3.73	4.27	16.88	46.54	28.52	8.06
Regions with Per Capita Income Less than 350 Yuan	86.04	6.57	7.40	37.71	31.86	24.16	6.26
Tibet	94.08	1.54	4.39	75.82	22.68	1.50	0.00
Guizhou	92.06	4.31	3.63	40.85	34.09	21.37	3.60
Shaanxi	81.83	10.22	7.94	27.09	32.64	31.53	8.74
Gansu	81.65	5.47	12.88	44.45	28.27	20.04	7.24

MAIN RURAL ECONOMIC INDICATORS BY REGIONAL ANNUAL PER CAPITA INCOME

(continued)

Region	Percentage Expenditure (total =100)			
	Living Expenditure	Productive Expenditure	Other Expenditure	Per Capita Cash Expenditure on Production (yuan/person)
Nationwide	**65.94**	**28.33**	**5.73**	**121.15**
Regions with Per Capita Income over 500 Yuan	67.03	27.18	5.79	160.93
Shanghai	76.20	18.36	5.44	168.99
Beijing	74.81	19.76	5.43	134.50
Tianjin	68.54	25.68	5.78	158.05
Zhejiang	72.72	23.23	4.06	169.59
Guangdong	65.54	29.19	5.27	200.80
Jiangsu	69.81	25.60	4.60	157.13
Liaoning	63.74	29.26	7.00	154.00
Jilin	57.14	33.66	9.20	175.82
Shandong	63.51	28.99	7.50	128.56
Regions with Per Capita Income 350-500 Yuan	65.56	28.74	5.70	109.49
Fujian	69.39	25.96	4.65	131.34
Heilongjiang	53.51	34.54	11.94	155.47
Hunan	68.02	27.59	4.39	116.39
Hubei	68.80	24.23	6.97	105.50
Xinjiang	53.51	40.66	5.83	202.99
Hebei	64.80	30.57	4.62	123.45
Jiangxi	70.06	24.42	5.52	100.29
Anhui	62.77	31.08	6.15	133.60
Qinghai	68.94	25.17	5.90	76.44
Inner Mongolia	61.38	33.30	5.33	108.13
Ningxia	63.10	32.26	4.63	131.32
Henan	64.86	27.94	7.21	94.41
Shanxi	69.96	22.66	7.65	79.18
Sichuan	65.02	29.86	5.13	99.18
Yunnan	67.34	28.70	3.96	85.82
Guangxi	68.22	28.62	3.16	98.84
Regions with Per Capita Income Less than 350 Yuan	67.60	28.18	4.22	75.29
Tibet	68.74	29.21	2.05	49.57
Guizhou	68.77	27.00	4.23	65.87
Shaanxi	66.92	29.08	4.00	90.78
Gansu	66.53	28.70	4.77	69.79

Section XI

SELECTED INDICATORS AT COUNTY LEVEL

11.1 *TOTAL OUTPUT VALUE OF RURAL SOCIETY BY COUNTY GROUP 1987*

Item		Counties by Total Output Value of Rural Society		
		Over 800,000,000 Yuan	400-800,000,000 Yuan	Less than 400,000,000 Yuan
Number of Counties		299	495	1563
Rural Population	1,000,000 person	225.91	281.45	347.98
Rural Total Output Value of Society	1,000,000,000 yuan	434.1	274.7	229.0
Gross Output Value of Ariculture	1,000,000,000 yuan	161.5	160.3	150.6
Gross Output Value of Industry	1,000,000,000 yuan	204.0	71.4	44.3
Gross Output Value of Construction	1,000,000,000 yuan	36.8	19.9	22.3
Gross Output Value of Trade	1,000,000,000 yuan	13.7	10.3	9.0
Gross Output Value of Commerce	1,000,000,000 yuan	18.0	12.9	10.2

11.2 *GROSS OUTPUT VALUE OF AGRICULTURE BY COUNTY GROUP 1987*

Item		Counties by Gross Output Value of Agriculture		
		Over 400,000,000 Yuan	200-400,000,000 Yuan	Less than 200,000,000 Yuan
Number of Counties		105	473	1779
Rural Population	1,000,000 person	103.64	320.51	431.18
Gross Output Value of Agriculture	1,000,000,000 yuan	51.1	129.1	139.7
Crop Farming Output Value	1,000,000,000 yuan	33.2	85.3	79.7
Forestry Output Value	1,000,000,000 yuan	0.9	3.3	7.8
Animal Husbandry Output Value	1,000,000,000 yuan	9.3	23.7	26.5
Sideline Output Value	1,000,000,000 yuan	4.3	4.6	1.3
Fishery Output Value	1,000,000,000 yuan	1.4	1.5	0.9
	1,000,000,000 yuan			

11.3 TOTAL OUTPUT VALUE OF GRAIN BY COUNTY GROUP 1987

Region		Counties by Total Output of Grain		
		Over 400,000 Tns	200-400,000 Tns	Less than 200,000 Tns
Number of Counties		240	502	1615
Rural Population	1,000,000 Person	205.92	288.60	360.81
Sown Area of Grain Crops	1,000,000 mu*	442.99	545.31	733.00
Total Output of Grain	1,000,000 tns	134.85	141.66	119.22
Grain Output per Mu*	kg/mu*	304	260	163
Volume of Grain Sold	1,000,000 tns	39.65	33.90	23.09

Note:
* 1 mu = 1/15 hectare.

11.4 OUPUT INDICATORS BY COUNTY GROUP BY PER CAPITA CULTIVATED LAND

Item		Counties by Per Capita Cultivated Land		
		Over 3 Mu*	1-3 Mu*	Less than 1 Mu*
Number of Counties		28.3	130.4	77.0
Rural Total Output Value of Society	1,000,000,000 yuan	54.7	525.5	357.5
Gross Output Value of Agriculture	1,000,000,000 yuan	28.1	192.5	99.3
Crop Farming Output Value	1,000,000,000 yuan	20.0	125.5	52.8
Animal Husbandry Output Value	1,000,000,000 yuan	5.0	32.9	21.6
Total Output of Grain	1,000,000 tns	44.19	239.20	112.34
Purchase Value of Farming and Sideline Products	1,000,000,000 yuan	16.2	111.1	64.6

Note:
* 1 mu = 1/15 hectare.

11.5 RANKING OF 297 COUNTIES WITH TOTAL OUTPUT VALUE OF RURAL SOCIETY AT CURRENT PRICES ABOVE 800,000,000 YUAN 1987

(1,000 yuan)

County	Total Output Value	County	Total Output Value
Wuxi County	7700580	Area under Yancheng City's Jurisdiction	2030600
Jiangyin County	5870710	Area under Jinan City's Jurisdiction	2028880
Changshu City	5633590	Qingpu County	1993760
Shazhou County	5585440	Yuyao City	1988070
Wujin County	5036000	Haining County	1958010
Area under Shengyang City's Jurisdiction	4869590	Songjiang County	1946790
Dongguan City	4753340	Area under Chongqing City's Jurisdiction	1944920
Wuxian County	4494950	Wuqing County	1933310
Shaoxing County	4174750	Linyi City	1931900
Xiaoshan County	4074760	Area under Ningpo City's Jurisdiction	1919190
Yixing County	4057670	Shunyi County	1892310
Area under Dalian City's Jurisdiction	3821470	Area under Chengdu City's Jurisdiction	1890410
Nanhai County	3762990	Baoshan County	1867530
Area under Zibo city's Jurisdiction	3723970	Rongcheng County	1851330
Shunde County	3468350	Congming County	1846290
Zhongshan City	3358380	Haimen County	1842570
Jinxian County	3255500	Xinhui County	1818750
Wujiang County	3011100	Jinjiang County	1816480
Chuansha County	2938630	Tongxiang County	1806680
Danyang County	2898410	Dongtai County	1791850
Taixing County	2734230	Area under Xi'an City's Jurisdiction	1772170
Nanhui County	2722290	Rudong County	1769130
Jiading County	2700920	Rugao County	1736460
Yuhang County	2663250	Jinjiang County	1730110
Haicheng County	2648850	Zhangqiu County	1726230
Haicheng City	2648850	Jiangning County	1722670
Cixi County	2646400	Area under Hangzhou City's Jurisdiction	1676440
Area under Huzhou City's Jurisdiction	2596730	Taishan County	1672640
Nantong County	2570590	Panyu County	1666140
Area under Guangzhou City's Jurisdiciton	2533310	Gaoyao County	1659780
Jiangdu County	2483420	Taixian County	1656680
Area under Wuxi City's Jurisdiction	2369490	Jimuo County	1640250
Qidong County	2296850	Liyang County	1603030
Shanghai County	2280410	Xiantao City	1600230
Kunshan County	2243270	Jinhai County	1591150
Xinghua County	2182790	Tongxian County	1575900
Pingdu County	2173980	Zhucheng County	1568300
Area under Zaozhuang City's Jurisdiction	2123980	Tengxian County	1564720
Taicang County	2107180	Anqiu County	1556500
Fengxian County	2074990	Area under Jiaxing City's Jurisdiction	1517930
Ganyu County	2052500	Changping County	1515380
Tongshan County	2043710	Jinshan County	1512310

RANKING OF 297 COUNTIES WITH TOTAL OUTPUT VALUE OF RURAL SOCIETY AT CURRENT PRICES ABOVE 800,000,000 YUAN 1987

(1,000 yuan) (continued)

County	Total Output Value	County	Total Output Value
Wafangdian City	1483130	Jintan County	1195170
Shangyu County	1482810	Area under Tai'an City's Jurisdiction	1192010
Shouguang County	1470740	Gongzhuling City	1190630
Putian County	1469970	Huai'an County	1190480
Tianmen County	1467870	Dafeng County	1181910
Wenling County	1436490	Area under Changchun City's Jurisdiction	1177220
Area under Wuhan City's Juridiction	1433040	Xinjin County	1176810
Yexian County	1425450	Sheyang County	1176280
Laoshan County	1424170	Yangzhong County	1174220
Hai'an County	1414350	Zhongxiang County	1169360
Jiaoxian County	1411560	Gaixian County	1151780
Gaoyou County	1394550	Leqing County	1145220
Zhuji County	1392210	Shuanliu County	1145150
Huangyan County	1386370	Lixian County	1141060
Changyi County	1368060	Huangxian County	1136240
Chaoyang County	1364160	Baodi County	1126780
Wendeng County	1360960	Jiurong County	1126250
Area under Nanjing City's Jurisdiction	1359250	Xiaogan City	1125420
Jianli County	1358770	Xinzhou County	1122710
Yangjiang County	1337030	Rezhou City	1119100
Pixian County	1336700	Kaiping County	1115010
Yingkou County	1333560	Changde County	1114330
Area under Weifang City's Jurisdiction	1326760	Area under Fuzhou City's Jurisdiction	1113350
Xiangyang County	1326610	Yi'an County	1106830
Bao'an County	1295790	Qingzhou City	1103430
Donghai County	1295050	Laiwu City	1103280
Yushu County	1288930	Haozhou City	1092990
Gaomi County	1287490	Baxian County	1090890
Jiaonan County	1278430	Lianjiang County	1090320
Hanjiang County	1272790	Jiangling County	1089180
Changtu County	1253680	Muping County	1087750
Gongxian County	1246360	Haikang County	1085950
Chaozhou City	1245520	Yanshi County	1079650
Shuqian County	1236060	Taoyuan County	1077240
Area under Changzhou City's Jurisdiction	1229420	Liling City	1073300
Zhaoyuan County	1223130	Changnan County	1071300
Area under Shijiazhuang City's Jurisdiction	1212880	Dongyang County	1069020
Laixi County	1207970	Huaiyuan County	1067530
Jieyang County	1207300	Daxing County	1058680
Dianbai County	1206710	Jianhu County	1058300
Shuyang County	1205680	Gaocheng County	1057580
Suizhou City	1204070	Zhuanghe County	1054150

RANKING OF 297 COUNTIES WITH TOTAL OUTPUT VALUE OF RURAL SOCIETY AT CURRENT PRICES ABOVE 800,000,000 YUAN *1987*

(1,000 yuan) (continued)

County	Total Output Value	County	Total Output Value
Guanghan County	1053990	Li'an County	945550
Dantu County	1052560	Area under Suzhou City's Jurisdiction	945540
Huangpo County	1047280	Feicheng County	941300
Fengren County	1044560	Nancang County	938620
Xinyi County	1043210	Jinxian County	936030
Peixian County	1041660	Xinji City	934520
Lanxi City	1032240	Suining County	934330
Liuyang County	1029560	Pinghu County	931950
Rui'an County	1028410	Mengcheng County	931460
Yuxian County	1023590	Woyang County	929020
Laiyang County	1019720	Luxian County	928840
Donggou County	1016730	Fenghua County	926800
Changqing County	1016580	Haiyan County	924150
Baxian County	1016150	Fenglai County	923610
Xintai City	1013750	Deqing County	920900
Xinmin County	1011960	Yiwu County	920580
Area under Yantai City's Jurisdiction	1007830	Zaoyang County	919240
Area under Pingxiang City's Jurisdiction	1002910	Putuo County	918610
Changsha County	1000750	Shaodong County	917830
Lianshui County	1000470	Renshou County	916310
Area under Taiyuan City's Jurisdiction	999600	Ninghai County	909280
Ningxiang County	992430	Longhai County	906890
Changle County	986380	Wuwei County	904320
Qingyuan County	982250	Anyang County	900690
Weiyuan County	980790	Hanchuan County	900100
Dingzhou City	978180	Hanyang County	899890
Fuyang County	977230	Lixian County	899160
Huazhou County	976870	Shuxian County	897920
Hechuan County	976490	Fuyu County	896130
Nanyang County	974750	Dengxian County	891110
Mixian County	974550	Linhai City	890770
Daye County	970770	Xiangshan County	886630
Haifeng County	965450	Area under Tanshan City's Jurisdiction	884900
Huixian County	964060	Xiangtang County	883780
Area under Harbin City's Jurisdiction	961190	Changshan County	881950
Area under Jining City's Jurisdiction	958840	Area under Deyang City's Jurisdiction	881540
Zhunhua County	956780	Linru County	880750
Fengcheng County	953940	Rushan County	879670
Zouxian County	952230	Linqu County	875980
Shengxian County	947860	Luxian County	875580
Lishu County	947620	Taihe County	875190
Dangtu County	946220	Jiashan County	874140

RANKING OF 297 COUNTIES WITH TOTAL OUTPUT VALUE OF RURAL SOCIETY AT CURRENT PRICES ABOVE 800,000,000 YUAN 1987

(1,000 yuan) (continued)

County	Total Output Value	County	Total Output Value
Gaozhou County	874090	Dingyuan County	842780
Shiyang County	873510	Fuyang County	841000
Yulin County	873170	Yingde County	840500
Nanxian County	871100	Jiangjin County	837030
Funing County	869670	Qixia County	834420
Honghu County	867910	Haiyang County	833850
Sanshui County	867450	Lingxian County	831780
Feidong County	867380	Liaocheng City	829550
Wucang County	865360	Guanyun County	826290
Linquan County	863890	Luoding County	824570
Lunan County	862270	Sanhe County	821250
Ouhai County	860310	Changxing County	818520
Yuanjiang County	854720	Yishui County	817710
Gong'an County	853700	Liaozhong County	810430
Area under Zhanjiang City's Jurisdiction	852530	Fengxian County	809210
Nan'an County	852320	Tianchang County	808290
Xianyou County	851490	Pinggu County	808030
Engping County	850410	Nangong City	805720
Baoying County	848730	Fuqing County	804730
Tanghe County	847890	Pengxian County	804290
Xindu County	846060	Qinyang County	801940
Puning County	845110	Chang'an County	801880
Luhe County	843680	Area under Zhengzhou City's Jurisdiction	801820

11.6 *RANKING OF 98 COUNTIES WITH TOTAL OUTPUT VALUE ABOVE 400,000,000 YUAN* 1987

(1,000 yuan)

County	Total Output Value	County	Total Output Value
Pingdu County	7827500	Baxian County	5034000
Xinghua County	7345280	Taixing County	5020670
Dongguan City	7237430	Rugao County	5001110
Ganyu County	6929990	Sheyang County	4971970
Area under Dalian City's Jurisdiction	6715300	Zhucheng County	4963900
Tongshan County	6491150	Changde County	4949400
Yushu County	6425770	Renshou County	4929600
Rongcheng County	6376700	Shouguang County	4892300
Donghai County	6345600	Hechuan County	4861000
Nantong County	6311400	Jiangling County	4830050
Wuxian County	6204920	Yixing County	4796150
Dongtai County	6200010	Yangjiang County	4773710
Area under Shengyang City's Jurisdiction	6081900	Area under Jinan City's Jurisdiction	4751000
Jianli County	6040400	Gaoyao County	4724150
Area under Zaozhuang City's Jurisdiction	6010700	Huaiyuan County	4696200
Wujin County	5969330	Linyi City	4676900
Suizhou City	5748730	Ningxiang County	4667800
Xiantao City	5737360	Area under Chongqing City's Jurisdiction	4633900
Gongzhuling City	5675760	Gaoyou County	4549090
Tianmen County	5665450	Jiangjin County	4544800
Xiangyang County	5639690	Dafeng County	4531260
Fuyu County	5592910	Qidong County	4529430
Rudong County	5503350	Rezhao City	4501800
Cangtu County	5496500	Zaoyang County	4500200
Shuyang County	5492580	Zhongxiang County	4458700
Anqiu County	5400800	Lishu County	4458260
Area under Huzhou City's Jurisdiction	5399200	Haozhou City	4440700
Dingzhou City	5358200	Rui'an County	4432900
Zhongshan City	5341800	Lianshui County	4426440
Pixian County	5280270	Tengxian County	4376600
Area under Zibo City's Jurisdiction	5181400	Changshu City	4360500
Area under Yancheng City's Jurisdiction	5174230	Taoyuan County	4343500
Weiyuan County	5130300	Yanyang County	4332900

RANKING OF 98 COUNTIES WITH TOTAL OUTPUT VALUE ABOVE 400,000,000 YUAN *1987*

(1,000 yuan) (continued)

County	Total Output Value
Luxian County	4314300
Fengcheng County	4301500
Haicheng City	4299500
Shuxian County	4294000
Woyang County	4278200
Shuangcheng County	4269400
Dengxian County	4263000
Wujiang County	4258890
Wuwei County	4200600
Yi'an County	4198400
Jiaonan County	4185800
Area under Tai'an City's Jurisdiction	4147800
Mengcheng County	4138700
Suining County	4130140
Huarong County	4125500
Area under Chengdu City's Jurisdiction	4120100
Huai'an County	4113810
Fengxian County	4113700
Wuxi County	4108430
Santai County	4096000
Taikang County	4092500
Jiangyin County	4083670
Wuqing County	4057780
Linquan County	4055300
Wendeng County	4052500
Xiangtan County	4047200
Zunyi County	4033100
Gaomi County	4022000
Tanghe County	4021000
Nanhai County	4020700
Guanyun County	4014610
Lu'an County	4013600

11.7 RANKING OF 238 COUNTIES WITH OUTPUT OF GRAIN ABOVE 400,000 TONS 1987

(tn)

County	Output of Grain
Gongzhuling City	1727355
Yushu County	1607500
Fuyu County	1538801
Cangtu County	1346176
Lishu County	1269062
Xinghua County	1089551
Tongshan County	1001212
Dehui County	956651
Jianli County	945462
Pingdu County	928230
Area under Shengyang City's Jurisdiction	899319
Shuyang County	870110
Donghai County	866716
Shuangcheng County	864002
Suizhou City	850004
Ningxiang County	840143
Yi'an County	839521
Zhaodong County	796419
Xiangyang County	768226
Xiantao County	759017
Nancang County	756853
Wujin County	752821
Pixian County	749851
Hechuan County	744525
Huaiyuan County	739657
Area under Zaozhuang City's Jurisdiction	731910
Shuxian County	730393
Xiangtan County	712406
Changde County	701637
Gaoyou County	699563
Huai'an County	691267
Jiutai County	690355
Zhongxiang County	688911
Suining County	682540
Weiyuan County	678819
Baxian County	678264
Zaoqiang County	676735
Janyang County	667015
Area under Yancheng City's Jurisdiction	665551
Luxian County	661191
Jiangling County	658524
Lingpi County	653615

County	Output of Grain
Area under Zibo City's Jurisdiction	647635
Haozhou City	645174
Nahe County	640149
Baoying County	633925
Anqiu County	633358
Xinmin County	628371
Yixing County	627811
Laishui County	625269
Jiangjin County	625064
Dongtai County	624906
Liuyang County	623391
Rudong County	622147
Zhucheng County	621656
Wuxian County	620888
Suixi County	620688
Woyang County	620320
Fengcheng County	610030
Hengyang County	606287
Wucang County	605665
Funing County	605620
Jianhu County	604492
Shouxian County	603089
Mengcheng County	602569
Renshou County	601585
Dengxian County	597657
Bayan County	595756
Taixing County	595203
Sheyang County	595001
Ganyu County	594738
Rugao County	592597
Huaxian County	590204
Changsha County	589383
Xinyi County	588884
Shihong County	587556
Linquan County	586350
Area under Jiaxing City's Jurisdiction	585090
Dingyuan County	585020
Tengxian County	582740
Xuyi County	579862
Tianchang County	577702
Huoqiu County	574913
Taoyuan County	571795

RANKING OF 238 COUNTIES WITH OUTPUT OF GRAIN ABOVE 400,000 TONS 1987

(tn) (continued)

County	Output of Grain	County	Output of Grain
Santai County	569789	Hengnan County	502806
Zhongshan City	567576	Dongfeng County	501985
Fuyang County	564818	Haicheng City	501051
Linyi City	557887	Guang'an County	500980
Yongjin County	555649	Dongliao County'	500855
Jiangdu County	555122	Area under Tai'an City's Jurisdiction	500823
Nantong County	553706	Yitong County	500281
Qian Gorlos County	553289	Yongchuan County	498644
Tanghe County	552122	Bazhong County	497356
Area under Huzhou City's Jurisdiciton	551949	Hancheng County	497279
Changling County	550336	Feixi County	496903
Daxian County	550145	Fengxi County	496737
Lixin County	549031	Danyang County	496019
Shuangyang County	545422	Changshan County	495160
Taihe County	545014	Gao'an County	494022
Shouguang County	543943	Shangshui County	493104
Wuwei County	543125	Shiyang County	492422
Peixian County	541967	Boyang County	491982
Lu'an County	541659	Hailun County	490587
Tianmen County	541044	Fengyang County	490226
Lujiang County	540852	Wuxi County	486300
Area under Chongqing City's Jurisdiction	537809	Lezhi County	486034
Guanyun County	535390	Yingshang County	485139
Taikang County	534862	Suihua City	481658
Zhuqian County	533993	Xishui County	479518
Tongliao City	533603	Qianjiang County	478761
Nenjiang County	533564	Jimuo County	476533
Jingshan County	529781	Xiangxiang City	476530
Changfeng County	528203	Zhaozhou County	474851
Fengxian County	526684	Changshu County	474703
Nancong County	522256	Shunyi County	469123
Baoqing County	518582	Dongguan County	464750
Xiaogan City	516137	Area under Suining City's Jurisdiction	464632
Wujiang County	515154	Linchuan County	463143
Dingzhou City	513276	Fushun County	462191
Gaomi County	513057	Zhuji County	461601
Taixian County	512726	Kaixian County	459987
Faku County	510850	Tancheng County	459038
Feidong County	510197	Honghu County	458718
Huangpo County	508845	Yueyang County	458637
Shaoxing County	506483	Yongcheng County	458237
Zhongjiang County	504012	Jiangning County	458022

RANKING OF 238 COUNTIES WITH OUTPUT OF GRAIN ABOVE 400,000 TONS *1987*

(tn) (continued)

County	Output of Grain	County	Output of Grain
Pingjiang County	457811	Laiwu County	416741
Xiaoshan County	457537	Yancheng County	414685
Shengqiu County	456907	Shangcai County	413821
Yuncheng County	455233	Huaiyang County	413291
Liling City	453950	Jiangyin County	412912
Rongxian County	453790	Yiyang County	412398
Area under Chengdu City's Jurisdiction	453722	Dazhu County	412312
Fengxian County	451103	Tongxian County	412227
Huarong County	448054	Fujin County	412009
Wangcheng County	447310	Liaozong County	411916
Binhai County	446003	Guixian County	411767
Gaocheng County	445475	Hulan County	411283
Feicheng County	444081	Mishan County	410795
Luhe County	443495	Quxian County	410602
Taishan County	442601	Jinxian County	410025
Shuangfeng County	441471	Heze City	409629
Nanyang County	441340	Luyi County	408863
Luxian County	440670	Bobai County	408509
Haihekou City	438827	Qiyang County	408414
Zouxian County	435263	Area under Weifang City's Jurisdiction	407360
Guzhen County	432403	Keshan County	407058
Liyang County	429221	Guang'an County	406802
Shixian County	427253	Hejiang County	406580
Kunshan County	427203	Xiangyin County	406515
Wuhe County	427066	Milou City	405574
Wuqing County	425000	Changyi County	405548
Chaoyang County	424712	Qingyuan County	403540
Baiquan County	422972	Xintai City	403238
Xinzhou County	422968	Laiyang City	403092
Dafeng County	422426	Huangmei County	402686
Hai'an County	421788	Hanshou County	402378
Rezhao City	419353	Anyue County	402194
Macheng County	418252	Poling County	401788
Fangcheng County	418148	Shuangliao County	401350
Yuechi County	417398	Laixi County	400086

11.8 *RANKING OF 127 COUNTIES WITH OUTPUT OF OIL-BEARING CROPS ABOVE 25,000 TONS* *1987*

(tn)

County	Output of Oil-Bearing Crops	County	Output of Oil-Bearing Crops
Pingdu County	145395	Yinan County	42492
Laixi County	105090	Biyang County	42465
Lunan County	104934	Tongyu County	42209
Changling County	100910	Jiaoxian County	42165
Rongcheng County	98110	Feixian County	42017
Rezhao City	91919	Mengcheng County	41359
Wendeng County	87265	Weiyuan County	41358
Donghai County	87240	Quanjiao County	41332
Jiaonan County	77062	Lingbi County	41192
Dingyuan County	76034	Zhengyang County	41098
Laiyang County	75804	Kaifeng County	40273
Ganyu County	69716	Guanghan County	39617
Feidong County	66732	Wujiang County	39577
Jimuo County	66223	Zhongjiang County	39477
Zunyi County	65599	Tanghe County	39298
Haiyang County	64677	Luanxian County	38470
Feixi County	64406	Urad Front Banner	38459
Zhaoyuan County	62748	Guzhen County	37626
Linshu County	59859	Zouxian County	37591
Santai County	58683	Area under Suining City's Jurisdiction	37477
Wuyuan County	58644	Tianchang County	37380
Luxian County	58018	Taoyuan County	36660
Muping County	57520	Xintai City	36540
Qixia County	56680	Funan County	36352
Fenglai County	55307	Yibin City	36229
Yexian County	54795	Area under Mianyang City's Jurisdiction	36159
Fengxi County	54367	Caohu City	35731
Fengxian County	54046	Linquan County	35720
Hanggin Rear Banner	53950	Liyang County	35544
Linhe City	53571	Lu'an County	35459
Qi'an County	53370	Pingyi County	35145
Runan County	53164	Yishui County	34727
Wuwei County	50660	Jianping County	34313
Zhongshan City	48742	Fangcheng County	33550
Rushan County	46294	Renshou County	32973
Horqin Left Middle Banner	46116	Dingzhou City	32942
Changfeng County	46031	Dali County	32769
Suining County	45279	Huaiyuan County	32433
Shuxian County	44568	Lujiang County	31958
Shouxian County	44501	Anyue County	31954
Hexian County	43522	Huaiyin County	31897
Wulian County	43420	Jinshan County	31828

RANKING OF 127 COUNTIES WITH OUTPUT OF OIL-BEARING CROPS ABOVE 25,000 TONS 1987

(ton) (continued)

County	Output of Oil-Bearing Crops	County	Output of Oi-Bearing Crops
Xianyang County	31653	Anqiu County	28488
Lixin County	31540	Xincai County	28059
Nantong County	31267	Changde County	28024
Xuyi County	31116	Queshan County	27675
Lankao County	30948	Janyang County	27606
Area under Deyang City's Jurisdiction	30502	Lianshui County	27467
Gaotai County	30443	Weishi County	27174
Pinghu County	30441	Xinyi County	27055
Kunshan County	30259	Longchang County	26349
Da'an County	30007	Xindu County	26260
Dengxian County	29968	Zhucheng County	26257
Suixi County	29952	Huoqiu County	26172
Haimen County	29648	Lezhi County	26134
Huaiyang County	29614	Poyang County	26062
Shuangliu County	29613	Qian Gorlos County	26005
Qidong County	29360	Yinshang County	25852
Area under Zaozhuang City's Jurisdiction	29358	Congming County	25826
Mianzhu County	28971	Tengxian County	25817
Qian'an County	28908	Tongxu County	25804
Tumd Right Banner	28628	Dongtai County	25588
Shihong County	28607	Pengxian County	25421
		Area under Huzhou City's Jurisdiction	25093

11.9 *RANKING OF 76 COUNTIES WITH OUTPUT OF SUGAR ABOVE 150,000 TONS* 1987
(tn)

County	Output of Sugar	County	Output of Sugar
Panyu County	1530382	Liujiang County	237931
Suixi County	1441571	Fusui County	237924
Doumen County	1363180	Bobai County	229679
Guixian County	1271404	Ledong County	223258
Haikang County	1194155	Taishan County	221407
funing County	942556	Linhe City	218148
Xuwen County	871525	Longzhou County	217891
Hengxian County	849505	Yuhang County	212660
Lianjiang County	728336	Neijiang County	209176
Xianyou County	653633	Boluo County	204131
Shunde County	639210	Ningming County	202795
Guiping County	536407	Zhao'an County	199800
Laibin County	530589	Area under Xiamen City's Jurisdiction	194842
Binyang County	500516	Nanjin County	193704
Area under Zhanjiang City's Jurisdiction	395677	Area under Zhangzhou City's Jurisdiction	191733
Liucheng County	394619	Area under Guangzhou City's Jurisdiction	191159
Dongguan County	378094	Nankang County	190812
Wuming County	367595	Hanggin Rear Banner	186245
Zanxian County	366434	Bei'an City	185138
Yangchun County	352534	Lezhi County	184840
Qinzhou County	342233	Tianyang County	184540
Qiongshan County	342208	Ding'an County	184066
Congzhuo County	330953	Yingde County	182958
Area under Nanning City's Jurisdcition	323347	Miyi County	177325
Yangjiang County	321941	Shangshi County	174210
Zangpu County	311655	Baisha County	170734
Xinhui County	300000	Lingshan County	170146
Nan'an County	284602	Weiyuan County	168444
Changtai County	281507	Pinghe County	168313
Luzai County	278164	Zhaozhou County	167716
Longhai County	270976	Hexian County	166642
Putain County	268060	Jiuquan City	165406
Yishan County	258934	Huazhou County	164533
Fuqing County	257411	Tumd Left Banner	157692
Dengmai County	256078	Ganxian County	157302
Wuxuan County	246581	Ningnan County	155460
Xingguo County	244115	Daxin County	152305
Nanxian County	237962	Jinjiang County	151927

11.10 *RANKING OF 176 COUNTIES WITH OUTPUT OF COTTON ABOVE 7,000 TONS* *1987*

(tn)

County	Output of Cotton	County	Output of Cotton	County	Output of Cotton
Tianmen County	53795	Rudong County	21628	Suizhou County	15538
Lingxian County	45120	Pingdu County	21305	Cixi County	15362
Fugou County	45000	Weiyuan County	21104	Pengze County	15330
Xiajin County	44157	Shangxian County	20850	Xinxiang County	15302
Linqing City	40086	Nangong City	20837	Zhongxiang County	15174
Qihe County	36039	Dong'e County	20799	Susong County	14882
Sheyang County	35782	Yanling County	20723	Xihua County	14805
Chiping County	35534	Shouguang County	20669	Xinye County	14803
Xinxian County	35492	Fengxian County	20497	Shangqiu County	14463
Gaotang County	35000	Neihuang County	20201	Linxi County	13959
Liaocheng County	34642	Wuqiao County	19970	Huaxian County	13840
Xinghua County	34508	Jixian County	19941	Qiuxian County	13309
Guanxian County	33957	Weishi County	19837	Huangmei County	13156
Nanyang County	33905	Gaomi COunty	19511	Nantong County	13066
Caoxian County	31956	Jiangling County	19499	Feixiang County	12977
Pingyuan County	31844	Dongguang County	19495	Lijin County	12835
Huimin County	31401	Zhijiang County	19416	Honghu County	12789
Shanghe County	30927	Tongshan County	19412	Cheng'an County	12785
Dafeng County	30625	Gaoqing County	18880	Dengxian County	12751
Linyi County	29475	Dingtao County	18383	Jianli County	12742
Dongtai County	29228	Qianjiang County	18345	Suning County	12599
Yanggu County	29012	Zhanhua County	18301	Changshu County	12424
Juye County	28544	Gucheng County	18104	Dancheng County	12316
Weixian County	27570	Cangyi County	17784	Tanghe County	12273
Xiantao City	27525	Yucheng County	17657	Dangshan County	12266
Yucheng County	27037	Jiaxiang County	17622	Jingxian County	12113
Jiyang County	26978	Shache County	17467	Zaoqiang County	12006
Yuncheng County	26724	Binzhou City	17428	Ningjin County	11980
Wucheng County	25614	Jingxiang County	17383	Wangjiang County	11939
Taikang County	25545	Hanchuan County	17215	Lankao County	11845
Area Under Yancheng City's Jurisdiction	25204	Guangrao County	16550	Dongming County	11751
Zhouping County	25031	Luyi County	16432	Yongji County	11732
Xinzhou County	24823	Renshou County	16431	Weinan County	11646
Qixian County	24785	Heze County	16285	Tongxu County	11635
Chengwu County	24441	Songci County	16181	Shenxian County	11335
Wenshan County	24118	Guangyun County	15949	Fucheng County	11289
Leling County	23815	Xiangyang County	15783	Gaoyou County	11236
Dali County	22697	Zaoyang County	15750	Huaiyang County	11146
Dong'an County	22692	Yangxin County	15750	Liangshan County	11007
Ningjin County	22267	Boxing County	15703	Wuwei County	10993
Xinji County	22095	Pixian County	15578	Hejian County	10989
		Qidong County	15554	Longyao County	10892

RANKING OF 176 COUNTIES WITH OUTPUT OF COTTON ABOVE 7,000 TONS 1987

(tn) (continued)

County	Output of Cotton
Peixian County	10852
Jinxian County	10790
Markit County	10776
Shanzhou County	10764
Quzhou County	10448
Linyi County	10419
Qinghe County	10309
Guantao County	10300
Sixian County	10298
Lixian County	10240
Huarong County	10228
Dingzhou County	10216
Wudi County	10210
Dingxing County	10155
Suxian County	10151
Bachu County	10000
Zhucheng County	9934
Anyang County	9816
Xiaoxian County	9853
Xiayi County	9542
Area under Dongying City's Juristdiction	9516
Zhangqiu County	9338
Jiujiiang County	9234
Langfang City	9064
Macheng City	9049
Nanle County	8942
Area under Wuhan City's Jurisdiction	8883
Zhecheng County	8829
Shehong County	8780
Raoyang County	8730
Wuqing County	8720
Shishou City	8633
Juancheng County	8594
Binhai County	8567
Lixian County	8559
Dongzhi County	8525
Suining County	8482
Pengxi County	8352
Yecheng County	8298
Gaocheng County	8270
Nanpi County	8261
Qingfen County	8151
Anqiu County	8064
Xiangfen County	7920
Longchang County	7904
Fengqiu County	7652
Anxiang County	7635
Jingshan County	7605
Taicang County	7567
Yutai County	7535
Yanjin County	7525

11.11 RANKING OF 117 COUNTIES WITH OUTPUT OF PORK, BEEF AND MUTTON ABOVE 27,000 TONS 1987

(tn)

County	Output of Pork, Beef and Mutton	County	Output of Pork, Beef and Mutton
Wugong County	79276	Tongnan County	33741
Hechuan County	71801	Dongguan City	33339
Baxian County	69374	Nanbu County	33174
Area under Chongqing City's Jurisdiction	65706	Guang'an County	33139
Weiyuan County	64665	Shehong County	33083
Jiangjin County	63079	Anyue County	33013
Renshou County	60893	Hai'an County	33012
Taixing County	60873	Wusheng County	32932
Janyang County	58956	Hejiang County	32781
Ningxiang County	50120	Liuyang County	32538
Luxian County	49524	Area under Suining City's Jurisdiction	32527
Lezhi County	48234	Shuangliu County	32457
Area under Chengdu City's Jurisdiction	47725	Yushu County	32210
Zhongjiang County	47167	Lunan County	32052
Changsha County	46326	Yuechi County	31826
Nancong County	43971	Qiuxian County	31467
Rugao County	43882	Shuyang County	31417
Pengxi County	40916	Congqing County	31125
Rongxian County	40823	Tongshan County	31002
Fushun County	39438	Changshou County	30754
Xiangtan County	38046	Taoyuan County	70736
Xiangxiang City	37558	Yilong County	30731
Area under Zaozhuang City's Jurisdiction	37124	Zizhong County	30725
Daxian County	37043	Lianyuan County	30496
Zunyi County	36567	Pingnan County	30408
Wanxian County	36331	Tengxian County	30358
Xuanhan County	36186	Jianli County	30353
Santai County	36108	Gaozhou County	30291
Wujin County	36038	Fengcheng County	30035
Jinagbei County	35746	Area under Yancheng City's Jurisdiction	29803
Yongchuan County	35594	Yi'an County	29744
Area under Leshan City's Jurisdiction	35593	Shunyi County	29648
Rudong County	35304	Shuangfeng County	29569
Dongtai County	35247	Shanghai County	29518
Tianmen County	34994	Yueyang County	29440
Yibin County	34865	Nanhai County	29438
Tongliang County	34618	Dazu County	29420
Kaixian County	34557	Yangjiang County	29331
Bazhong County	34270	Area under Deyang City's Jurisdiction	29170
Hengyang County	34242	Wangcheng County	29136
Changde County	34237	Xintai County	29120
	33828	Zhucheng County	29090

RANKING OF 117 COUNTIES WITH OUTPUT OF PORK, BEEF AND MUTTON ABOVE 27,000 TONS 1987

(tn) (continued)

County	Output of Pork, Beef and Mutton
Qiyang County	28889
Suizhou County	28784
Lixian County	28640
Neijiang County	28621
Nanchang County	28618
Hengxian County	28607
Kangjiang County	28563
Donghai County	28503
Pengxian County	28471
Langzhong County	28292
Area under Pingxiang City's Jurisdiction	28249
Qionglai County	28174
Liling City	28160
Gaoyao County	28099
Yunyang County	28061
Anqiu County	28056
Guanghan County	27991

County	Output of Pork, Beef and Mutton
JiangJiang County	27948
Cangtu County	27862
Rezhao City	27839
Shunde County	27746
Pingjiang County	27703
Zunhua County	27694
Shiyang County	27629
Linchuan County	27619
Weining Autonomous County	27594
Yixing County	27436
Changxi County	27429
Suqian County	27349
Huazhou County	27324
Taojiang County	27282
Meishan County	27281
Fengjie County	27115

11.12 *RANKING OF 83 COUNTIES WITH OUTPUT OF AQUATIC PRODUCTS ABOVE 25,000 TONS* *1987*

(ton)

County	Output of Aquatic Products
Area under Dalian City's Jurisdiction	389723
Rongcheng County	301920
Putuo County	173159
Yangjiang County	149930
Changhai County	144354
Shunde County	131662
Lianjiang County	125946
Daishan County	105426
Jinjiang County	104312
Dianbai County	95833
Area under Yantai City's Jurisdiction	89897
Area under Beihai City's Jurisdiction	88740
Haifeng County	86569
Hui'an County	83464
Wenling County	77340
Yuhua County	75941
Shengshi County	75487
Area under Qingtao City's Jurisdiction	68706
Pingtan County	67637
Putian County	62940
Qidong County	60491
Zhongshan County	57815
Suixi County	57492
Changle County	55308
Changdao County	54905
Rezao City	54106
Wuxian County	53291
Area under Xiamen City's Jurisdiction	52724
Zhuanghe County	51498
Rudong County	51477
Xiapu County	51404
Xinhui County	50600
Nanhai County	50479
Dongshang County	50219
Tongtou County	50159
Taishan County	49613
Area under Zhanjiang City's Jurisdiction	47471
Huanghua County	47460
Lufeng County	46923
Haikang County	46914
Dongguan City	44616
Fuding County	43769
Changnan County	43399
Xiangshan County	43391
Area under Ningbo City's Jurisdiction	43260
Longhai County	42950
Area under Fuzhou City's Jurisdiction	42220
Wujiang County	41618
Honghu County	41432
Liaoshan County	40912
Wafangdian City	39568
Fenglai County	39527
Fuqing County	38930
Chaoyang County	38853
Area under Huzhou City's Jurisdiction	38065
Anji County	38065
Xiantao City	37704
Weihai City	37643
Yaoping County	37562
Wendeng County	37313
Dinghai County	36127
Area under Wuhan City's Jurisdiction	35548
Yexian County	34247
Jianli County	33813
Zhangpu County	32855
Luannan County	30894
Area under Lianyungang City's Jurisdiction	30297
Congming County	29190
Leqing County	29773
Shouguang County	29286
Donggou County	29141
Area under Guangzhou City's Jurisdiction	29031
Huilai County	28701
Sheyang County	28523
Haiyang County	27615
Ganyu County	27010
Shengxian County	26924
Jiaonan County	26692
Changshu County	26600
Sanmen County	26596
Panyu County	26360
Ninghai County	26061
Wudi County	25808

11.13 *RANKING OF 209 COUNTIES WITH PER CAPITA CULTIVATED LAND ABOVE 3.5 MU** *1987*

(mu*/person)

County	Per Capita Cultivated Land	County	Per Capita Cultivated Land	County	Per Capita Cultivated Land
Fuyuan County	21.1	Hutubi County	6.9	Hailun County	5.1
Tongjiang County	20.8	Tongyu County	6.7	Yilan County	5.1
Raohe County	18.7	Kangbao County	6.6	Baicheng County	5.0
Ergun Right Banner	18.0	Zhaosu County	6.6	Huining County	5.0
Xunke County	17.5	Baiquan County	6.6	Xinghe County	5.0
Suibin County	15.0	Keshan County	6.5	Gangca County	4.9
Gusum County	13.8	Wuzhai County	6.5	Tongwei County	4.9
Shengda County	13.8	Pengyang County	6.4	Tangyuan County	4.9
Hulin County	12.7	Shangyi County	6.4	Lanxi County	4.9
Luobei County	11.7	Huachuan County	6.4	Qinggang County	4.8
Darhan Joint Banner	11.3	Huade County	6.4	Zhaozhou County	4.8
Siziwang Banner	10.4	Mori County	6.3	Mingshui County	4.8
Youyi County	10.2	Pinglu County	6.3	Qahar Right Wing Front Banner	4.8
Heihe City	10.2	Dingbian County	6.3	Fuyu County	4.7
Nenjiang County	10.0	Pianguan County	6.2	Qing'an County	4.7
Baoqing County	9.9	Qitai County	6.1	Qapqal County	4.7
Dedu County	9.7	Zuoyun County	6.1	Boli County	4.7
Fujin County	9.4	Zhangbei County	5.9	Chongxin County	4.7
Yumin County	9.3	Yi'an County	5.9	Fugu County	4.7
Wuchuan County	9.2	Nehe County	5.9	Tailai County	4.7
Kure Banner	9.0	Shangdu County	5.9	Jalaid Banner	4.7
Jiayin County	9.0	Taibus Banner	5.8	Habahe County	4.7
Wenquan County	9.0	Manas County	5.7	Fuhai County	4.7
Emin County	8.7	Tongxin County	5.7	Wuqi County	4.7
Youyu County	8.5	Kelan County	5.7	Tao'an County	4.6
Guyang County	8.2	Linyou County	5.6	Urad Middle Banner	4.6
Sunwu County	8.2	Horinger County	5.5	Dulan County	4.6
Tacheng City	8.1	Arun Banner	5.5	Jimsar County	4.6
Chen Barag Banner	8.1	Qingshuihe County	5.5	Qianan County	4.6
Guinan County	8.0	Shawan County	5.5	Horqin Left Wing Middle Banner	4.6
Wudalianchi City	7.9	Qahar Right Wing Rear Banner	5.4	Linxi County	4.6
Duolun County	7.7	Bei'an City	5.4	Lingtai County	4.6
Huma County	7.7	Lindian County	5.4	Horqin Left Wing Rear Banner	4.6
Guyuan County	7.6	Kedong County	5.3	Haiyuan County	4.5
Shenchi County	7.5	Shilou County	5.3	Tuquan County	4.5
Gannan County	7.5	Liangcheng County	5.3	Huanan County	4.5
Jixian County	7.4	Meixian County	5.3	Wangkui County	4.5
Mishan County	7.3	Zhenlai County	5.2	Minle County	4.5
Morin Dawa Banner	7.2	Changling County	5.2	Fengzhen County	4.5
Qahar Right Wing Middle Banner	7.1	Longjiang County	5.2	Horqin Right Wing Middle Banner	4.4
Yanchi County	6.9	Zhuozi County	5.1	Fuyu County	4.4
		Huanxian County	5.1		

Note:
* 1 mu = 1/15 hectare.

*RANKING OF 209 COUNTIES WITH PER CAPITA CULTIVATED LAND ABOVE 3.5 MU** *1987*

(mu*/person) (continued)

County	Per Capita Cultivated Land
Dingxi County	4.4
Shanyin County	4.3
Nongan County	4.3
Guyuan County	4.3
Dorbod County	4.3
Qian Gorlos Banner	4.2
Bayan County	4.2
Bole City	4.2
Mulan County	4.2
Barkol Autonomous County	4.2
Suileng County	4.1
Hexigten Banner	4.1
Tongde County	4.1
Shuangliao County	4.1
Jarud Banner	4.1
Horqin Right Wing Front Banner	4.1
Zhenyuan County	4.1
Huachi County	4.0
Shuangcheng County	4.0
Jidong County	4.0
Zhaodong County	4.0
Wuyuan County	4.0
Nilka County	4.0
Jingbian County	4.0
Yonghe County	4.0
Wensu County	4.0
Dehui County	4.0
Yangqu County	4.0
Yushu County	3.9
Datong County	3.9
Ongniud Banner	3.9
Binxian County	3.9
Hoxud County	3.9
Jalaid City	3.9
Jungar Banner	3.9
Zhidan County	3.9
Burqin County	3.9
Fuxin Autonomous County	3.9
Henshan County	3.9
Jingning County	3.9
Zhangwu County	3.8
Shouyang County	3.8
Qingjiang County	3.8
Xingxian County	3.8
Minqin County	3.7
Ar Horqin Banner	3.7
Faku County	3.7
Garze County	3.7
Qianyang County	3.7
Awat County	3.7
Hulan County	3.7
Lanxian County	3.7
Kangping County	3.7
Fukang County	3.7
Yangyuan County	3.7
Shenmu County	3.7
Bohu County	3.7
Yining County	3.6
Changtu County	3.6
Anda County	3.6
Qingshui County	3.6
Aohan Banner	3.6
Jinle County	3.6
Yanshou County	3.6
Menyuan Autonomous County	3.6
Zhaoyuan County	3.6
Lishu County	3.6
Yanchuan County	3.6
Longde County	3.6
Yijun County	3.6
Xiahe County	3.6
Jingtai County	3.6
Gongzhuling City	3.6
Chunhua County	3.5
Naiman Banner	3.5
Gulang County	3.5
Longxian County	3.5
Guangling County	3.5
Kailu County	3.5
Wusu County	3.5
Togtoh County	3.5
Urad Front Banner	3.5
Xayar County	3.5
Xinhe County	3.5
Suihua City	3.5

Note:
* 1 mu = 1/15 hectare.

11.14 BASIC STATISTICS ON 60 AGRICULTURAL PRODUCTION BASE COUNTIES WITH STATE PRIORITY INVESTMENT* 1987

County	Rural Population (1,000)	Total Crop Grown Area (1,000 mu**)	Output of Grain (tn)	Grain Purchased by State (tn)
Muolidawa Banner	190	1786	240387	149815
Tuquan County	242	1324	104938	22020
Wuyuan County	204	959	130676	37768
Urad Front Banner	234	876	99274	19563
Xinmin County	583	2203	628371	357940
Changtu County	790	3467	1346176	88850
Faku County	379	1618	510850	306450
Yushu County	1055	4371	1607500	763801
Yi'an County	917	4395	839521	504099
Dehui County	714	3213	956651	574589
Gongzhuling City	684	3308	1727355	1001950
Lishu County	610	2796	1269062	766563
Fuyu County	728	3995	1538801	741587
Naihe County	548	3958	640149	190121
Bayan County	533	2716	595756	182447
Suihua City	553	2617	481658	135334
Hailun County	652	3956	490587	108982
Heihe City	47	962	64192	19839
Xunke County	43	1026	92094	35988
Tongshan County	1432	3722	1001212	280978
Pixian County	1200	2823	749851	169300
Donghai County	849	2836	866716	239657
Shuyang County	1207	3253	870110	176295
Lianshui County	777	2330	625269	128150
Sihong County	777	2743	587556	167351
Changfeng County	761	2425	528203	158548
Feixi County	785	2230	496903	173324
Tianchang County	472	1645	577702	208810
Fengyang County	504	1914	490226	176505
Lu'an County	1324	3034	541659	206708
Shouxian County	1023	3384	603089	166221
Huoqiu County	1333	3504	574913	186701
Lujiang County	986	2760	540852	153770
Nancang County	764	3092	756853	403705
Fengcheng County	874	3533	610030	199773
Gao'an County	575	2608	494022	142800
Yugan County	632	1752	292783	125111
Taihe County	419	1414	218452	75786
Anfu County	275	1006	191640	69743
Shangshui County	903	2664	493104	126366
Dancheng County	971	2763	497279	108773

Note:
* These 60 counties are the first group of counties included in the state priority investment program to build agricultural bases. The agricultural production base counties will become major agricultural product suppliers after finishing the program.

** 1 mu = 1/15 hectare.

BASIC STATISTICS ON 60 AGRICULTURAL PRODUCTION BASE COUNTIES WITH STATE PRIORITY INVESTMENT* 1987

County	Rural Population (1,000)	Total Crop Grown Area (1,000 mu**)	Output of Grain (tn)	Grain Purchased by State (tn)
Huaiyang County	1031	2604	413291	135000
Tanghe County	1057	3710	552122	128156
Dengxian County	1239	4119	597657	229952
Huangchuan County	565	1588	324545	127559
Xiantao County	1114	3378	759017	256163
Jiangling County	616	2747	658524	395284
Jianli County	1015	4048	945462	354434
Honghu County	576	1918	458718	142920
Jinshan County	454	1800	529781	343003
Yueyang County	718	2098	458637	134554
Huarong County	603	2284	448054	148955
Yiyang County	685	1573	412398	98244
Yuanjinag County	547	1501	287855	152148
Changde County	874	3502	701637	204709
Anxiang County	458	1761	302890	108250
Sanya City	200	408	59767	4612
Ledong County	316	847	116930	15661
Lingshui County	212	471	65819	6087

Note:
* These 60 counties are the first group of counties included in the state priority investment program to build agricultural bases. The agricultural production base counties will become major agricultural product suppliers after finishing the program.

** 1 mu = 1/15 hectare.

11.15 BASIC STATISTICS ON 111 KEY GRAIN PRODUCTION BASE COUNTIES WITH STATE PRIORITY INVESTMENT* 1986-1990

County	Rural Population (1,000)	Cultivated Land (1,000 mu**)	Total Crop Grown Area (1,000 mu**)	Output of Grain (tn)	Grain Purchased by State (tn)
Qingyuan County	561	975	1593	270224	35882
Daming County	593	1102	1710	209813	51200
Yongnian County	633	963	1463	241780	59920
Ningjin County	577	1234	1803	247169	51940
Xinji City	490	1058	1642	279920	76501
Gaocheng County	605	833	1415	445475	106304
Zhaoxian County	434	777	1315	341146	86549
Dingzhou County	883	1259	2076	513276	79364
Xiangfen County	376	907	1058	145262	40536
Yuncheng City	356	958	1107	137330	53162
Ruicheng County	296	780	865	148818	46263
Linyi County	431	1508	1730	257961	84012
Horqin Left Wing Middle Banner	405	2171	2210	385150	206826
Kailu County	287	1220	1291	315461	177090
Xinmin County	583	2120	2203	628371	357940
Yingkou County	529	780	771	320584	169500
Dawa County	265	685	692	378778	192500
Suining County	978	1529	2589	682540	135219
Wujin County	1164	1349	2387	752821	201261
Huaiyin County	671	988	1528	390875	51379
Jinhu County	282	523	1171	385391	175716
Xiangshui County	413	652	1144	251153	49433
Gaoyou County	715	1089	2252	699563	261030
Baoying County	793	911	1903	633925	258109
Nanling County	451	511	1327	268504	50400
Wuhe County	500	1162	1892	427066	153487
Dangtu County	550	657	1589	376808	87637
Suixi County	878	1989	3450	620688	120580
Fuyang County	1146	1597	2914	564818	100597
Shenhe County	502	1074	1494	312966	54533
Xinxian County	737	1296	2158	396304	53498
Tancheng County	766	993	1735	459038	84025
Cangshan County	943	1284	2154	495160	61640
Heze City	883	1272	2164	409629	107855
Dingtao County	451	767	1318	254764	60487
Chengwu County	461	750	1321	229776	55576
Shanxian County	881	1474	2432	339300	79624
Dongming County	542	1036	1926	246707	60484
Qixian County	794	1275	2270	280050	68042
Weishi County	652	1197	2046	350679	59593
Linru County	699	983	1524	249925	34784
Xiangcheng County	671	827	1420	262117	55595

Note:
*** These 111 counties are included in the state priority investment program during the 7th five-year plan (1986-1990), to build key grain production base counties. They will become major grain suppliers after finishing the program.**

**** 1 mu = 1/15 hectare.**

BASIC STATISTICS ON 111 KEY GRAIN PRODUCTION BASE COUNTIES WITH STATE PRIORITY INVESTMENT * 1986 -1990

(continued)

County	Rural Population (1,000)	Cultivated Land (1,000 mu**)	Total Crop Grown Area (1,000 mu**)	Output of Grain (tn)	Grain Purchased by State (tn)
Anyang County	933	1272	2069	307609	50736
Huaxian County	920	1645	2894	590204	160053
Neihuang County	564	938	1538	205044	53641
Jixian County	341	588	1001	205174	55314
Huixian County	615	900	1560	261956	30466
Jiyuan County	477	606	979	215512	50336
Yuxian County	931	1182	1897	386648	46233
Area under Luohe City's Jurisdiction	19	41	78	18518	4100
Yucheng County	824	1417	2526	355605	72172
Shangqiu County	841	1514	2526	373245	87799
Yongcheng County	995	1616	2813	458237	179096
Fugou County	549	1135	1895	227199	57332
Luyi County	853	1245	2268	408863	116984
Nanyang County	977	1618	2533	441340	95761
Xinye County	622	1020	1739	269454	62330
Area under Xiangfan City's Jurisdiction	103	105	204	48474	17215
Suizhou City	1135	1509	2688	850004	406540
Laohekou City	317	600	1009	233488	62490
Xiangyang County	997	1775	3216	768226	333670
Zaoyang County	817	1620	2871	676735	357980
Yicheng County	399	691	1313	389795	160400
Xiaogan City	1089	1005	2421	516137	143975
Yingcheng City	459	592	1423	334609	150176
Anlu County	463	519	1058	336514	131136
Gong'an County	830	1200	2660	500980	175250
Zhongxiang County	772	1308	2654	688911	406410
Ningxiang County	1202	1167	2731	840143	108095
Liling County	791	575	1423	453950	49342
Xiangtan County	1004	1037	2268	712406	135520
Hengdong County	556	511	1164	305166	92771
Linli County	379	564	1416	282745	121683
Shuangfeng County	768	620	1459	441471	48842
Lingui County	389	520	910	160342	27288
Quanzhou County	676	717	1420	316674	65822
Pengxian County	649	669	1442	309278	62032
Baxian County	1098	1267	2725	678264	112397
Rongxian County	799	931	1665	453790	82670
Jiangyou County	638	697	1269	315349	68869
Nancong County	1305	1238	2392	522256	61731
Daxian County	1143	1080	2251	550145	91909
Songming County	262	342	118040	10166	
Lufeng County	316	357	95949	11749	

Note:
* These 111 counties are included in the state priority investment program during the 7th five-year plan (1986-1990), to build key grain production base counties. They will become major grain suppliers after finishing the program.

** 1 mu = 1/15 hectare.

BASIC STATISTICS ON 111 KEY GRAIN PRODUCTION BASE COUNTIES WITH STATE PRIORITY INVESTMENT* 1986 -1990

(continued)

County	Rural Population (1,000)	Cultivated Land (1,000 mu**)	Total Crop Grown Area (1,000 mu**)	Output of Grain (tn)	Grain Purchased by State (tn)
Pucheng County	513	717	1138	239280	30732
Fuping County	584	1160	1514	268334	37360
Zhouzhi County	427	853	1075	200111	33349
Baoji County	431	1015	1183	206355	43560
Fengxian County	619	1720	1953	227171	90380
Qianxian County	600	1199	1526	218188	69785
Linquan County	1390	1775	3326	586350	66428
Taihe County	1163	1872	3161	545014	115750
Woyang County	989	1980	3279	620320	220179
Mengcheng County	849	1903	3268	602569	258212
Funan County	1113	1589	2778	397240	63175
Xiaoxian County	948	1463	2471	320684	87651
Taihu County	479	323	795	173074	54161
Jianyang County	231	458	928	208975	82504
Pucheng County	320	585	1197	254047	
Xinjian County	443	832	1969	336245	141570
De'an County	116	160	391	83803	38605
Ningdu County	535	667	1461	243805	47769
Fengxin County	208	429	1015	221001	118283
Yifeng County	187	376	856	174174	51690
Yiyang County	250	350	963	165122	57978
Boyang County	961	1135	2789	491982	43820
Jishui County	381	660	1384	253906	101044
Nancheng County	214	287	750	201174	84700
Pingdu County	1157	266	3787	928230	208144
Area under Zaozhang City's Jurisdiction	1323	1762	3067	731910	268899
Laiyang County	791	1209	1895	398053	54654
Anqiu County	950	1505	2315	633358	89720
Zhucheng County	981	1635	2425	621656	109357
Area under Jining City's Jurisdiction	550	817	1418	385784	61701
Yanzhou County	398	650	1129	306938	54275
Yutai County	312	589	931	244396	70991
Jinxiang County	458	883	1597	349678	77987
Area under Tai'an City's Jurisdiction	134	1209	1985	500823	61137
Feicheng County	753	982	1637	444081	98530
Linyi County	406	865	1183	213941	45049

Note:
* These 111 counties are included in the state priority investment program during the 7th five-year plan (1986-1990), to build key grain production base counties. They will become major grain suppliers after finishing the program.

** 1 mu = 1/15 hectare.

11.16 BASIC INDICATORS OF AGRICULTURE IN FOURTEEN COASTAL CITIES BY COUNTY

County	Population (year-end figure 1,000 persons)	Rural Total Output Value of Society (1,000 yuan)	Grain Output (tn)	Total Value of Farm and Sideline Products Purchase (1,000 yuan)
Area under Tianjin City's Jurisdiction	311	126940	89028	3510
Ninghe County	306	539680	160820	128070
Wuqing County	749	1933310	425000	119020
Jinghai County	446	1591160	172166	104250
Baodi County	570	1126790	294861	78920
Jinxian County	691	936030	299483	128030
Area under Qinghuangdao City's Jurisdiction	464	307850	37713	130060
Qinglong County	496	259270	71362	44050
Changli County	510	458100	259695	107750
Funing County	500	457350	192488	87610
Lulong County	384	395840	218420	56430
Area under Dalian City's Jurisdiction	2276	3821470	180766	258410
Wafangdian City	973	1483130	277158	301030
Xinjin County	792	1176810	273385	233330
Changhai County	77	382750	6530	74260
Zhuanghe County	870	1054150	230122	206630
Shanghai County	410	2280410	137111	295600
Jiading County	504	2700920	184011	152790
Baoshan County	342	1867530	120053	118440
Chuansha County	621	2938630	161450	136910
Nanhui County	685	2722300	262797	121870
Fengxian County	493	2074990	253816	116530
Songjiang County	492	1946790	285174	139300
Jinshan County	466	1512310	271147	186160
Qingpu County	448	1993760	253503	301330
Congming County	649	1846290	298138	101170
Area under Nantong City's Jurisdiction	145	796110	27656	5270
Hai'an County	959	1414360	421788	280720
Rugao County	1402	1736470	592597	252200
Rudong County	1108	1769130	622147	310960
Nantong County	1525	257059	533706	202660
Haimen County	1003	1842570	234184	132340
Qidong County	1133	2296850	303161	274460
Area under Lianyungang City's Jurisdiction	485	378340	92598	212120
Ganyu County	858	2052500	594738	212790
Donghai County	913	1295060	866716	275660
Guanyun County	861	826390	535390	200480
Area under Ningbo City's Jurisdiction	1048	1919190	349434	453040
Yuyao City	789	1988070	343805	205870
Cixi County	937	2646400	193197	218770
Fenghua County	466	0926800	198911	98310

BASIC INDICATORS OF AGRICULTURE IN FOURTEEN COASTAL CITIES BY COUNTY

(continued)

County	Population (year-end figure 1,000 persons)	Rural Total Output Value of Society (1,000 yuan)	Grain Output (tn)	Total Value of Farm and Sideline Products Purchase (1,000 yuan)
Xiangshan County	514	0886630	199464	116170
Ninghai County	548	909280	189091	94860
Jinxian County	679	3255500	378422	154860
Area under Wenzhou City's Jurisdiction	544	452170	45439	247460
Ouhai County	510	860310	144554	78950
Tongtou County	121	172190	4819	17780
Leqing County	973	1145220	256999	64210
Yongjia County	790	604780	176920	53900
Rui'an County	1076	1028410	290514	134070
Pingyang County	735	717660	192400	69960
Changnan County	1028	1071300	251404	90610
Wencheng County	348	148460	74054	15250
Taishun County	315	157550	79071	32990
Area under Fuzhou City's Jurisdiction	1236	113350	79467	461870
Minhou County	564	505680	186392	113340
Lianjiang County	569	624120	112195	88080
Luoyuan County	221	193100	75024	26120
Minqing County	270	241390	116522	28010
Yongtai County	310	179050	103111	49920
Changle County	611	986380	148573	128300
Fuqing County	1011	804730	267985	119450
Pingtan County	299	260900	20512	13710
Area under Qingdao City's Jurisdiction	1296	366870	27778	36850
Laoshan County	676	1424170	100748	88480
Jimuo County	1005	1640250	476533	177160
Jiaonan County	822	1278430	380066	22802
Jiaoxian County	687	1411560	354244	178460
Laixi County	680	1207970	400086	195660
Pingdu County	1250	2170550	928230	397140
Area under Yantai City's Jurisdiction	754	1007830	94354	105290
Penglai County	485	923610	200792	158660
Huangxian County	578	1136240	216034	171060
Zhaoyuan County	554	1223130	268214	178630
Yexian County	863	1425450	365808	242790
Liayang County	863	1019720	398053	213590
Qixia County	664	834420	294354	192800
Haiyang County	700	833850	357116	132620
Muping County	569	1087750	237351	138060
Changdao County	41	224380	1027	25790
Weihai City	233	563710	47357	72060
Rushan County	630	879760	261945	168760

BASIC INDICATORS OF AGRICULTURE IN FOURTEEN COASTAL CITIES BY COUNTY
(continued)

County	Population (year-end figure 1,000 persons)	Rural Total Output Value of Society (1,000 yuan)	Grain Output (tn)	Total Value of Farm and Sideline Products Purchased (1,000 yuan)
Wendeng County	715	1360960	335261	239810
Rongcheng County	748	1851330	342248	381920
Area under Guangzhou City's Jurisdiction	1218	2533310	179733	140750
Huaxian County	469	721700	222070	158920
Conghua County	410	402020	157012	93700
Xinfeng County	205	125200	61882	26300
Longmen County	272	223740	117383	52670
Zengcheng County	630	712340	263752	213570
Panyu County	724	1666150	326823	209710
Qingyuan County	971	982250	403541	199210
Fugang County	256	195830	113361	31620
Area under Zhanjiang city's Jurisdiction	968	852560	112971	123780
Wuchuan County	683	751820	155467	155900
Lianjiang County	1086	1090360	283420	217680
Suixi County	676	795960	175435	235580
Haikang County	1039	1085920	255336	202870
Xuwen County	514	450390	91622	114720
Area under Beihai City's Jurisdiction	185	238280	15574	157480

www.ingramcontent.com/pod-product-compliance
Ingram Content Group UK Ltd.
Pitfield, Milton Keynes, MK11 3LW, UK
UKHW050950290926
15470UKWH00005B/1751

9 780275 933463